THE
ESSENTIAL
D. L. Moody
COLLECTION

THE
ESSENTIAL
D. L. Moody
COLLECTION

SECRET POWER, THE OVERCOMING LIFE, AND PREVAILING PRAYER

Dwight L. Moody
James Spencer, ed.

Revell

a division of Baker Publishing Group
Grand Rapids, Michigan

© 2024 by James Spencer

Published by Revell
a division of Baker Publishing Group
Grand Rapids, Michigan
RevellBooks.com

Printed in the United States of America

Library of Congress Cataloging-in-Publication Data
Names: Moody, Dwight Lyman, 1837–1899, author. | Moody, Dwight Lyman,
  1837–1899. Secret power. | Moody, Dwight Lyman, 1837–1899. Overcoming
  life. | Moody, Dwight Lyman, 1837–1899. Prevailing prayer. | Spencer, James,
  1977– editor.
Title: The essential D. L. Moody collection / Dwight L. Moody ; James Spencer, ed.
Description: 3-in-1 edition. | Grand Rapids, Michigan : Revell, a division of Baker
  Publishing Group, [2024] | Three volumes in one physical volume: Secret power,
  The overcoming life and Prevailing prayer. | Includes bibliographical references.
Identifiers: LCCN 2024013326 | ISBN 9780800746186 (paper) | ISBN 9780800746421
  (casebound) | ISBN 9781493447220 (ebook)
Subjects: LCSH: Evangelistic sermons. | Sermons, American. | Evangelistic work.
Classification: LCC BV3797.M7 E88 2024 | DDC 248.4—dc23/eng/20240506
LC record available at https://lccn.loc.gov/2024013326

Cover design by Jonathan Lewis.

Baker Publishing Group publications use paper produced from sustainable forestry practices and postconsumer waste whenever possible.

24   25   26   27   28   29   30   7   6   5   4   3   2   1

Contents

Introduction

When we look back on those God has used in the past, the Bible is (as always!) a helpful guide. In Hebrews 11, we find a list of those who served the Lord "by faith." The faith of Noah, Abraham, Moses, Rahab, and others are presented as examples for us to follow. They form "so great a cloud of witnesses" that we should "lay aside every weight, and sin which clings so closely" so that we may "run with endurance the race that is set before us" (Heb. 12:1 ESV). As inspiring as those in Hebrews 11 may be, when we look at other parts of Scripture, we see that many of those referenced in the so-called hall of faith were not always particularly faithful. Abraham passed Sarah off as his sister to avoid being killed in Egypt (Gen. 12:10–20; 20:1–18) and slept with Hagar to secure an heir (Gen. 16). Moses's anger kept him from entering the promised land (Num. 20:10–13). Rahab was a prostitute (Josh. 2:1). The Bible presents the good with the bad. It does so because the heroes of the Bible's story are always faithful and flawed. The world does not run on the righteousness of women and men but on the grace and will of God.

As we consider the life and work of Dwight L. Moody, we would do well to remember that Moody, like the rest of us, made an incomplete and imperfect contribution to the world. He was faithful and flawed.

To dismiss Moody for his flaws is as foolish as venerating him for his faithfulness. Moody's story is God's story. Dwight Moody was a man used by God. Yet he was also a man of his time. As such, it is important to understand his time as we approach his work. It is similarly important to have some sense of Moody's life experiences. His early childhood and various other experiences colored and constrained the scope of his work, the topics he covered, and the issues he chose to address in his writing. While a full survey of Moody's context, early life, and ministry are not possible in a brief introduction, the following seeks to provide a sketch of some of the major challenges Moody faced in the nineteenth century, in his own personal and family life, and in his various ministry endeavors.

Moody's Context

To call the United States in the nineteenth century "tumultuous" is an understatement. Moody experienced an era in United States history that was not wholly different from our own. Prosperity and opportunity were often accompanied by corruption and tragedy. The good was mixed with the bad. The nation was divided. Racial tensions reached a boiling point. As the United States struggled to live up to the high expectations its founders had set for the new republic, new technologies, people, and problems were shaping the character of the nation and its citizens. Between his birth in 1837 and death in 1899, Moody witnessed (1) the difficulties associated with urbanization, industrialization, and immigration; (2) the horrors of the Civil War; and (3) the challenges of Reconstruction before and after the assassination of Abraham Lincoln. Moody was not a passive onlooker to the events shaping the United States. He was active in ministering to the urban and rural poor, served as a relief worker and chaplain during the Civil War, and sought to minister in the South after the war ended. For much of his life, he worked in a nation divided. While the Union victory had sustained the formal connection between North and South, the political and ideological divides persisted after the Civil War. Even though the war had resolved the issue of slavery in principle, it could not eliminate the ongoing mistreatment of Black people, especially in the Southern states.

The quest for equal rights would become one of the most significant issues of Moody's day. It would also serve as the backdrop for the most controversial aspect of Moody's ministry: his segregated meetings in the South. The Civil War provided an opening to address slavery and racism, but slavery and racism were only part of America's problem. Consumer capitalism continued to create problems for the working class after the Civil War. As historian Mark Noll suggests,

> After the shooting stopped, two great problems in practical theology confronted the United States. One was the enduring reality of racism, which displayed its continuing force almost as virulently through the mob and the rope as it had in the chain and the lash. The other was the expansion of consumer capitalism, in which unprecedented opportunities to create wealth were matched by large-scale alienation and considerable poverty in both urban and rural America.[1]

Regarding the first of the "two great problems," Black people in the South continued to experience discrimination, intimidation, and violence. For instance, while Black men were afforded the right to vote via the Fifteenth Amendment, ratified in 1870, exercising their right to vote became problematic when federal troops were no longer available to police the polls and ensure they were not kept from casting their ballots. Various Southern states curtailed Black voting through poll taxes and literacy tests. Violence and other forms of intimidation were also used to keep Black men from the polls.

Though the issue of consumer capitalism became more problematic after the Civil War, dynamics prior to the war contributed to the problem. For instance, historian James Findlay notes that evangelical convictions regarding the use of wealth and the importance of work had forged an odd relationship between "evangelical denominations and the business leaders" in the 1850s.[2] This relationship, according to Findlay, led to many "constructive" endeavors while also creating an "economic dependency [that] made it difficult for evangelical leaders to criticize the business community, even if they so desired, in any terms other than through judgments on personal morality and individual actions taken in the business world."[3] Intertwined with business, the church became less capable of addressing consumer capitalism, the second of Noll's "two great problems."

Beyond the convergence of evangelicals and business, transportation and communication technologies also contributed to the problem of consumer capitalism. The railroad had allowed for the development of large, centralized firms with national reach.[4] According to historian Rosanne Currarino, the issue of labor relations arose during this period "because of workers' real and highly visible suffering, because of high unemployment, and because of the widespread distress of the manufacturing industry."[5]

The various problems facing the United States in the nineteenth century would ultimately spill into the religious realm. Whereas many in the North and among the Black population saw emancipation and Reconstruction as evidence of God's providential hand and favor, the South struggled to reorient its religious understandings post-slavery. Many questions remained for Christians and Americans who had expected the war and the abolition of slavery to usher in something approximating utopia. Historian Edward J. Blum writes,

> As prophetic visions, providential promises, and millennial dreams failed
> to be realized fully, all types of Americans recast their faiths. Southern
> whites found new explanations for slavery and race. Many northern
> whites became religiously tentative.[6]

Noll comments that the turmoil in the religious realm and the rifts reinforced between the North and South after the Civil War explain "why one interpretation of God's dealing shaped southern white resistance to Republican Reconstruction, [and] another led northern white abolitionists to prioritize national reconciliation over Black liberation."[7] Beyond the differing perspectives within the religious community, the approaches taken by various religious figures of the day also created a degree of confusion. Some, like Moody, offered a more individual message calling for personal consecration. Others were more concerned with social issues such as labor practices, women's suffrage, civil rights, and temperance. The religious vision that seemed relatively uniform at the beginning of the nineteenth century became more diverse after the Civil War. The Bible "remained central" to a Protestant vision of a healthy social order, but in the 1870s it was "now speaking in confusion from a once cohesive Protestant world."[8]

Less than a century after its founding, the United States was experiencing something of an identity crisis on numerous fronts. The growing pains were evident in at least three areas: (1) labor practices associated with industrialization and urbanization, (2) sociopolitical rifts that led to the Civil War and continued during Reconstruction, and (3) religious confusion prompted by differing conceptions of God and His authorization of practices such as slavery. These and other major national events provide a sense of the context in which Dwight Moody sought to proclaim the gospel.

Moody's Early Life and Conversion

Born in 1837, Dwight L. Moody had an early life that grounded him in the harsher realities of the world. After the death of his father, Edwin, Dwight and his family lived in poverty. While they were able to keep their home in Northfield, Massachusetts, the Moody family often depended on the kindness of family members and neighbors for their basic necessities. Young Dwight stopped attending school after the fifth grade to support his family. His early life was a formative time. As he notes, "When I was young, I thought it was hard that I had lost my father but now I believe I would not be where I am if I had not been thrown on to myself early in life."[9]

Similar to many other young men and women at the time, Dwight Moody left the rural setting of Northfield for the urban opportunities of Boston. At seventeen, he was off to seek his fortune. After having difficulty finding employment, Moody approached his uncle Samuel for a job in his shoe store. Moody quickly became an effective salesman. For instance, William Moody writes,

> [Dwight] was not satisfied with the ordinary methods of the salesman, and, like the merchants of old, he cried his wares before the door, and actually went out into the street to persuade uninterested passers that they wanted to buy. Nothing delighted him so much as a success of this kind, and that he had many is not surprising.[10]

His ability to sell revealed aspects of his personality that would serve him in his evangelistic and preaching efforts.

When his uncle hired Dwight, he set certain conditions on his employment: Moody had to attend church.[11] While attending the Mount Vernon Congregational Church, Dwight met Edward Kimball. Kimball taught Moody's Sunday school class and would eventually lead Dwight Moody to Christ in 1855. After his conversion, Moody continued working in his uncle's shoe store while participating in his church and the Young Men's Christian Association (YMCA). Moody's faith was growing, but he still wanted to pursue his business interests.

It was those interests that led Moody to Chicago in 1856. From 1856 to 1861, Moody split his time between building up a reputation in business and working in Christian ministry. Some of Moody's most memorable ministry occurred while he was still working as a shoe salesman. In 1858, for example, Moody earned the nickname "crazy Moody" after beginning a Sunday school for children in "an abandoned freight car on North State Street."[12] By 1861, Moody had determined to go into full-time ministry. He left his business behind. While he had been making good progress toward his business goals and had also been developing a romantic relationship with his future wife, Emma Revell, he set aside shoe sales to serve the Lord. His decision to step away from a blossoming professional life would have implications.[13] As he notes,

> When I came to Jesus Christ, I had a terrible battle to surrender my will, and to take God's will. When I gave up business, I had another battle for three months; I fought against it. It was a terrible battle. But oh! How many times I have thanked God that I gave up my will and took God's will.[14]

Moody's Preaching

People rightly refer to Dwight Moody as an evangelist. Throughout the course of his ministry Moody reached more than one hundred million people with the gospel message.[15] Yet it would be a mistake to limit Moody's work to that of evangelism. Moody was consistently driven by the gospel, which would lead him to share the gospel with unbelievers and challenge Christians to do the same.

In both exhortation and evangelism, Moody was an effective communicator. In part, his ability to convey the gospel to the masses was a function of his own self-perception. Moody didn't think of himself as a scholar but as a student learning the Word of God so that he could share the Word of God. His end goal was not making Christians more knowledgeable. Knowledge was important, but Moody sought to encourage Christians to a life of usefulness. To do so, God's people could not settle for being merely nominal Christians. They had to "seek to be vessels meet for the Master's use, that God, the Holy Spirit, may shine fully through us." As early as his work in the Civil War, Moody's preaching was "direct and effective, and multitudes responded with a promise to follow Christ."[16] Moody's direct approach became the hallmark of his preaching. He did not mince words. Instead, he was "strikingly free from all pretense and parade" and spoke "as one who thoroughly believes what he says, and who is downright earnest in delivering his message."[17] Moody seldom won people over with his eloquence or the complexity of his thought. He was compelling because he spoke plainly and without an agenda. Commenting on Moody's presentation during his missions in England, Lord Shaftesbury writes,

> In his intense earnestness they go along with him: the simplicity of his message—Christ crucified—the evident fact that he has no special Church purposes, nor, on the surface at least, any interested consideration. All seems natural, easy, almost necessary to him. It appears the dictate of the moment, without previous thought, or any form of preparation! Yet how to account for the effect on every station and degree? Workpeople, shopkeepers, merchants, lawyers, clergy and laity, alike, confess the power and cannot explain it.[18]

Shaftesbury's comments summarize well Moody's preaching style. They also point to the reason for Moody's effectiveness. He was without any agenda other than to point people to Christ. His sermons were full of power not because he was particularly convincing but because he had owned the message so that God's power became evident.

Despite his straightforward style, Moody quickly realized the value of music. Beginning in the late 1850s, much of Moody's preaching was accompanied by music, but he would not find a consistent partner in music ministry until recruiting Ira Sankey to the work in 1873. The significance of music in Moody's ministry is illustrated in a letter to fellow evangelist Daniel W. Whittle in which Moody writes, "I would make a specialty of advertising in the city and country that Bliss will sing the Gospel and let him sing a good deal. God has honored that wonderfully in this country."[19] Singing and music had become a crucial part of Moody's presentation of the gospel. Moody's preaching was also rich with illustrations. When asked why he used stories, Moody said he did so "to touch the heart and while it is soft, send right in the arrow of truth."[20] Looking through Moody's sermon notes reinforces the way illustrations flowed from his readings of biblical texts and topics. For instance, while exploring the topic of deliverance, Moody made note of various deliverances made by lawyers for their clients and doctors for their patients, "but Christ can do all at once and not leave a hoof behind."[21]

If Moody's illustrations feel seamless, it is, at least in part, because they were not an afterthought. Moody did not see the Bible as separate from daily living but as an integral part of it. As such, when he looked out on the world, he could not help but see parallels between mundane day-to-day events and profound spiritual realities. His presentation of the gospel was powerful. Not only did he have a deep, experiential understanding of the message he was conveying but he also had the ability to speak plainly about the gospel. In addition, he learned to create a context that would prepare his audience to receive that message. In many ways, Moody was a master at getting people to let down their guard so that they became open to the message of the Scriptures.

Moody's Ministry

One of Moody's earliest ministry posts involved serving as a relief worker and chaplain in the Civil War. Moody got a "taste of what it was like when men and women from every sect and denomination, pulled together to take on the common foe."[22] The unity of the church became one of his central concerns. Unfortunately, as he would find out during his Southern campaigns, uniting disparate groups of Christians was no simple task.

Moody's Chicago ministry expanded after the war. He began his work as a missionary with the YMCA of Chicago and was elected its president in 1866. He also helped found the Illinois Street Independent Church in 1864. Moody's ministry in Chicago was flourishing. However, by 1867 the stress of ministry was beginning to take its toll on both him and his wife, Emma. As his friend Major Whittle commented,

> [Moody] had become mixed up with building Farwell Hall and was on committees for every kind of work and in his ambition to make his enterprises succeed because they were his, had taken his eyes off the Lord and had been burdened in Soul and unfruitful in his work for months.[23]

Ultimately, on the advice of Emma's doctor, the couple decided to take a trip to the United Kingdom. During their four-month trip, "evangelicals in the United Kingdom reinforced many of Moody's developing ideas about theology and social action."[24] He returned to Chicago refreshed, yet he continued to struggle spiritually. In 1871, Moody "realized more and more how little he was fitted by personal acquirements for his work. An intense hunger and thirst for spiritual power were aroused in him by two young women who used to attend the meetings and sit on the front seat."[25] These women told Moody they were praying for him to receive the power of the Holy Spirit. Initially confused and resistant, Moody encouraged them to pray for others. The women, however, would not be stopped. Moody would ultimately come to realize his need for the Holy Spirit's power. As he later admitted, "I really felt that I did not want to live if I could not have this power for service."[26]

After the Great Chicago Fire in October 1871, Moody was no longer tethered to Chicago. Still, he refused to abandon the YMCA or the Illinois Street Church. He sought to raise funds to assist in rebuilding what the fire had destroyed. However, as he said, "My heart was not in the work of begging. I could not appeal. I was crying all the time that God would fill me with His Spirit."[27] God would ultimately answer Moody's cries in an incident described by R. A. Torrey:

> The power of God fell upon him as he walked up the street and he had to hurry off to the house of a friend and ask that he might have a room

16

by himself, and in that room he stayed alone for hours; and the Holy Ghost came upon him filling his soul with such joy that at last he had to ask God to withhold His hand, lest he die on the spot from very joy.[28]

Following his experience with the Holy Spirit, Moody would go on to preach in England, Ireland, Scotland, and surrounding areas from 1872 to 1875. He then continued his campaigns back in the States, preaching in Brooklyn, Philadelphia, and Georgia. His trip to Georgia represented a turning point in Moody's ministry because it "demonstrated the limits of his commitment to [racial] integration."[29] Moody had intended to have integrated meetings but met resistance from White pastors in Augusta. Recounting Moody's confrontation with the Southern pastors, one article notes,

> When he [Moody] first began holding his open-air meetings here [in Georgia], negroes mingled so indiscriminately with the audience that it became disagreeable to the whites, and a dividing fence was put up. Mr. Moody did not like this, and spoke of it, when one of our pastors informed him that it was impossible for blacks and whites to mingle even in a religious audience. Mr. Moody then said, "I see you have not gotten over your rebellious feelings yet."[30]

Despite Moody's objections, his friend and adviser Major Whittle ultimately convinced him that holding segregated meetings was the only way to reach White audiences in the South. After Georgia, Moody would continue to hold segregated campaigns until his meeting in Texas in 1895. At that meeting, "Moody openly defied Jim Crow and racial discrimination. He became outraged when he saw physical barriers separating blacks from whites. . . . Moody thrust his 270-pound frame against the wooden railings."[31] Moody's intolerance for the racial divide was evident, yet, even after the 1895 Texas meeting, Moody tolerated segregation.[32]

Despite ultimately shifting his practices, Moody did hold segregated meetings in the South for a time and remained silent on matters such as lynching, both of which were controversial choices. While it seems likely that Moody was attempting to reform individual Southern White people through the proclamation of God's Word, his segregated meetings reinforced the ongoing practices of racial discrimination in the South. For instance, in 1886, the *Savannah Morning News* printed an article titled "Mr. Moody's Wise Course." The article notes that Moody "did not have sufficient confidence in himself to believe that he could settle it [the race issue] in a few days when years of constant agitation had failed to do so."[33] Concerning Moody's acquiescence to local committees, the article went on to suggest, "It would be a good thing for the country if some of the agitators of the race question at the North were equally as wise."[34]

The decision to preach the gospel in the South rather than refusing to hold segregated campaigns reflected one of Moody's central theological convictions: "the fundamental cause of the urban ills plaguing the United States and the United Kingdom was human sinfulness."[35] Moody focused on individual salvation rather than on political and social matters. If reform was possible, Moody believed it had to begin in the hearts of individual believers. As apolitical as Moody's preaching may have been, Moody's Southern campaigns did have a political effect. Blum notes,

> Although Moody endeavored to be apolitical in his ministry, his amazing American revivals in the mid-1870s had a profound political effect. They played a crucial role in reuniting the North and the South while religiously legitimating the northern retreat from radical Reconstruction.[36]

By participating in rather than speaking out against segregation, Moody showed himself to be a child of his time. Emancipation had been widely accepted, particularly among Republicans, yet "the Republicans could never agree on what southern reinstatement or freedom for slaves truly meant."[37] Despite the public challenges associated with his segregated campaigns, Moody continued to expand his ministry through formal educational efforts. He opened the Northfield Seminary for girls in 1879 and the Mount Hermon School for boys in 1881. These schools, along with the summer conferences held in Northfield, demonstrate Moody's ongoing interest in preparing God's people for service. While the Northfield schools trained students in traditional disciplines, "The motive presented for the pursuit of an education is the power it confers for Christian life and usefulness, not the means it affords to social distinction, or to the gratification of selfish ambition."[38] Moody viewed education as a means of equipping "Christian workers who could effectively reach all levels of society."[39] The Bible institutes in Northfield and Chicago were extensions of this educational ministry "by which he [Moody] could inject new life into the church."[40]

Moody's ministry has had a lasting impact in the United States and around the world. He was not perfect, but it is clear that God was working through this humble man from Northfield. Millions heard the gospel. Christian women and men were challenged to develop a "deeper sense of their responsibility" because "only when the rank and file of the Christian churches are enlisted in active service for Christ, will His kingdom advance as it ought."[41]

Moody's Thought

Dwight Moody was not an academic. He was, however, a theologian in the sense that he was a man uniquely gifted "to seek, speak, and show understanding of what God was doing in Christ for the sake of the world."[42] He was driven by basic theological convictions. These convictions shaped his understanding of Christian character, Christian community, and Christian practice. While influenced by the various movements of his day, Moody's work does not reflect any single theological system or tradition. He did lean toward dispensationalism. He also emerged as a prominent figure in revivalism. Yet theological systems were never a reason for excluding one group or another. As Moody notes,

Too frequently when Christians get together, they seek for points upon which they differ, and then go at it. . . . The Christian denominations too often present a spectacle of a political party split into factions and unable to make an effective fight.[43]

Dwight Moody was interested in Bible study and theology. That interest was often shaped by his commitment to the building up of Christ's body. His life was devoted not simply to evangelism but to the building up of the church. Moody understood that the church would not be built through evangelism alone. God's people need to be useful to God. For the church to prosper, it needed to be guided by the Holy Spirit so that God was determining the direction of His people and empowering them for service.

While Moody's thoughts are well organized, his writings are not systematic. It may be helpful to think of Moody's work through three key concepts, often referred to as the "three R's," that tend to guide his beliefs and practices: (1) ruined by the fall, (2) redeemed by the blood, and (3) regenerated by the Spirit. Moody recognized that the ruin of the fall persists after our redemption. The Spirit's regeneration is not instant, but "Scripture teaches that in every believer there are two natures warring against each other." As such, the believer has an internal and external struggle. Christians needed to engage in a constellation of practices to help them overcome not only the world but their own old nature. Moody did not believe the world would get better through human effort. It was ruined by the fall. Those unredeemed by the blood of the Lamb and without the regeneration of the Spirit would ultimately repeat the fallen world's patterns. Without Christ, the world has no alternative pattern to follow. Moody's emphasis on individual salvation reflects his conviction that new life in Christ was a prerequisite to good works. Giving life is "the first work of the Spirit," and without life "there can be no power." Moody was aware of society's various ills. He simply believed those ills could not be sufficiently addressed by people who had dismissed "the eternal future by reason of love for passing things." Loving the world and its ways would not fix the world. The world needed Christ.

Secret Power

The books included in this collection reflect Moody's three core convictions in a variety of ways. *Secret Power* addresses the Holy Spirit, the Spirit's work in the lives of believers, and the ways believers can realize or hinder the Spirit's power for service. Once regenerated by the Holy Spirit, Christians need to tap into the Spirit's power. Without regeneration, humans are lost. They are incapable of overcoming sin's "ruin." Moody believed "the only cure for the accursed appetite is regeneration—a new life—the power of the risen Christ within us." He often highlighted the necessity of the Holy Spirit for Christian life and work. *Secret Power* begins by affirming "the Holy Spirit of God" as the needed source of the power. Later in the book, Moody notes,

> I believe this is a mistake a great many of us are making; we are trying to do God's work with the grace God gave us ten years ago. . . . Now what we want is a fresh supply, a fresh anointing and fresh power, and if we seek it, and seek it with all our hearts, we will obtain it.

Torrey also highlights Moody's interest in the Holy Spirit, noting, "Time and again Mr. Moody would come to me and say: 'Torrey, I want you to preach on baptism with the Holy Ghost.'"[44] In Moody's work, the Holy Spirit was an animating presence from whom Christians received the power for ministry. Following his experience in New York, Moody was convinced that all Christians needed the Holy Spirit's empowerment. Moody highlighted the difference between receiving the Holy Spirit and being fueled by Him, suggesting, "The Holy Spirit dwelling in us, is one thing . . . and the Holy Spirit upon us for service, is another thing." To be filled or anointed by the Holy Spirit was separate from the indwelling of the Holy Spirit at the point of salvation. Not everyone had the Spirit's power for service. One who has lost hope is "out of communion with God" and does not have "the Spirit of God resting upon him for service; he may be a son of God, and disheartened so that he cannot be used of God."

While the general focus of *Secret Power* concerns the Holy Spirit's work in the lives of individual Christians, Moody also believed that the Spirit worked in the body of Christ as a whole. For instance, Moody spoke to the danger of church division, saying that a divided church "cannot grow in divine things." In fact, "The Spirit of God does not work where there is division, and what we want today is the spirit of unity amongst God's children, so that the Lord may work." When God's people detach themselves from the Spirit and His sword, which is the Word of God, they become incapable of resisting the world because "the Church can not overcome the enemy [if] she don't know how to use the sword of the Spirit."

The Overcoming Life

In *The Overcoming Life*, Moody begins by dispelling a myth about Christian victory:

> When I was converted, I made this mistake: I thought the battle was already mine, the victory already won, the crown already in my grasp. . . . But I found out . . . conversion was only like enlisting in the army, that there was a battle on hand, and that if I was to get a crown, I had to work for it and fight for it.

Throughout the rest of the book, Moody describes the internal and external foes against which Christians do battle. He also discusses the characteristics believers must cultivate to overcome the world and their own flesh. The flesh and the world press us to work apart from God, but, as Moody says, "if we are going to overcome the world, we have got to work with God." Moody's perspective in *The Overcoming*

Life reminds Christians of the freedom that comes through regeneration. Left to our own devices, humans tend to give in to our desire to "shine above our fellows." As Christians align their lives to be guided by the Holy Spirit, they no longer need to compete to be the best because "not only can *one* obtain the prize, but *all* may have it if they will." God does not require us to be the best or strongest because "in the kingdom of God the very least and the very weakest may shine." In Christ, believers are freed from the burdens of competition and the trappings of worldly success.

Freedom ultimately involves repentance. God's people need to move beyond "the low standard of Christian living" that is "keeping a good many in the world and in their sins." The overcoming life is not lived on one's own terms or on terms set by the world. Moody believed Christians "must often go against the customs of the world." It is a life characterized by humility because "the lower we get, the higher God will lift us." In humility, we also "find rest on the bosom of the Son of God." The rest that is found in Christ comes as we "follow the will of God." Victory comes to the Christian in the same way it came to Christ: through the cross. Those who "want the crown but not the cross" don't understand that "if we are to be disciples of Jesus Christ, we have to take up our crosses daily." Victory is found in our willingness to conform our lives to Him because "the way of obedience is always the way of blessing."

Prevailing Prayer

Prevailing Prayer: What Hinders It? is perhaps the most practical of the three books included in this volume. While prayer is addressed in the first chapter, the book's focus is on "nine elements which are essential to true prayer." These essentials form a constellation of practices. Practicing prayer in isolation is, in Moody's mind, problematic because prayer alone is not an avenue to spiritual heights unknown but an activity made possible by other Christian practices. Moody addresses (1) the adoration of God, (2) confession of sin, (3) restitution for wrongs done, (4) thanksgiving for God's blessings, (5) forgiveness of sin, (6) unity of the church, (7) faith that God is present and active among us, (8) petition for the needs that are apparent to us, and (9) submission to God's will even if His will opposes our own. Prayer, as D. L. Moody recognized, is a point of individual and communal interaction with God comprehensible when practiced within a life of repentance. Such a life, in Moody's thought, is characterized by conviction, contrition, confession, conversion, and confession of Christ before the world.

As tempting as it may be to call prayer the cornerstone of Moody's life and thought, there is little evidence to suggest that Moody understood prayer to sit atop a hierarchy of Christian practices. For instance, at one point in *Prevailing Prayer*, he highlights the connection between Bible study and prayer, noting that without the Scriptures, "we shall be ignorant of the mind and will of God and become mystical and fanatical, and liable to be blown about by every wind of doctrine," whereas "if we read the Word and do not pray, we may become puffed up with knowledge, without the love that buildeth up." Prayer is not an isolated practice. Like one star within a constellation, it is part of a broader pattern comprised of other Christian practices. While unique and distinct, prayer gains intelligibility and power in relation to adoration, confession, restitution, thanksgiving, forgiveness, unity, faith, petition, and submission. It also offers intelligibility and power to these other practices. Prayer, in other words, arises from and contributes to a life of discipleship. That life of discipleship cannot be fully constituted by prayer alone.

At its worst, prayer can become an empty show of piety that manipulates others in an attempt to shape the world according to one's own image. At its best, however, prayer showcases our willingness to set aside our desire for control and to follow God even when we don't understand where He is going. Prayer nested within a life of discipleship is a means to express our gratitude to the God worthy of our complete devotion and to open ourselves up to His guidance so that our longings align ever more closely with those of the Master.

Conclusion

Dwight L. Moody was a faithful and flawed servant of the Lord. His description of the Christian life can be both convicting and comforting. His work pushes Christians toward small, consistent acts of obedience. Moody's simplicity is profound, and his insights into God and the Christian life are invaluable. As you read the works included in this volume, expect to be challenged by his words.

Moody was not some spiritual giant. He was a man used by God. He would not want anyone who reads his work to venerate him. Speaking to several pastors at a meeting in Northfield, Dwight Moody said, "Don't go away and talk so much about these meetings as about Christ; the world needs him."[45]

Secret Power

CONTENTS

Preface

One man may have "zeal without knowledge," while another may have knowledge without zeal. If I could have only the one, I believe I should choose the first; but, with an open Bible, no one need be without knowledge of God's will and purpose; and the object of this book is to help others to know the source of true power, that both their zeal and their knowledge may be of increased service in the Master's work. Paul says, "All Scripture is given by inspiration of God, and is profitable"; but I believe one portion, and that the subject of this book, has been too much overlooked, as though it were not practical, and the result is lack of power in testimony and work. If we would work, "not as one that beateth the air," but to some definite purpose, we must have this power from on high. Without this power, our work will be drudgery. With it, it becomes a joyful task, a refreshing service. May God make this book a blessing to many. This is my prayer.

D. L. Moody, Northfield, Massachusetts, May 1, 1881

1

Power—Its Source

Moody was concerned that God's people were ignorant of the Holy Spirit. In many ways, it isn't clear that the church's awareness of and dependence on the Holy Spirit is better today than it was in D. L. Moody's time. The Holy Spirit appears in doctrinal statements and becomes a flashpoint in debates about the cessation of sign gifts, but it isn't clear that the church today gives a great deal of time or energy to pursuing the empowerment of the Holy Spirit.

The talents and resources God has given to Christians, and the rest of humanity, allow us to accomplish great things without God—as, for instance, those who built the tower of Babel illustrate. However, in *Secret Power*, Moody rightly recognizes that any great things humans can accomplish pale in comparison to what humans can do when empowered by the Holy Spirit.

Writing before some of the more modern debates concerning the Holy Spirit that arose in the twentieth century, Dwight Moody's understanding of the Spirit was free from some of the baggage contemporary Christians might carry. As such, we need to take care to read

Moody on his own terms rather than importing our understandings onto his work. For instance, Moody speaks about being filled with the Spirit. This filling is, in Moody's thought, an empowerment for service. It allows believers to wield "the sword of the Spirit, which is the Word of God" (Eph. 6:17 ESV). Today the notion of being "filled with the Spirit" can often conjure up images of more extreme experiences such as being slain in the Spirit or speaking in tongues. Moody, as far as I am aware, does not reference these sorts of experiences but focuses on the more general point of the Spirit's role of empowering believers for the tasks God has set for them.

In this initial chapter, Moody focuses on the connection between the Holy Spirit and love. Referencing Romans 5:5 and the appearance of love in the fruit of the Spirit (Gal. 5:22), Moody fuses the work of the Holy Spirit with the cultivation of love. This emphasis on the connection between the Spirit and love is somewhat unique. Despite the importance of love in the Bible (e.g., Matt. 22:34–40), it often gets lost in considering other aspects of theology. Moody's emphasis on the Holy Spirit's role of producing love in our hearts points to his conviction that love of God and love of neighbor are crucial to the life of the believer.

———✳———

Without the soul, divinely quickened and inspired, the observances of the grandest ritualism are as worthless as the motions of a galvanized corpse.

Anonymous

I quote this sentence, as it leads me at once to the subject under consideration. What is this quickening and inspiration? What is this power needed? From whence its source? I reply: the Holy Spirit of God. I am a full believer in the Apostles' Creed, and therefore "I believe in the Holy Ghost."

A writer has pointedly asked: "What are our souls without His grace?—as dead as the branch in which the sap does not circulate. What is the Church without Him?—as parched and barren as the fields without the dew and rain of heaven."

There has been much inquiry of late on the subject of the Holy Spirit. In this and other lands thousands of persons have been giving attention to the study of this grand theme. I hope it will lead us all to pray for a greater manifestation of His power upon the whole Church of God.

How much we have dishonored Him in the past! How ignorant of His grace, love, and presence we have been. True, we have heard of Him and read of Him, but we have had little intelligent knowledge of His attributes, His offices, and His relations to us. I fear He has not been to many professed Christians an actual existence, nor is He known to them as a personality of the Godhead.

The first work of the Spirit is to give life; spiritual life. He gives it and He sustains it. If there is no life, there can be no power; Solomon says: "A living dog is better than a dead lion." When the Spirit imparts this life, He does not leave us to droop and die, but constantly fans the flame. He is ever with us. Surely we ought not to be ignorant of His power and His work.

Identity and Personality

In 1 John 5:7, we read: "There are three that bear record in heaven, the Father, the Word, and the Holy Ghost, and these three are one." By the Father is meant the first Person; Christ, the Word, is the second; and the Holy Spirit, perfectly fulfilling His own office and working in union with the Father and the Son, is the third. I find clearly presented in my Bible that the One God who demands my love, service, and worship has there revealed Himself, and that each of those three names of Father, Son, and Holy Ghost has personality attached to them.

Therefore we find some things ascribed to God as Father, some to God as Savior, and some to God as Comforter and Teacher. It has been remarked that the Father plans, the Son executes, and the Holy Spirit applies. But I also believe they plan and work together. The distinction of persons is often noted in Scripture. In Matthew 3:16–17, we find Jesus submitting to baptism, the Spirit descending upon Him, while the Father's voice of approval is heard saying: "This is My beloved Son in whom I am well pleased." Again in John 14:16, we read: "I [Jesus] will pray the Father, and He shall give you another Comforter." Also in Ephesians 2:18: "Through Him [Christ Jesus] we both [Jews and Gentiles] have access by one Spirit unto the Father." Thus we are taught the distinction of persons in the Godhead, and their inseparable union. From these and other Scriptures also we learn the identity and actual existence of the Holy Spirit.

If you ask do I understand what is thus revealed in Scripture, I say "no." But my faith bows down before the inspired Word, and I unhesitatingly believe the great things of God when even reason is blinded and the intellect confused.

In addition to the teaching of God's Word, the Holy Spirit in His gracious work in the soul declares His own presence. Through His agency we are "born again," and through His indwelling we possess superhuman power. Science, falsely so called, when arrayed against the existence and presence of the Spirit of God with His people, only exposes its own folly to the contempt of those who have become "new creatures in Christ Jesus." The Holy Spirit who inspired prophets and qualified apostles continues to animate, guide, and comfort all true believers.

To the actual Christian, the personality of the Holy Spirit is more real than any theory science has to offer, for so-called science is but calculation based on human observation and is constantly changing its inferences. But the existence of the Holy Spirit is to the child of God a matter of Scripture revelation and of actual experience.

Some skeptics assert that there is no other vital energy in the world but physical force, while contrary to their assertions, thousands and tens of thousands who cannot possibly be deceived have been quickened into spiritual life by a power neither physical or mental. Men who were dead in sins—drunkards who lost their will, blasphemers who lost their purity, libertines sunk in beastliness, infidels who published their shame to the world—have in numberless instances become the subjects of the Spirit's power and are now walking in the true nobility of Christian manhood, separated by an infinite distance from their former life.

Let others reject if they will, at their own peril, this imperishable truth. I believe, and am growing more into this belief, that divine, miraculous creative power resides in the Holy Ghost. Above and beyond all natural law, yet in harmony with it, creation, providence, the divine government, and the upbuilding of the Church of God are presided over by the Spirit of God. His ministration is the ministration of life more glorious than the ministration of law (2 Cor. 3:6–10). And like the eternal Son, the eternal Spirit, having life in Himself, is working out all things after the counsel of His own will, and for the everlasting glory of the Triune Godhead.

The Holy Spirit has all the qualities belonging to a person: the power to understand, to will, to do, to call, to feel, to love. This cannot be said of a mere influence. He possesses attributes and qualities which can only be ascribed to a person, as acts and deeds are performed by Him which cannot be performed by a machine, an influence, or a result.

Agent and Instrument

The Holy Spirit is closely identified with the words of the Lord Jesus: "It is the spirit that quickeneth; the flesh profiteth nothing: the words that I speak unto you, they are spirit, and they are life" (John 6:63). The gospel proclamation cannot be divorced from the Holy Spirit. Unless He attend the Word in power, vain will be the attempt in preaching it. Human eloquence or persuasiveness of speech are the mere trappings of the dead, if the living Spirit be absent; the prophet may preach to the bones in the valley, but it must be the breath from heaven which will cause the slain to live.

In 1 Peter 3:18 it reads, "For Christ also hath once suffered for sins, the just for the unjust, that He might bring us to God, being put to death in the flesh, but quickened by the Spirit." Here we see that Christ was raised up from the grave by this same Spirit, and the power exercised to raise Christ's dead body must raise our dead souls and quicken them. No other power on earth can quicken a dead soul but the same power that raised the body of Jesus Christ out of Joseph's sepulcher.

And if we want that power to quicken our friends who are dead in sin, we must look to God, and not be looking to man to do it. If we look alone to ministers, if we look alone to Christ's disciples to do this work, we shall be disappointed; but if we look to the Spirit of God and expect it to come from Him and Him alone, then we shall honor the Spirit, and the Spirit will do His work.

Secret of Efficiency

I cannot help but believe there are many Christians who want to be more efficient in the Lord's service, and the object of this book is to take up this subject of the Holy Spirit, that they may see from whom to expect this power. In the teaching of Christ, we find the last words recorded in the Gospel of Matthew: "Go ye, therefore, and teach all nations, baptizing them in the name of the Father, and of the Son, and of the Holy Ghost" (28:19). Here we find that the Holy Spirit and the Son are equal with the Father—are one with Him, "teaching them in the name of the Father, and of the Son, and of the Holy Ghost."

Christ was now handing His commission over to His apostles. He was going to leave them. His work on earth was finished, and He was now just about ready to take His seat at the right hand of

God, and He spoke unto them and said: "All power is given unto Me in heaven and on earth" (Matt. 28:18). All power, so then He had authority.

If Christ was mere man, as some people try to make out, it would have been blasphemy for Him to have said to the disciples, go and baptize all nations in the name of the Father, and in His own name, and in that of the Holy Ghost, making Himself equal with the Father.

There are three things: *All power* is given unto Me; go *teach all* nations. Teach them what? To *observe all* things. There are a great many people now that are willing to observe what they like about Christ, but the things that they don't like they just dismiss and turn away from. But His commission to His disciples was, "Go teach all nations to observe all things whatsoever I have commanded you." And what right has a messenger who has been sent of God to change the message?

If I had sent a servant to deliver a message, and the servant thought the message didn't sound exactly right—a little harsh—and that servant went and changed the message, I should change servants very quickly; he could not serve me any longer. And when a minister or a messenger of Christ begins to change the message because he thinks it is not exactly what it ought to be, and thinks he is wiser than God, God just dismisses that man.

They haven't taught "all things." They have left out some of the things that Christ has commanded us to teach because they didn't correspond with man's reason. Now we have to take the Word of God just as it is; and if we are going to take it, we have no authority to take out just what we like, what we think is appropriate, and let dark reason be our guide.

It is the work of the Spirit to impress the heart and seal the preached Word. His office is to take of the things of Christ and reveal them unto us.

Some people have got an idea that this is the only dispensation of the Holy Ghost, that He didn't work until Christ was glorified.

Secret Power

But Simeon felt the Holy Ghost when he went into the temple. In 2 Peter 1:21, we read: "For the prophecy came not in old time by the will of man: but holy men of God spake as they were moved by the Holy Ghost." We find the same Spirit in Genesis as is seen in Revelation. The same Spirit that guided the hand that wrote Exodus inspired also the epistles, and we find the same Spirit speaking from one end of the Bible to the other. So holy men in all ages have spoken as they were moved by the Holy Ghost.

His Personality

I was a Christian a long time before I found out that the Holy Ghost was a person. Now this is something a great many don't seem to understand, but if you will just take up the Bible and see what Christ had to say about the Holy Spirit, you will find that He always spoke of Him as a person—never spoke of Him as an influence.

Some people have an idea that the Holy Spirit is an attribute of God, just like mercy—just an influence coming from God. But we find in John 14:16 these words: "And I will pray the Father, and He shall give you another Comforter, that He may abide with you forever." That He may abide with you forever. And, again, in the same chapter, verse 17: "Even the Spirit of truth; whom the world cannot receive, because it seeth Him not, neither knoweth Him: but ye know Him; for He dwelleth with you, and shall be in you." Again, in verse 26: "But the Comforter, which is the Holy Ghost, whom the Father will send in my name, He shall teach you all things, and bring all things to your remembrance whatsoever I have said unto you."

Observe the pronouns "He" and "Him." I want to call attention to this fact that whenever Christ spoke of the Holy Ghost He spoke of Him as a person, not a mere influence; if we want to honor the Holy Ghost, let us bear in mind that He is one of the Trinity, a personality of the Godhead.

38

The Reservoir of Love

We read that the fruit of the Spirit is love. God is love, Christ is love, and we should not be surprised to read about the love of the Spirit. What a blessed attribute is this. May I call it the dome of the temple of the graces. Better still, it is the crown of crowns worn by the Triune God. Human love is a natural emotion which flows forth toward the object of our affections. But divine love is as high above human love as the heaven is above the earth. The natural man is of the earth, earthy, and however pure his love may be, it is weak and imperfect at best. But the love of God is perfect and entire, wanting nothing. It is as a mighty ocean in its greatness, dwelling with and flowing from the Eternal Spirit.

In Romans 5:5, we read: "and hope maketh not ashamed; because the love of God is shed abroad in our hearts by the Holy Ghost which is given unto us." Now if we are coworkers with God, there is one thing we must possess, and that is love. A man may be a very successful lawyer and have no love for his clients, and yet get on very well. A man may be a very successful physician and have no love for his patients, and yet be a very good physician; a man may be a very successful merchant and have no love for his customers, and yet he may do a good business and succeed; but no man can be a coworker with God without love. If our service is mere profession on our part, the quicker we renounce it the better. If a man takes up God's work as he would take up any profession, the sooner he gets out of it the better.

We cannot work for God without love. It is the only tree that can produce fruit on this sin-cursed earth that is acceptable to God. If I have no love for God nor for my fellow man, then I cannot work acceptably. I am like sounding brass and a tinkling cymbal. We are told that "the love of God is shed abroad in our hearts by the Holy Ghost." Now, if we have had that love shed abroad in our hearts, we are ready for God's service; if we have not, we are not ready. It is so easy to reach a man when you love him; all barriers are broken down and swept away.

Paul, when writing to Titus, tells him to be sound in faith, in charity, and in patience (2:1). Now in this age, ever since I can remember, the Church has been very jealous about men being unsound in the faith. If a man becomes unsound in the faith, they draw their ecclesiastical sword and cut at him; but he may be ever so unsound in love, and they don't say anything. He may be ever so defective in patience; he may be irritable and fretful all the time, but they never deal with him.

Now the Bible teaches us that we are not only to be sound in the faith but in charity and in patience. I believe God cannot use many of his servants because they are full of irritability and impatience; they are fretting all the time, from morning until night. God cannot use them; their mouths are sealed; they cannot speak for Jesus Christ, and if they have not love, they cannot work for God. I do not mean love for those that love me; it doesn't take grace to do that. The rudest person in the world can do that; the greatest heathen that ever lived can do that; the vilest man that ever walked the earth can do that. It doesn't take any grace at all. I did that before I ever became a Christian. Love begets love; hatred begets hatred. If I know a man loves me first, I know my love will be going out toward him.

Suppose a man comes to me, saying, "Mr. Moody, a certain man told me today that he thought you were the meanest man living." Well, if I didn't have a good deal of the grace of God in my heart, then I know there would be hard feelings that would spring up in my heart against that man, and it would not be long before I would be talking against him. Hatred begets hatred. But suppose a man comes to me and says, "Mr. Moody, do you know that such a man that I met today says that he thinks a great deal of you?" and though I may never have heard of him, there would be love springing up in my heart. Love begets love, we all know that; but it takes the grace of God to love the man that lies about me, the man that slanders me, the man that is trying to tear down my character; it takes the grace of God to love that man. You may hate the sin he has committed; there is a difference between the sin and the sinner; you may hate the one with a perfect hatred, but you must love the sinner. I cannot otherwise do him any good. Now you know the first impulse of a young convert is to love. Do you remember the day you were converted? Was not your heart full of sweet peace and love?

The Right Overflow

I remember the morning I came out of my room after I had first trusted Christ, and I thought the old sun shone a good deal brighter than it ever had before; I thought that the sun was just smiling upon me, and I walked out upon Boston Common, and I heard the birds in the trees, and I thought that they were all singing a song for me. Do you know I fell in love with the birds? I never cared for them before; it seemed to me that I was in love with all creation.

I had not a bitter feeling against any man, and I was ready to take all men to my heart. If a man has not the love of God shed abroad in his heart, he has never been regenerated. If you hear a person get up in prayer meeting, and he begins to speak and find fault with everybody, you may know that his is not a genuine conversion, that it is counterfeit; it has not the right ring, because the impulse of a converted soul is to love and not to be getting up and complaining of everyone else and finding fault.

But it is hard for us to live in the right atmosphere all the time. Someone comes along and treats us wrongly, perhaps we hate him; we have not attended to the means of grace and kept feeding on the Word of God as we ought. A root of bitterness springs up in our hearts, and perhaps we are not aware of it, but it has come up in our hearts; then we are not qualified to work for God. The love of God is not shed abroad in our hearts as it ought to be by the Holy Ghost.

But the work of the Holy Ghost is to impart love. Paul could say, "For the love of Christ constraineth us" (2 Cor. 5:14). He could not help going from town to town and preaching the gospel. Jeremiah at one time said: "I will speak no more in the Lord's name; I have suffered enough; these people don't like God's Word."

They lived in a wicked day, as we do now. Infidels were creeping up all around him who said the Word of God was not true; Jeremiah had stood like a wall of fire, confronting them, and he boldly proclaimed that the Word of God was true. At last they put him in prison, and he said: "I will keep still; it has cost me too much." But a little while after, you know, he could not keep still. His bones caught fire; he had to speak. And when we are so full of the love of God we are compelled to work for God, then God blesses us. If our work is sought to be accomplished by the lash, without any true motive power, it will come to nought.

Now the question comes up, Have we the love of God shed abroad in our hearts, and are we holding the truth in love? Some people hold the truth, but in such a cold, stern way that it will do no good. Other people want to love everything, and so they give up much of the truth; but we are to hold the truth in love. We are to hold the truth even if we lose all, but we are to hold it in love, and if we do that, the Lord will bless us.

There are a good many people trying to get this love; they are trying to produce it of themselves. But therein all fail. The love implanted deep in our new nature will be spontaneous. I don't have to learn to love my children. I cannot help loving them.

I said to a young miss some time ago, in an inquiry meeting, who said that she could not love God; that it was very hard for her to love Him—I said to her, "Is it hard for you to love your mother? Do you have to learn to love your mother?"

And she looked up through her tears, and said, "No; I can't help it; that is spontaneous." "Well," I said, "when the Holy Spirit kindles love in your heart, you cannot help loving God; it will be spontaneous."

When the Spirit of God comes into your heart and mine, it will be easy to serve God.

The fruit of the Spirit, as you find it in Galatians, begins with love. There are nine graces spoken of in the sixth chapter, and of the nine different graces Paul puts love at the head of the list; love is the first thing—the first in that precious cluster of fruit. Someone has put it in this way: that all the other eight can be put in the word *love*. Joy is love exulting; peace is love in repose; longsuffering is love on trial; gentleness is love in society; goodness is love in action; faith is love on the battlefield; meekness is love at school; and temperance is love in training.

So it is love all the way: love at the top, love at the bottom, and all the way along down these graces; and if we only just brought forth the fruit of the Spirit, what a world we would have. There would be no need of any policemen; a man could leave his overcoat around without someone stealing it; men would not have any desire to do evil.

Says Paul, "Against such there is no law"; you don't need any law. A man who is full of the Spirit doesn't need to be put under law, doesn't need any policemen to watch him. We could dismiss all our policemen; the lawyers would have to give up practicing law, and the courts would not have any business.

The Triumphs of Hope

In Romans 15:13, the apostle says: "Now the God of hope fill you with all joy and peace in believing, that you may abound in hope through the power of the Holy Ghost." The next thing then is hope.

Did you ever notice this, that no man or woman is ever used by God to build up His kingdom who has lost hope? Now, I have been observing this throughout different parts of the country, and wherever I have found a worker in God's vineyard who has lost hope, I have found a man or woman not very useful.

Now, just look at these workers. Let your mind go over the past for a moment. Can you think of a man or woman whom God has used to build His kingdom who has lost hope? I don't know of any; I never heard of such a one. It is very important to have hope in the Church; and it is the work of the Holy Ghost to impart hope.

Let Him come into some of the churches where there have not been any conversions for a few years, and let Him convert a score of people, and see how hopeful the Church becomes at once. He imparts hope; a man filled with the Spirit of God will be very hopeful. He will be looking out into the future, and he knows that it is all bright, because the God of all grace is able to do great things. So it is very important that we have hope.

If a man has lost hope, he is out of communion with God; he has not the Spirit of God resting upon him for service; he may be a son of God, and disheartened so that he cannot be used of God. Do you know, there is no place in the Scriptures where it is recorded that God ever used even a discouraged man.

Some years ago, in my work I was quite discouraged, and I was ready to hang my harp on the willow. I was very much cast down and depressed. I had been for weeks in that state, when one Monday morning a friend who had a very large Bible class came into my study. I used to examine the notes of his Sunday school lessons, which were equal to a sermon, and he came to me this morning and said, "Well, what did you preach about yesterday?" and I told him.

I said, "What did you preach about?" and he said that he preached about Noah.

"Did you ever preach about Noah?"

"No, I never preached about Noah."

"Did you ever study his character?"

"No, I never studied his life particularly."

"Well," says he, "he is a most wonderful character. It will do you good. You ought to study up that character."

When he went out, I took down my Bible and read about Noah; and then it came over me that Noah worked 120 years and never had a convert, and yet he did not get discouraged; and I said, "Well, I ought not to be discouraged," and I closed my Bible, got up, and walked downtown, and the cloud had gone. I went down to the noon prayer meeting, and heard of a little town in the country where they had taken into the church one hundred young converts, and I said to myself, *I wonder what Noah would have given if he could have heard that.* And yet he worked 120 years and didn't get discouraged.

And then a man right across the aisle got up and said, "My friends, I wish you to pray for me; I think I'm lost"; and I thought to myself, *I wonder what Noah would have given to hear that.* He never heard a man say, "I wish you to pray for me; I think I am lost," and yet he didn't get discouraged!

Oh, children of God, let us not get discouraged; let us ask God to forgive us, if we have been discouraged and cast down; let us ask God to give us hope, that we may be ever hopeful. It does me good sometimes to meet some people and take hold of their hands, they are so hopeful; while other people throw a gloom over me because they are all the time cast down, and looking at the dark side, and looking at the obstacles and difficulties that are in the way.

The Boon of Liberty

The next thing the Spirit of God does is to give us liberty. He first imparts love; He next inspires hope and then gives liberty, and that is about the last thing we have in a good many of our churches at the present day. And I am sorry to say there must be a funeral in a good many churches before there is much work done; we shall have to bury the formalism so deep that it will never have any resurrection. The last thing to be found in many a church is liberty.

If the gospel happens to be preached, the people criticize as they would a theatrical performance. It is exactly the same, and many a professed Christian never thinks of listening to what the man of God has to say. It is hard work to preach to carnally minded critics, but "Where the Spirit of the Lord is, there is liberty" (2 Cor. 3:17).

Very often a woman will hear a hundred good things in a sermon, and there may be one thing that strikes her as a little out of place, and she will go home and sit down to the table and talk right out before her children and magnify that one wrong thing, and not say a word about the hundred good things that were said. That is what people do who criticize.

God does not use men in captivity. The condition of many is like Lazarus when he came out of the sepulcher bound hand and foot. The bandage was not taken off his mouth, and he could not speak. He had life, and if you had said Lazarus was not alive, you would have told a falsehood, because he was raised from the dead. There are a great many people, the moment you talk to them and insinuate they are not doing what they might, they say, "I have life. I am a Christian." Well, you can't deny it, but they are bound hand and foot.

May God snap these fetters and set His children free, that they may have liberty. I believe He comes to set us free and wants us to work for Him and speak for Him. How many people would like to get up in a social prayer meeting to say a few words for Christ, but there is such a cold spirit of criticism in the church that they dare not do it. They have not the liberty to do it. If they get up, they are so frightened with these critics that they begin to tremble and sit down. They cannot say anything. Now, that is all wrong.

The Spirit of God comes just to give liberty, and wherever you see the Lord's work going on, you will see that Spirit of liberty. People won't be afraid of speaking to one another. And when the meeting is over they will not get their hats and see how quickly they can get out of the church but will begin to shake hands with one another, and there will be liberty there. A good many go to the prayer meeting out of a mere cold sense of duty. They think *I must attend because I feel it is my duty.* They don't think it is a glorious privilege to meet and pray, and to be strengthened, and to help someone else in the wilderness journey.

What we need today is love in our hearts. Don't we want it? Don't we want hope in our lives? Don't we want to be hopeful? Don't we want liberty? Now, all this is the work of the Spirit of God, and let us pray God daily to give us love, and hope, and liberty. We read in Hebrews 10:19, "Having, therefore, brethren, boldness to enter into the holiest by the blood of Jesus." If you will turn to the passage and read the margin, it says: "Having, therefore, brethren, *liberty* to enter into the holiest." We can go into the holiest, having freedom of access, and plead for this love and liberty and glorious hope, that we may not rest until God gives us the power to work for Him.

If I know my own heart today, I would rather die than live as I once did, a mere nominal Christian, and not used by God in building up His kingdom. It seems a poor empty life to live for the sake of self.

Let us seek to be useful. Let us seek to be vessels meet for the Master's use, that God, the Holy Spirit, may shine fully through us.

> Know, my soul, thy full salvation;
> Rise o'er sin, and fear, and care;
> Joy to find, in every station,
> Something still to do or bear.
>
> Think what Spirit dwells within thee;
> Think what Father's smiles are thine;
> Think that Jesus died to win thee:
> Child of heaven, canst thou repine?
>
> Haste thee on from grace to glory,
> Armed by faith, and winged by prayer,
> Heaven's eternal day's before thee:
> God's own hand shall guide thee there.
>
> Soon shall close thy earthly mission,
> Soon shall pass thy pilgrim days,

Hope shall change to glad fruition,
Faith to sight, and prayer to praise.

I am so weak, dear Lord! I cannot stand
One moment without Thee;
But oh, the tenderness of Thy enfolding,
And oh, the faithfulness of Thine upholding,
And oh, the strength of Thy right hand!
That strength is enough for me.

I am so needy, Lord! and yet I know
All fullness dwells in Thee;
And hour by hour that never-failing treasure
Supplies and fills in overflowing measure
My last and greatest need. And so
Thy grace is enough for me.

It is so sweet to trust Thy Word alone!
I do not ask to see
The unveiling of Thy purpose, or the shining
Of future light on mysteries untwining;
Thy promise-roll is all my own—
Thy Word is enough for me.

There were strange soul-depths, restless, vast, and broad,
Unfathomed as the sea,
An infinite craving for some infinite stilling;
But now Thy perfect love is perfect filling!
Lord Jesus Christ, my Lord, my God,
Thou, Thou art enough for me!

2

Power "In" and "Upon"

After his experience with the Holy Spirit in New York, Moody knew the Holy Spirit in a different way. The Spirit fueled and guided him. He did not simply have the Holy Spirit "in" him, but "upon" him. Moody makes this distinction in a number of ways and at a number of different points. For Moody, the indwelling of the Holy Spirit was a consequence of faith in Christ, yet being empowered by the Holy Spirit was a separate matter.

Moody sees a difference between having the Holy Spirit's indwelling and having the Spirit upon us for service. The Spirit's power is not given so that we can pursue our own interests. It is given so that we can pursue the interests of God's kingdom. For Moody, this power for service is, to some large degree, driven by our knowledge of and conformity to God's Word. We may see examples of this in differentiation in biblical passages such as Ephesians 5:13 and various Old Testament references to the Holy Spirit coming upon, for instance, the biblical judges (Judg. 3:10; 6:34; 11:29; 13:25; 14:6, 19; 15:14). Whether or not Moody's "in" and "upon" paradigm is the best way to describe it, the ministry of the Spirit certainly seems to involve more than just indwelling. There is a discernible differentiation between indwelling and empowerment. Under the new covenant, the Holy Spirit dwells within individual believers and in the body of Christ collectively. Moody does not deny that. He does, however, highlight the further work of the Holy Spirit that seems to be distinct from indwelling. The empowerment for service is a distinct activity that, in Moody's view, is to be sought after by all Christians.

Perhaps the most controversial aspect of Moody's teachings in this chapter to our modern ears involves waiting for the Holy Spirit. Citing Luke 24:49, Moody makes the point that moving forward without the empowerment of the Holy Spirit is a mistake. Waiting for the Holy Spirit to empower one for service is not a waste of time. This emphasis highlights Moody's conviction that the church can do more with the Holy Spirit's power (the Spirit being "upon" believers) than we ever could working in our own power (having the Spirit "in" us but not "upon" us). While we may wish to debate the finer points of his interpretation or his theology, it is important to hear his basic message rather than losing the proverbial forest for the trees. God's people need the Holy Spirit. They need to know how to avoid quenching the Spirit and how to go about being empowered by the Holy Spirit. The Holy Spirit needs to be a part of the church's life if we are to be empowered for ministry.

———*———

You remember that strange, half-involuntary "forty years" of Moses in the "wilderness" of Midian, when he had fled from Egypt. You remember, too, the almost equally strange years of retirement in "Arabia" by Paul, when, if ever, humanly speaking, instant action was needed. And preeminently you remember the amazing charge of the ascending Lord to the disciples, "Tarry at Jerusalem." Speaking after the manner of men, one could not have wondered if outspoken Peter or fervid James had said: "Tarry, Lord! How long?" "Tarry, Lord! Is there not a perishing world, groaning for the 'good news'?" "Tarry! Did we hear Thee aright, Lord? Was the word not haste?" "Nay;" "Being assembled together with them, He commanded them that they should not depart from Jerusalem, but wait for the promise of the Father." (Acts 1:4)

Grosart

The Holy Spirit dwelling in us is one thing; I think this is clearly brought out in Scripture; and the Holy Spirit upon us for service is another thing. Now there are only three places we find in Scripture that are dwelling places for the Holy Ghost.

In Exodus 40:33–35 are these words:

And he reared up the court round about the tabernacle and the altar, and set up the hanging of the court gate. So Moses finished the work.

Then a cloud covered the tent of the congregation, and the glory of the LORD filled the tabernacle.

And Moses was not able to enter into the tent of the congregation, because the cloud abode thereon, and the glory of the LORD filled the tabernacle.

The moment that Moses finished the work, the moment that the tabernacle was ready, the cloud came, the Shekinah glory came and filled it so that Moses was not able to stand before the presence of the Lord. I believe firmly that the moment our hearts are emptied of pride and selfishness and ambition and self-seeking, and everything that is contrary to God's law, the Holy Ghost will come and fill every corner of our hearts; but if we are full of pride and conceit, and ambition and self-seeking, and pleasure and the world, there is no room for the Spirit of God; and I believe many a man is praying to God to fill him when he is full already with something else. Before we pray that God would fill us, I believe we ought to pray Him to empty us.

There must be an emptying before there can be a filling; and when the heart is turned upside down, and everything is turned out that is contrary to God, then the Spirit will come, just as He did in the tabernacle, and fill us with His glory. We read in 2 Chronicles 5:13–14:

> It came even to pass, as the trumpeters and singers were as one to make one Sound, to be heard in praising and thanking the LORD, and when they lifted up their voice with the trumpets and cymbals and instruments of musick, and praised the LORD, saying, For He is good; for His mercy endureth forever: that then the house was filled with a cloud, even the house of the LORD. So that the priests could not stand to minister by reason of the cloud: for the glory of the LORD had filled the house of God.

Praising with One Heart

We find, the very moment that Solomon completed the temple, when all was finished, they were just praising God with one heart—the choristers and the singers and the ministers were all one; there was not any discord; they were all praising God, and the glory of God came and just filled the temple as the tabernacle.

Now, as you turn over into the New Testament, you will find, instead of coming to tabernacles and temples, believers are now the temple of the Holy Ghost. When, on the day of Pentecost, before Peter preached that memorable sermon, as they were praying, the Holy Ghost came, and came in mighty power. We now pray for the Spirit of God to come, and we sing:

> Come, Holy Spirit, heavenly dove,
> With all Thy quickening power;
> Kindle a flame of heavenly love
> In these cold hearts of ours.

I believe, if we understand it, it is perfectly right; but if we are praying for Him to come out of heaven down to earth again, that is wrong, because He is already here; He has not been out of this earth for 1,800 years; He has been in the Church, and He is with all believers; the believers in the Church are the called-out ones; they are called out from the world, and every true believer is a temple for the Holy Ghost to dwell in.

In John 14:17, we have the words of Jesus: "Even the Spirit of truth; whom the world cannot receive, because it seeth Him not, neither knoweth Him: but ye know Him; for He dwelleth with you, and shall be in you."

"Greater is He that is in you than he that is in the world" (1 John 4:4). If we have the Spirit dwelling in us, He gives us power over the flesh and the world, and over every enemy. He is dwelling with you, and shall be in you.

Read 1 Corinthians 3:16: "Know ye not that ye are the temple of God, and that the Spirit of God dwelleth in you?"

There were some men burying an aged saint some time ago, and he was very poor, like many of God's people, poor in this world. But they are very rich; they have all the riches on the other side of life—they have them laid up there where thieves cannot get them, and where sharpers cannot take them away from them, and where moth cannot corrupt—so this aged man was very rich in the other world, and they were just hastening him off to the grave, wanting to get rid of him, when an old minister, who was officiating at the grave, said, "Tread softly, for you are carrying the temple of the Holy Ghost." Whenever you see a believer, you see a temple of the Holy Ghost.

In 1 Corinthians 6:19–20, we read again: "Know ye not that your body is the temple of the Holy Ghost which is in you, which ye have of God, and ye are not your own? For ye are bought with a price: therefore glorify God in your body, and in your spirit, which are God's." Thus are we taught that there is a divine resident in every child of God.

I think it is clearly taught in Scripture that every believer has the Holy Ghost dwelling in him. He may be quenching the Spirit of God, and he may not glorify God as he should, but if he is a believer on the Lord Jesus Christ, the Holy Ghost dwells in him. But I want to call your attention to another fact. I believe today, that though Christian men and women have the Holy Spirit dwelling in them, yet He is not dwelling within them in power; in other words, God has a great many sons and daughters without power.

What Is Needed

Nine-tenths, at least, of church members never think of speaking for Christ. If they see a man, perhaps a near relative, just going right down to ruin, going rapidly, they never think of speaking to him about his sinful course and of seeking to win him to Christ. Now certainly there must be something wrong. And yet when you talk with them, you find they have faith, and you cannot say they are not children of God; but they have not the power, they have not the liberty, they have not the love that real disciples of Christ should have.

A great many people are thinking that we need new measures, that we need new churches, that we need new organs, and that we need new choirs, and all these new things. That is not what the Church of God needs today. It is the old power that the apostles had; that is what we want, and if we have that in our churches, there will be new life. Then we will have new ministers—the same old ministers renewed with power; filled with the Spirit.

I remember when in Chicago many were toiling in the work, and it seemed as though the car of salvation didn't move on, when a minister began to cry out from the very depths of his heart, "Oh, God, put new ministers in every pulpit." On next Monday I heard two or three men stand up and say, "We had a new minister last Sunday—the same old minister, but he had got new power."

I firmly believe that is what we want today all over America. We want new ministers in the pulpit and new people in the pews. We want people quickened by the Spirit of God, and the Spirit coming down and taking possession of the children of God and giving them power.

Then a man filled with the Spirit will know how to use "the sword of the Spirit." If a man is not filled with the Spirit, he will never know how to use the Book. We are told that this is the sword of the Spirit; and what is an army good for that does not know how to use its weapons? Suppose a battle was going on, and I were a general and had a hundred thousand men—great, able-bodied men, full of life—but they could not one of them handle a sword, and not one of them knew how to use his rifle. What would that army be good for? Why, one thousand well-drilled men, with good weapons, would rout the whole of them.

The reason why the Church cannot overcome the enemy is because she doesn't know how to use the sword of the Spirit. People will get up and try to fight the devil with their experiences, but he doesn't care for that, he will overcome them every time. People are trying to fight the devil with theories and pet ideas, but he will get the victory over them likewise. What we want is to draw the sword of the Spirit. It is that which cuts deeper than anything else.

Turn in your Bibles to Ephesians 6:14–17:

Stand therefore, having your loins girt about with truth, and having on the breastplate of righteousness;

And your feet shod with the preparation of the gospel of peace;

Above all, taking the shield of faith, wherewith ye shall be able to quench all the fiery darts of the wicked.

And take the helmet of salvation, and the sword of the Spirit, which is the word of God.

The Greatest Weapon

The sword of the Spirit is the Word of God, and what we need specially is to be filled with the Spirit, so we shall know how to use the Word.

There was a Christian man talking to a skeptic, who was using the Word, and the skeptic said, "I don't believe, sir, in that Book." But the man went right on and he gave him more of the Word; and the man again remarked, "I don't believe the Word," but he kept giving him more, and at last the man was reached.

And the brother added, "When I have proved a good sword which does the work of execution, I would just keep right on using it." That is what we want.

Skeptics and infidels may say they don't believe in it. It is not our work to make them believe in it; that is the work of the Spirit. Our work is to give them the Word of God, not to preach our theories and our ideas about it but just to deliver the message as God gives it to us.

We read in the Scriptures of the sword of the Lord and Gideon. Suppose Gideon had gone out without the Word; he would have been defeated. But the Lord used Gideon, and I think you find all through the Scriptures, God takes up and uses human instruments.

You cannot find, I believe, a case in the Bible where a man is converted without God calling in some human agency—using some human instrument; not but what He can do it in His independent sovereignty, there is no doubt about that. Even when by the revealed glory of the Lord Jesus, Saul of Tarsus was smitten to the earth, Ananias was used to open his eyes and lead him into the light of the gospel. I heard a man once say, if you put a man on a mountain peak, higher than one of the alpine peaks, God could save him without a human messenger, but that is not His way, that is not His method; it is "the sword of the Lord and Gideon," and the Lord and Gideon will do the work, and if we are just willing to let the Lord use us, He will.

None of Self

Then you will find all through the Scriptures, when men were filled with the Holy Spirit, they preached Christ and not themselves.

They preached Christ and Him crucified. It says in Luke 1:67–70, speaking of Zacharias, the father of John the Baptist:

> And his father, Zacharias, was filled with the Holy Ghost, and prophesied, saying:
> Blessed be the Lord God of Israel, for He hath visited and redeemed His people,
> And hath raised up an horn of salvation for us in the house of His servant David.
> As He spake by the mouth of His holy prophets, which have been since the world began.

See, he is talking about the Word. If a man is filled with the Spirit, he will magnify the Word; he will preach the Word and not himself; he will give this lost world the Word of the living God.

> And thou, child, shalt be called the prophet of the Highest; for thou shalt go before the face of the Lord to prepare His ways;
> To give knowledge of salvation unto His people by the remission of their sins,
> Through the tender mercy of our God, whereby the dayspring from on high hath visited us,
> To give light to them that sit in darkness and in the shadow of death, to guide our feet into the way of peace.
> And the child grew, and waxed strong in spirit, and was in the deserts till the day of his shewing unto Israel. (1:76–80)

And so we find again that when Elizabeth and Mary met, they talked of the Scriptures, and they were both filled with the Holy Ghost, and at once began to talk of their Lord.

We also find that Simeon, as he came into the temple and found the young child Jesus there, at once began to quote the Scriptures, for the Spirit was upon him. And when Peter stood up on the day of Pentecost, and preached that wonderful sermon, it is said he was filled with the Holy Ghost and began to preach the Word to the multitude, and it was the Word that cut them.

It was the sword of the Lord and Peter, the same as it was the sword of the Lord and Gideon. And we find it says of Stephen, "They were not able to resist the spirit and wisdom by which he spake" (Acts 6:10). Why? Because he gave them the Word of God. And we are told that the Holy Ghost came on Stephen, and none could resist his Word. And we read, too, that Paul was full of the Holy Spirit, and that he preached Christ and Him crucified, and that many people were added to the Church. Barnabas was full of faith and the Holy Ghost; and if you will just read and find out what he preached, you will find it was the Word, and many were added to the Lord. So that when a man is full of the Spirit, he begins to preach not himself but Christ, as revealed in the Holy Scriptures.

The disciples of Jesus were all filled with the Spirit, and the Word was published. And when the Spirit of God comes down upon the Church, and we are anointed, the Word will be published in the streets, in the lanes, and in the alleys; there will not be a dark cellar nor a dark attic, nor a home where the gospel will not be carried by some loving heart, if the Spirit comes upon God's people in demonstration and in power.

Spiritual Irrigation

It is possible a man may just barely have life and be satisfied, and I think that a great many are in that condition. In John 3 we find that Nicodemus came to Christ and that he received life. At first this life was feeble. You don't hear of him standing up confessing Christ boldly, or of the Spirit coming upon him in great power, though possessing life through faith in Christ. And then turn to chapter 4 of John, and you will find it speaks of the woman coming to the well of Samaria, and Christ held out the cup of salvation to her and she took it and drank, and it became in her "a well of water springing up into everlasting life" (v. 14). That is better than in chapter 3 of John; here it came down in a flood into her soul. As someone has said, it came down from the throne of God, and like a mighty current carried her back to the throne of God. Water always rises to its level, and if we get the soul filled with water from the throne of God it will bear us upward to its source.

But if you want to get the best class of Christian life portrayed, turn to chapter 7 and you will find that it says he that receiveth the Spirit, through trusting in the Lord Jesus, "out of him shall flow rivers of living water" (v. 38).

Now there are two ways of digging a well. I remember, when a boy upon a farm in New England, they had a well, and they put in an old wooden pump, and I used to have to pump the water from that well upon washday, and to water the cattle; and I had to pump and pump and pump until my arm got tired, many a time. But they have a better way now; they don't dig down a few feet and brick up the hole and put the pump in, but they go down through the clay and the sand and the rock, and on down until they strike what they call a lower stream, and then it becomes an artesian well, which needs no labor, as the water rises spontaneously from the depths beneath.

Now I think God wants all His children to be a sort of artesian well; not to keep pumping, but to flow right out. Why, haven't you seen ministers in the pulpit just pumping and pumping and pumping? I have, many a time, and I have had to do it too. I know how it is. They stand in the pulpit and talk and talk and talk, and the people go to sleep; they can't arouse them. What is the trouble? Why, the living water is not there; they are just pumping when there is no water in the well.

You can't get water out of a dry well; you have to get something in the well, or you can't get anything out. I have seen these wooden pumps where you had to pour water into them before you could pump any water out, and so it is with a good many people; you have to get something in them before you can get any out.

People wonder why it is that they have no spiritual power. They stand up and talk in meeting, and don't say anything. They say they haven't anything to say, and you find it out soon enough; they need not state it, but they just talk because they feel it is a duty, and say nothing.

Now I tell you when the Spirit of God is on us for service, resting upon us, we are anointed, and then we can do great things. "I will pour water on him that is thirsty," says God (Isa. 44:3). O, blessed thought—"He that hungers and thirsts after righteousness shall be filled!"

Outflowing Streams

I would like to see someone just full of living water, so full that they couldn't contain it; that they would have to go out and publish the gospel of the grace of God. When a man gets so full that he can't hold any more, then he is just ready for God's service.

When preaching in Chicago, Dr. Gibson remarked in the inquiry meeting, "Now, how can we find out who is thirsty?" Said he, "I was just thinking how we could find out. If a boy should come down the aisle, bringing a good pail full of clear water, and a dipper, we would soon find out who was thirsty; we would see thirsty men and women reach out for water; but if you should walk down the aisle with an empty bucket, you wouldn't find it out. People would look in and see that there was no water, and say nothing." So said he, "I think that is the reason we are not more blessed in our ministry; we are carrying around empty buckets, and the people see that we have not anything in them, and they don't come forward."

I think that there is a good deal of truth in that. People see that we are carrying around empty buckets, and they will not come to us until the buckets are filled. They see we haven't any more than they have. We must have the Spirit of God resting upon us, and then we will have something that gives the victory over the world, the flesh, and the devil; something that gives the victory over our tempers, over our conceits, and over every other evil. When we can trample these sins under our feet, then people will come to us and say, "How did you get it? I need this power; you have something that I haven't got; I want it."

Oh, may God show us this truth. Have we been toiling all night? Let us throw the net on the right side; let us ask God to forgive our sins and anoint us with power from on high. But remember, He is not going to give this power to an impatient man; He is not going to give it to a selfish man; He will never give it to an ambitious man whose aim is selfish, till first emptied of self, emptied of pride and of all worldly thoughts. Let it be God's glory and not our own that we seek, and when we get to that point, how speedily the Lord will bless us for good. Then will the measure of our blessing be full.

Do you know what heaven's measure is? "Good measure, pressed down, shaken together, and running over" (Luke 6:38). If we get our heart filled with the Word of God, how is Satan going to get in? How is the world going to get in, for heaven's measure is good measure, full measure, running over. Have you this fullness? If you have not, then seek it; say by the grace of God you will have it, for it is the Father's good pleasure to give us these things.

He wants us to shine down in this world; He wants to lift us up for His work; He wants us to have the power to testify for His Son. He has left us in this world to testify for Him. What did He leave us for? Not to buy and sell and to get gain, but to glorify Christ. How are you going to do it without the Spirit? That is the question. How are you to do it without the power of God?

Why Some Fail

We read in John 20:22: "And when He had said this, He breathed on them, and saith unto them, Receive ye the Holy Ghost."

Then see Luke 24:49: "And, behold, I send the promise of My Father upon you; but tarry ye in the city of Jerusalem until ye be endued with power from on high."

The first passage tells us He had raised those pierced and wounded hands over them and breathed upon them and said, "Receive ye the Holy Ghost." And I haven't a doubt they received it then, but not in such mighty power as afterward when qualified for their work. It was not in fullness that He gave it to them then, but if they had been like a good many now, they would have said, "I have enough now; I am not going to tarry, I am going to work."

Some people seem to think they are losing time if they wait on God for His power, and so away they go and work without unction; they are working without any anointing, they are working without any power. But after Jesus had said "Receive ye the Holy Ghost," and had breathed on them, He said: "Now you tarry in Jerusalem until you be endued with power from on high." Read Acts 1:8: "But ye shall receive power, after that the Holy Ghost is come upon you: and ye shall be witnesses unto Me both in Jerusalem, and in all Judaea, and in Samaria, and unto the uttermost part of the earth."

Now, the Spirit had been given them certainly or they could not have believed, and they could not have taken their stand for God and gone through what they did, and endured the scoffs and frowns of their friends, if they had not been converted by the power of the Holy Ghost. But now just see what Christ said: "ye shall receive power, after that the Holy Ghost is come upon you: and ye shall be witnesses unto Me both in Jerusalem, and in all Judaea, and in Samaria, and unto the uttermost part of the earth" (Acts 1:8).

Then, the Holy Spirit *in us* is one thing, and the Holy Spirit *on us* is another; and if these Christians had gone out and went right to preaching then and there, without the power, do you think that scene would have taken place on the day of Pentecost? Don't you think that Peter would have stood up there and beat against the air, while these Jews would have gnashed their teeth and mocked him? But they tarried in Jerusalem; they waited ten days.

"What!" you say. "What, the world perishing and men dying! Shall I wait?" Do what God tells you. There is no use in running before you are sent; there is no use in attempting to do God's work without God's power. A man working without this unction, a man working without this anointing, a man working without the Holy Ghost upon him, is losing his time after all.

So we are not going to lose anything if we tarry till we get this power. That is the object of true service, to wait on God, to tarry till we receive this power for witness-bearing. Then we find that on the day of Pentecost, ten days after Jesus Christ was glorified, the Holy Spirit descended in power. Do you think that Peter and James and John and those apostles doubted it from that very hour? They never doubted it. Perhaps some question the possibility of having the power of God now, and that the Holy Spirit never came afterward in similar manifestation, and will never come again in such power.

Fresh Supplies

Turn to Acts 4:31, and you will find He came a second time, and at a place where they were, so that the earth was shaken, and they were filled with this power. The fact is, we are leaky vessels, and we have to keep right under the fountain all the time to keep full of Christ, and so have a fresh supply.

I believe this is a mistake a great many of us are making; we are trying to do God's work with the grace God gave us ten years ago. We say, if it is necessary, we will go on with the same grace. Now, what we want is a fresh supply, a fresh anointing and fresh power, and if we seek it, and seek it with all our hearts, we will obtain it.

The early converts were taught to look for that power. Philip went to Samaria, and news reached Jerusalem that there was a great work being done in Samaria, and many converts; and John and Peter went down, and they laid their hands on them, and they received the Holy Ghost for service. I think that is what we Christians ought to be looking for—the Spirit of God for service—that God may use us mightily in the building up of His Church and hastening His glory.

In Acts 19 we read of twelve men at Ephesus, who, when the inquiry was made if they had received the Holy Ghost since they believed, answered: "We have not so much as heard whether there be any Holy Ghost." I venture to say there are very many, who, if you were to ask them, "Have you received the Holy Ghost since you believed?" would reply, "I don't know what you mean by that." They would be like the twelve men down at Ephesus, who had never understood the peculiar relation of the Spirit to the sons of God in this dispensation.

I firmly believe that the Church has just laid this knowledge aside, mislaid it somewhere, and so Christians are without power. Sometimes you can take one hundred members into the Church, and they don't add to its power. Now that is all wrong. If they were only anointed by the Spirit of God, there would be great power if one hundred saved ones were added to the Church.

Green Fields

When I was out in California, the first time I went down from the Sierra Nevada Mountains and dropped into the Valley of the Sacramento, I was surprised to find on one farm that everything about it was green—all the trees and flowers, everything was blooming, and everything was green and beautiful, and just across the hedge everything was dried up, and there was not a green thing there, and I could not understand it. I made inquiries, and I found that the man that had everything green, irrigated; he just poured the water right on, and he kept everything green, while the fields that were next to his were as dry as Gideon's fleece without a drop of dew; and so it is with a great many in the

Church today. They are like these farms in California—a dreary desert, everything parched and desolate, and apparently no life in them. They can sit next to a man who is full of the Spirit of God, who is like a green bay tree, and who is bringing forth fruit, and yet they will not seek a similar blessing. Well, why this difference? Because God has poured water on him that was thirsty; that is the difference. One has been seeking this anointing, and he has received it; and when we want this above everything else God will surely give it to us.

The great question before us now is, *Do* we want it? I remember when I first went to England and gave a Bible reading, I think about the first that I gave in that country; a great many ministers were there, and I didn't know anything about English theology, and I was afraid I should run against their creeds, and I was a little hampered, especially on this very subject, about the gift of the Holy Spirit for service. I remember particularly a Christian minister there who had his head bowed on his hand, and I thought the good man was ashamed of everything I was saying, and of course that troubled me. At the close of my address he took his hat and away he went, and then I thought, *Well, I shall never see him again.*

At the next meeting I looked all around for him and he wasn't there, and at the next meeting I looked again, but he was absent; and I thought my teaching must have given him offense. But a few days after that, at a large noon prayer meeting, a man stood up and his face shone as if he had been up in the mountain with God, and I looked at him, and to my great joy it was this brother. He said he was at that Bible reading, and he heard there was such a thing as having fresh power to preach the gospel; he said he made up his mind that if that was for him he would have it; he said he went home and looked to the Master, and that he never had such a battle with himself in his life.

He asked that God would show him the sinfulness of his heart that he knew nothing about, and he just cried mightily to God that he might be emptied of himself and filled with the Spirit, and he said, "God has answered my prayer."

I met him in Edinburgh six months from that date, and he told me he had preached the gospel every night during that time, that he had not preached one sermon but that some remained for conversation, and that he had engagements four months ahead to preach the gospel every night in different churches. I think you could have fired a cannonball right through his church and not hit anyone before he got this anointing, but it was not thirty days before the building was full and aisles crowded. He had his bucket filled full of fresh water, and the people found it out and came flocking to him from every quarter.

I tell you, you can't get the stream higher than the fountain. What we need very specially is power. There was another man whom I have in my mind, and he said, "I have heart disease, I can't preach more than once a week," so he had a colleague to preach for him and do the visiting. He was an old minister, and he couldn't do any visiting. He had heard of this anointing, and said, "I would like to be anointed for my burial. I would like before I go hence to have just one more privilege to preach the gospel with power." He prayed that God would fill him with the Spirit, and I met him not long after that, and he said, "I have preached on an average eight times a week, and I have had conversions all along." The Spirit came on him.

I don't believe that man broke down at first with hard work, so much as with using the machinery without oil, without lubrication. It is not the hard work breaks down ministers, but it is the toil of working without power.

Oh, that God may anoint His people! Not the ministry only, but every disciple. Do not suppose pastors are the only laborers needing it. There is not a mother but needs it in her house to regulate her family, just as much as the minister needs it in the pulpit or the Sunday school teacher needs it in his Sunday school. We all need it together, and let us not rest day nor night until we possess it; if that is the uppermost thought in our hearts, God will give it to us if we just hunger and thirst for it, and say, "God helping me, I will not rest until endued with power from on high."

Master and Servant

There is a very sweet story of Elijah and Elisha, and I love to dwell upon it. The time had come for Elijah to be taken up, and he said to Elisha, "You stay here at Gilgal, and I will go up to Bethel." There was a theological seminary there, and some young students, and he wanted to see how they were getting along; but Elisha said, "As the Lord liveth, and thy soul liveth, I will not leave thee" (2 Kings 2:2). And so Elisha just kept close to Elijah. They came to Bethel, and the sons of the prophets came out and said to Elisha, "Do you know that your master is to be taken away?" And Elisha said, "I know it; but you keep still." Then Elijah said to Elisha, "You remain at Bethel until I go to Jericho." But Elisha said, "As the Lord liveth and my soul liveth, I will not leave thee." "You shall not go without me," said Elisha.

And then I can imagine that Elisha just put his arm in that of Elijah, and they walked down together. I can see those two mighty men walking down to Jericho, and when they arrived there, the sons of the prophets came and said to Elisha, "Do you know that your master is to be taken away?" "Hush! Keep still," said Elisha, "I know it." And then Elijah said to Elisha, "Tarry here awhile; for the Lord hath sent me to Jordan." But Elisha said, "As the Lord liveth and my soul liveth, I will not leave thee. You shall not go without me." And then Elisha came right close to Elijah, and as they went walking down, I imagine Elisha was after something. When they came to the Jordan, Elijah took off his mantle and struck the waters, and they separated hither and thither, and the two passed through like giants, dry-shod, and fifty sons of the prophets came to look at them and watch them. They didn't know but Elijah would be taken up right in their sight. As they passed over Jordan, Elijah said to Elisha, "Now, what do you want?" He knew he was after something. "What can I do for you? Just make your request known." And he said, "I would like a double portion of thy Spirit."

I can imagine now that Elijah had given him a chance to ask, Elisha said to himself, *I will ask for enough*. Elisha had a good deal of the Spirit, but, said he, "I want a double portion of thy Spirit." "Well," said Elijah, "if you see me when I am taken up, you shall have it."

Do you think you could have enticed Elisha from Elijah at that moment? I can almost see the two arm in arm, walking along, and as they walked, there came along the chariot of fire, and before Elisha knew it, Elijah was caught up, and as he went sweeping toward the throne, the servant cried, "My Father! My Father! The chariot of Israel and the horsemen thereof!" Elisha saw him no more. He picked up Elijah's fallen mantle, and returning with that old mantle of his master's, he came to the Jordan and cried for Elijah's God, and the waters separated hither and thither, and he passed through dry-shod. Then the watching prophets lifted up their voices and said, "The Spirit of Elijah is upon Elisha," and so it was, a double portion of it.

May the Spirit of Elijah, beloved reader, be upon us. If we seek for it we will have it. Oh, may the God of Elijah answer by fire, and consume the spirit of worldliness in the churches, burn up the dross, and make us whole-hearted Christians.

May that Spirit come upon us; let that be our prayer in our family altars and in our closets. Let us cry mightily to God that we may have a double portion of the Holy Spirit, and that we may not rest satisfied with this worldly state of living; but let us, like Sampson, shake ourselves and come out from the world, that we may have the power of God.

3

Witnessing in Power

Moody's work on witness emphasizes the work of the Holy Spirit in testifying to Christ. At times, the witnessing work of the Spirit is done in tandem with God's people. Peter, for instance, preaches at Pentecost in the power of the Spirit. At other times, the Holy Spirit testifies on His own. While Moody is correct in pointing to the Holy Spirit's role of testifying to the truth, some of his examples seem to overread the Spirit's testimonial work into the text. For example, Moody suggests that by the time of Christ's baptism His birth has been forgotten. He then sees that the Spirit descending on Christ is a means of reminding the world of who Jesus is. This reading is somewhat problematic in that it assumes the Father's proclamation after Jesus's baptism functions to remind people of something they've forgotten. It isn't clear, however, that Jesus's birth had been forgotten or that the Gospel writers were seeking to emphasize that Jesus has been forgotten. Instead, the baptism marks the beginning of Jesus's ministry and God's authorization of Him as the "beloved Son" of the Father.

Regardless of this, and certain other instances in which Moody overreads the text, he provides an excellent overview of the notion of witness. As he addresses the issue of witness, Moody also reveals his preferences about various aspects of ministry. For instance, he critiques preachers for not preaching Christ in plain language, women and men for not allowing themselves to be guided by the Spirit, and Christians for being less than knowledgeable about the Word of God. For Christians to witness, they must do so in the power of the Spirit through the proclamation of the Word and the way they live, preaching and imitating Christ in all areas of their lives.

---*---

If we do not have the Spirit of God, it were better to shut the churches, to nail up the doors, to put a black cross on them, and say, "God have mercy on us!" If you ministers have not the Spirit of God, you had better not preach, and you people had better stay at home. I think I speak not too strongly when I say that a church in the land without the Spirit of God is rather a curse than a blessing. If you have not the Spirit of God, Christian worker, remember that you stand in somebody else's way; you are as a tree bearing no fruit standing where another fruitful tree might grow. This is solemn work; the Holy Spirit or nothing, and worse than nothing. Death and condemnation to a church that is not yearning after the Spirit, and crying and groaning until the Spirit has wrought mightily in her midst. He is here; He has never gone back since He descended at Pentecost. He is often grieved and vexed, for He is peculiarly jealous and sensitive, and the one sin never forgiven has to do with His blessed person; therefore let us be very tender towards Him, walk humbly before Him, wait on Him very earnestly, and resolve that about us there should be nothing knowingly continued which should prevent Him dwelling in us, and being with us henceforth and forever. Brethren, peace be unto you and your spirit!

Charles Spurgeon

The subject of witness-bearing in the power of the Holy Ghost is not sufficiently understood by the Church. Until we have more intelligence on this point, we are laboring under great disadvantage. Now, if you will take your Bible and turn to John 15:26, you will find these words: "But when the Comforter is come, whom I will send unto you from the Father, even the Spirit of Truth, which proceedeth from the Father, He shall testify of Me; and ye also shall bear witness, because ye have been with Me from the beginning."

Here we find what the Spirit is going to do, or what Christ said He would do when He came; namely, that He should testify of Him. And if you will turn over to the second chapter of Acts you will find that when Peter stood up on the day of Pentecost, and testified of what Christ had done, the Holy Spirit came down and bore witness to that fact, and men were convicted by hundreds and by thousands. So then man cannot preach effectively of himself. He must have the Spirit of God to give ability, and study God's Word in order to testify according to the mind of the Spirit.

What Is the Testimony?

If we keep back the gospel of Christ and do not bring Christ before the people, then the Spirit has not the opportunity to work. But the moment Peter stood up on the day of Pentecost and bore testimony to this one fact, that Christ died for sin, and that He had been raised again and ascended into heaven—the Spirit came down to bear witness to the Person and Work of Christ.

He came down to bear witness to the fact that Christ was in heaven, and if it was not for the Holy Ghost bearing witness to the preaching of the facts of the gospel, do you think that the Church would have lived during these last eighteen centuries? Do you believe that Christ's death, resurrection, and ascension would not have been forgotten as soon as His birth, if it had not been for the fact that the Holy Spirit had come? Because it is very clear that when John made his appearance on the borders of the wilderness, they had forgotten all about the birth of Jesus Christ.

Just thirty short years. It was all gone. They had forgotten the story of the shepherds; they had forgotten the wonderful scene that took place in the temple, when the Son of God was brought into the temple and the older prophets and prophetesses were there; they had forgotten about the wise men coming to Jerusalem to inquire where He was that was born King of the Jews. That story of His birth seemed to have just faded away; they had forgotten all about it, and when John made his appearance on the borders of the wilderness it was brought back to their minds. And if it had not been for the Holy Ghost coming down to bear witness to Christ, to testify of His death and resurrection, these facts would have been forgotten as soon as His birth.

Greater Work

The witness of the Spirit is the witness of power. Jesus said, "The works that I do shall ye do also, and greater works than these shall ye do because I go to the Father" (John 14:12). I used to stumble over that. I didn't understand it. I thought, *What greater work could any man do than Christ had done?* How could anyone raise a dead man who had been laid away in the sepulcher for days, and who had already begun to turn back to dust; how with a word could he call him forth?

But the longer I live, the more I am convinced it is a greater thing to influence a man's will, a man whose will is set against God—to have that will broken and brought into subjection to God's will. Or, in other words, it is a greater thing to have power over a living, sinning, God-hating man than to quicken the dead.

He who could create a world could speak a dead soul into life, but I think the greatest miracle this world has ever seen was the miracle at Pentecost. Here were men who surrounded the apostles, full of prejudice, full of malice, full of bitterness; their hands, as it were, dripping with the blood of the Son of God. And yet an unlettered man, a man whom they detested, a man whom they hated, stood up there and preached the gospel, and three thousand of them were immediately convicted and converted, and became disciples of the Lord Jesus Christ, and were willing to lay down their lives for the Son of God.

It may have been on that occasion that Stephen was converted, the first martyr, and some of the men who soon after gave up their lives for Christ. This seems to me the greatest miracle this world has ever seen. But Peter did not labor alone; the Spirit of God was with him, hence the marvelous results.

The Jewish law required that there should be two witnesses, and so we find that when Peter preached there was a second witness. Peter testified of Christ, and Christ said "When the Holy Spirit comes, He will testify of Me." And they both bore witness to the verities of our Lord's incarnation, ministry, death, and resurrection, and the result was that a multitude turned as with one heart unto the Lord.

Our failure now is that preachers ignore the cross and veil Christ with sapless sermons and superfine language. They don't just present Him to the people plainly, and that is why, I believe, the Spirit of God doesn't work with power in our churches. What we need is to preach Christ and present Him to a perishing world. The world can get on very well without you and me, but the world cannot get on without Christ, and therefore we must testify of Him, and the world, I believe, today is just hungering and thirsting for this divine, satisfying portion.

Thousands and thousands are sitting in darkness, knowing not of this great Light, but when we begin to preach Christ honestly, faithfully, sincerely, and truthfully; holding Him up, not ourselves; exalting Christ and not our theories; presenting Christ and not our opinions; advocating Christ and not some false doctrine; then the Holy Ghost will come and bear witness. He will testify that what we say is true.

When He comes, He will confirm the Word with signs following. This is one of the strongest proofs that our gospel is divine; that it is of divine origin; that not only did Christ teach these things but when leaving the world He said, "He shall glorify Me," and "He will testify of Me."

If you will just look at Acts 2:36—to that wonderful sermon that Peter preached—you read these words: "Therefore let all the house of Israel know assuredly, that God hath made the same Jesus, whom ye have crucified, both Lord and Christ." And when Peter said this the Holy Ghost descended upon the people and testified of Christ—bore witness in signal demonstration that all this was true.

And again, in verse 40, "And with many other words did he testify and exhort, saying, Save yourselves from this untoward generation." With many other words did he testify, not only these words that have been recorded but many other words.

The Sure Guide

Turn to John 16:13 and read: "Howbeit when He, the Spirit of truth, is come, He will guide you into all truth: for He shall not speak of Himself; but whatsoever He shall hear, that shall He speak: and He will shew you things to come." He will guide you into all truth.

Now there is not a truth that we ought to know but the Spirit of God will guide us into it if we will let Him; if we will yield ourselves up to be directed by the Spirit, and let Him lead us, He will guide us into all truth. It would have saved us from a great many dark hours if we had only been willing to let the Spirit of God be our counselor and guide.

Lot never would have gone to Sodom if he had been guided by the Spirit of God. David never would have fallen into sin and had all that trouble with his family if he had been guided by the Spirit of God.

There are many Lots and Davids nowadays. The churches are full of them. Men and women are in total darkness, because they have not been willing to be guided by the Spirit of God. "He shall guide you into all truth. He shall not speak of Himself." He shall speak of the ascended glorified Christ.

What would be thought of a messenger, entrusted by an absent husband with a message for his wife or mother who, on arrival, only talked of himself and his conceits, and ignored both the husband and the message? You would simply call it outrageous. What then must be the crime of the professed teacher who speaks of himself, or some insipid theory, leaving out Christ and His gospel? If we witness according to the Spirit, we must witness of Jesus.

The Holy Spirit is down here in this dark world to speak just of the Absent One, and He takes the things of Christ and brings them to our minds. He testifies of Christ; He guides us into the truth about Him.

Rappings in the Dark

I want to say right here that I think in this day a great many children of God are turning aside and committing a grievous sin. I don't know as they think it is a sin, but if we examine the Scriptures, I am sure we will find that it is a great sin. We are told that the Comforter is sent into the world to "guide us into all truth," and if He is sent for that purpose, do we need any other guide?

Need we hide in the darkness, consulting with mediums who profess to call up the spirits of the dead? Do you know what the Word of God pronounces against that fearful sin? I believe it is one of the greatest sins we have to contend with at the present day. It is dishonoring to the Holy Spirit for me to go and summon up the dead and confer with them, even if it were possible.

I would like you to notice 1 Chronicles 10:13–14:

So Saul died for his transgression which he had committed against the LORD, even against the Word of the LORD, which he kept not, and also for asking counsel of one that had a familiar spirit, to inquire of it;

And enquired not of the LORD: therefore He slew him, and turned the kingdom unto David the son of Jesse.

God slew him for this very sin. Of the two sins that are brought against Saul here, one is that he would not listen to the Word of God, and the second is that he consulted a familiar spirit. He was snared by this great evil and sinned against God.

Saul fell right here, and there are a great many of God's professed children today who think there is no harm in consulting a medium who pretends to call up some of the departed to inquire of them.

But how dishonoring is it to God who has sent the Holy Spirit into this world to guide us "into all truth"? There is not a thing that I need to know, there is not a thing that is important for me to know, there is not a thing that I ought to know but the Spirit of God will reveal it to me through the Word of God; and if I turn my back upon the Holy Spirit, I am dishonoring the Spirit of God, and I am committing a grievous sin.

You know we read in Luke, where that rich man in the other world wanted to have someone sent to his father's house to warn his five brothers, Christ said, "They have Moses and the prophets, and if they will not hear them, they will not hear one though he rose from the dead." Moses and the prophets, the part of the Bible then completed, that is enough. But a great many people now want something besides the Word of God, and are turning aside to these false lights.

Spirits That Peep and Mutter

There is another passage which reads, "And when they shall say unto you, seek unto them that have familiar spirits, and unto wizards that peep and mutter: Should not a people seek unto their

God? for the living to the dead?" (Isa. 8:19). What is that but table-rapping and cabinet-hiding? If it was a message from God, do you think you would have to go into a dark room and put out all the lights? In secret my Master taught nothing. God is not in that movement, and what we want, as children of God, is to keep ourselves from this evil.

And then notice the verse following, quoted so often out of its connection. "To the law and to the testimony; if they speak not according to this word, it is because there is no light in them" (v. 20). Any man, any woman, who comes to us with any doctrine that is not according to the law and the testimony, let us understand that they are from the evil one, and that they are enemies of righteousness. They have no light in them.

Now you will find these people who are consulting familiar spirits, first and last, attack the Word of God. They don't believe it. Still, a great many people say you must hear both sides—but if a man should write me a most slanderous letter about my wife, I don't think I would have to read it; I should tear it up and throw it to the winds. Have I to read all the infidel books that are written, to hear both sides? Have I to take up a book that is a slander on my Lord and Master, who has redeemed me with His blood? Ten thousand times no; I will not touch it.

"Now the Spirit speaketh expressly, that in the latter times some shall depart from the faith, giving heed to seducing spirits, and doctrines of devils" (1 Tim. 4:1). That is pretty plain language, isn't it? "Doctrines of devils." Again, "speaking lies in hypocrisy; having their consciences seared with a hot iron" (v. 2). There are other passages of Scripture warning against every delusion of Satan.

Let us ever remember the Spirit has been sent into the world to guide us into all truth. We don't want any other guide; He is enough. Some people say, "Is not conscience a safer guide than the Word and the Spirit?" No, it is not. Some people don't seem to have any conscience, and don't know what it means. Their education has a good deal to do with conscience. There are persons who will say that their conscience did not tell them they had done wrong until after the wrong was done; what we want is something to tell us a thing is wrong before we do it. Very often a man will go and commit some awful crime, and after it is done his conscience will wake up and lash and scourge him, and then it is too late, the act is done.

The Unerring Guide

I am told by people who have been over the Alps that the guide fastens them, if they are going in a dangerous place, right to himself, and he just goes on before; they are fastened to the guide.

And so should the Christian be linked to His unerring Guide, and be safely upheld. Why, if a man was going through the Mammoth Cave, it would be death to him if he strayed away from his guide—if separated from him he would certainly perish; there are pitfalls in that cave and a bottomless river, and there would be no chance for a man to find his way through that cave without a guide or a light.

So there is no chance for us to get through the dark wilderness of this world alone. It is folly for a man or woman to think that they can get through this evil world without the light of God's Word and the guidance of the divine Spirit. God sent Him to guide us through this great journey, and if we seek to work independent of Him, we shall stumble into the deep darkness of eternity's night.

But bear in mind the *Word* of the Spirit of God; if you want to be guided, you must study the Word; because the Word is the light of the Spirit. In John 14:26 we read: "But the Comforter, which is the Holy Ghost, whom the Father will send in my name, He shall teach you all things, and bring all things to your remembrance, whatsoever I have said unto you."

Again in John 16:13: "Howbeit when He, the Spirit of truth, is come, He will guide you into all truth: for He shall not speak of

Himself; but whatsoever He shall hear, that shall He speak: and He will shew you things to come."

He will show us things to come. A great many people seem to think that the Bible is out of date, that it is an old book, and they think it has passed its day. They say it was very good for the Dark Ages, and that there is some very good history in it, but then it was not intended for the present time. We are living in a very enlightened age, and men can get on very well without the old book; we have outgrown it. They think we have no use for it, because it is an old book.

Now you might just as well say that the sun, which has shone so long, is now so old that it is out of date, and that whenever a man builds a house he need not put any windows in it, because we have got a newer light and a better light; we have gaslight and this new electric light. These are something new; I would advise people, if they think the Bible is too old and worn out, when they build houses, not to put any windows in them but just to light them with this new electric light. That is something new, and this is what they are anxious for.

People talk about this Book as if they understood it; but we don't know much about it yet. The press gives us the daily news of what has taken place. This Bible, however, tells us what is about to take place. This *is* new; we have the news here in this Book; this tells us of the things that will surely come to pass, and that is a great deal newer than anything in the newspapers. It tells us that the Spirit shall teach us all things; not only guide us into all truth but teach us all things. He teaches us how to pray, and I don't think there has ever been a prayer upon this sin-cursed earth that has been indicted by the Holy Spirit but was answered. There is much praying that is not indicted by the Holy Spirit.

In former years I was very ambitious to get rich; I used to pray for one hundred thousand dollars; that was my aim, and I used to say, "God does not answer my prayer; He does not make me rich." I had no warrant for such a prayer, yet a good many people pray in that way; they think that they pray, but they do not pray according to the Scriptures. The Spirit of God has nothing to do with their prayers, and such prayers are not the product of His teaching.

It is the Spirit who teaches us how to answer our enemies. If a man strikes me, I should not pull out a revolver and shoot him. The Spirit of the Lord doesn't teach me revenge; He doesn't teach me that it is necessary to draw the sword and cut a man down in order to defend my rights.

Some people say you are a coward if you don't strike back. Christ says turn the other cheek to him who smites. I would rather take Christ's teaching than any other. I don't think a man gains much by loading himself down with weapons to defend himself. There has been life enough sacrificed in this country to teach men a lesson in this regard. The Word of God is a much better protection than the revolver. We had better take the Word of God to protect us, by accepting its teaching and living out its precepts.

An Aid to Memory

It is a great comfort to us to remember that another office of the Spirit is to bring the teaching of Jesus to our remembrance. This was our Lord's promise: "He shall teach you all things, and bring all things to your remembrance" (John 14:26).

How striking that is. I think there are many Christians who have had that experience. They have been testifying, and found that while talking for Christ the Spirit has just brought into mind some of the sayings of the Lord Jesus Christ, and their mind was soon filled with the Word of God. When we have the Spirit resting upon us, we can speak with authority and power, and the Lord will bless our testimony and bless our work.

I believe the reason why God makes use of so few in the Church is because there is not in them the power that God can use. He is not going to use our ideas; we must have the Word of God hid in our hearts, and then, the Holy Spirit inflaming us, we will have the testimony which will be rich, and sweet, and fresh, and the Lord's Word will vindicate itself in blessed results.

God wants to use us; God wants to make us channels of blessing, but we are in such a condition He does not use us. That is the trouble; there are so many men who have no testimony for the Lord; if they speak, they speak without saying anything, and if they pray, their prayer is powerless. They do not plead in prayer; their prayer is just a few set phrases that you have heard too often. Now what we want is to be so full of the Word that the Spirit coming upon us shall bring to mind—bring to our remembrance—the words of the Lord Jesus.

In 1 Corinthians 2:9, it is written: "Eye hath not seen, nor ear heard; neither have entered into the heart of man the things which God hath prepared for them that love Him."

We hear that quoted so often in prayer—many a man weaves it into his prayer and stops right there. And the moment you talk about heaven, they say, "Oh, we don't know anything about heaven, it hath not entered into the heart of man. Eye hath not seen; it is all speculation; we have nothing to do with it," and they say they quote it as it is written. "Eye hath not seen, nor ear heard; neither have entered into the heart of man the things which God hath prepared for them that love Him." What next— "but God hath revealed them unto us by His Spirit" (v. 10). You see, the Lord hath revealed them unto us: "For the Spirit searches all things—yea, the deep things of God" (v. 10). That is just what the Spirit does.

Long and Short Sight

He brings to our minds what God has in store for us. I heard a man, some time ago, speaking about Abraham. He said, "Abraham was not tempted by the well-watered plains of Sodom, for Abraham was what you might call a long-sighted man; he had his eyes set on the city which had foundation—'whose Builder and Maker is God' (Heb. 11:10)." But Lot was a short-sighted man.

And there are many people in the Church who are very short-sighted; they only see things right around them they think good. Abraham was long-sighted; he had glimpses of the celestial city. Moses was long-sighted, and he left the palaces of Egypt and identified himself with God's people—poor people, who were slaves. He had something in view yonder; he could see something God had in store.

Again there are some people who are sort of long-sighted and short-sighted too. I have a friend who has one eye that is long-sighted and the other is short-sighted, and I think the Church is full of this kind of people. They want one eye for the world and the other for the kingdom of God. Therefore everything is blurred, one eye is long and the other is short, all is confusion, and they "see men as trees walking." The Church is filled with that sort of people.

But Stephen was long-sighted; he looked clear into heaven; they couldn't convince him even when he was dying, that Christ had not ascended to heaven. "Look, look yonder," he said. "See Him over there; He is on the throne, standing at the right hand of God"; and he looked clear into heaven; the world had no temptation for him; he had put the world under his feet.

Paul was another of those long-sighted men; he had been caught up and seen things unlawful for him to utter, things grand and glorious. I tell you when the Spirit of God is on us the world looks very empty; the world has a very small hold upon us, and we begin to let go our hold of it. When the Spirit of God is on us we will just let go the things of time and lay hold of things eternal.

This is the Church's need today; we want the Spirit to come in mighty power and consume all the vile dross there is in us. Oh! That the Spirit of fire may come down and burn everything in us that is contrary to God's blessed Word and Will. In John 14:16, we read of the Comforter. This is the first time He is spoken of as the Comforter. Christ had been their Comforter. God had sent Him to comfort the sorrowing. It was prophesied of Him, "The Spirit of the Lord is upon Me, because He hath anointed Me to preach the Gospel to the poor; He has sent Me to heal the broken-hearted" (Luke 4:18).

You can't heal the brokenhearted without the Comforter, but the world would not have the first Comforter, and so they rose up and took Him to Calvary and put Him to death; but on going away, He said, "I will send you another Comforter; you shall not be comfortless. Be of good cheer, little flock; it is the Father's good pleasure to give you the kingdom." All these sweet passages are brought to the remembrance of God's people, and they help us to rise out of the fog and mist of this world. Oh, what a comforter is the Holy Spirit of God!

The Faithful Friend

The Holy Spirit tells a man of his faults in order to lead him to a better life. In John 16:8, we read: "He is to reprove the world of sin." Now, there are a class of people who don't like this part of the Spirit's work. Do you know why? Because He convicts *them* of sin; they don't like that.

What they want is someone to speak comforting words and make everything pleasant, keep everything all quiet, tell them there is peace when there is war, tell them it is light when it is dark, and tell them everything is growing better. That the world is getting on amazingly in goodness, that it is growing better all the time; that is the kind of preaching they seek for. Men think they are a great deal better than their fathers were. That suits human nature, for it is full of pride. Men will strut around and say, "Yes, I believe that; the world is improving. I am a good deal better man than my father was; my father was too strict; he was one of those old Puritanical men who was so rigid. Oh, we are getting on, we are more liberal; my father wouldn't think of going out riding on

Sunday, but we will; we will trample the laws of God under our feet, we are better than our fathers."

That is the kind of preaching which some dearly love, and there are preachers who tickle such itching ears. When you bring the Word of God to bear upon them, and when the Spirit drives it home, then men will say: "I don't like that kind of preaching; I will never go to hear that man again," and sometimes they will get up and stamp their way out of church before the speaker gets through; they don't like it. But when the Spirit of God is at work he convicts men of sin. "When He comes He will reprove the world of sin, of righteousness and of judgment; of sin"—not because men swear and lie and steal and get drunk and murder—"of sin because they believe not on Me" (John 16:8–9).

The Climax Sin

That is the sin of the world. Why, a great many people think that unbelief is a sort of misfortune, but do not know, if you will allow me the expression, it is the damning sin of the world today; that is what unbelief is, the mother of all sin. There would not be a drunkard walking the streets if it were not for unbelief; there would not be a harlot walking the streets if it were not for unbelief; there would not be a murderer if it were not for unbelief; it is the germ of all sin.

Don't think for a moment that it is a misfortune, but just bear in mind it is an awful sin, and may the Holy Spirit convict every reader that unbelief is making God a liar. Many a man has been knocked down on the streets because someone has told him he was a liar. Unbelief is giving God the lie; that is the plain English of it.

Some people seem to boast of their unbelief; they seem to think it is quite respectable to be an infidel and doubt God's Word, and they will vainly boast and say, "I have intellectual difficulties; I can't believe." Oh, that the Spirit of God may come and convict men of sin! That is what we need—His convicting power, and I am so thankful that God has not put that into our hands.

We have not to convict men; if we had I would get discouraged, and give up preaching, and go back to business within the next forty-eight hours. It is my work to preach and hold up the cross and testify of Christ; it is His work to convict men of sin and lead them to Christ.

One thing I have noticed, that some conversions don't amount to anything; that if a man professes to be converted without conviction of sin, he is one of those stony-ground hearers who don't bring forth much fruit. The first little wave of persecution, the first breath of opposition, and the man is back in the world again. Let us pray, dear Christian reader, that God may carry on a deep and thorough work, that men may be convicted of sin so that they cannot rest in unbelief. Let us pray God it may be a thorough work in the land.

I would a great deal rather see a hundred men thoroughly converted, truly born of God, than to see a thousand professed conversions where the Spirit of God has not convicted of sin. Don't let us cry, "Peace, peace," when there is no peace. Don't go to the man who is living in sin and tell him all he has to do is to stand right up and profess, without any hatred for sin. Let us ask God first to show every man the plague of his own heart, that the Spirit may convict them of sin. Then will the work in our hands be real, and deep, and abide the fiery trial which will try every man's labor.

Thus far, we have found the work of the Spirit is to impart life, to implant hope, to give liberty, to testify of Christ, to guide us into all truth, to teach us all things, to comfort the believers, and to convict the world of sin.

> Holy Spirit, faithful guide,
> Ever near the Christian's side;
> Gently lead us by the hand,
> Pilgrims in a desert land;
> Weary souls for e'er rejoice,

85

While they hear that sweetest voice,
Whisp'ring softly, wanderer come!
Follow Me, I'll guide thee home.

Ever present, truest Friend,
Ever near Thine aid to lend,
Leave us not to doubt and fear,
Groping on in darkness drear,
When the storms are raging sore,
Hearts grow faint, and hopes give o'er;
Whisp'ring softly, wanderer come!
Follow Me, I'll guide thee home.

When our days of toil shall cease,
Waiting still for sweet release,
Nothing left but heaven and prayer,
Wond'ring if our names were there,
Wading deep the dismal flood,
Pleading nought but Jesus' blood;
Whisp'ring softly, wanderer come!
Follow Me, I'll guide thee home.

———✳———

Oh! Spirit of God, whose voice I hear,
Sweeter than sweetest music, appealing
In tones of tenderness and love;
Whose comforts delight my soul, and
Fills the temple of my heart with joy beyond compare.
I need Thee day by day, and each day's moment, Lord.
I sigh for greater likeness
To Him who loved me unto death, and loves me still.
'Tis Thine to lead me to Him; 'tis Thine to ope the eye,
To manifest His royal glories to my longing heart;
'Tis Thine the slumbering saint to waken
And discipline this blood-touched ear
To hearken to my heavenly Lover's voice,

And quickly speed His summons to obey.
Oh! Spirit of the Mighty God, uplift my faith
Till heaven's precious light shall flood my soul,
And the shining of my face declare
That I have seen the face of God.

4

Power in Operation

Moody's discussion of "power in operation" in this chapter focuses on the fruit of the Spirit as the manifestation of power in the lives of believers. Clearly, the Holy Spirit works within God's people to produce fruit. Moody's threefold division of the nine fruits noted in Galatians is intended to be organizational rather than strictly theological. Though Moody divides the gifts into those that are "all to God" (love, peace, and joy), "toward man" (goodness, long-suffering, and gentleness), and "in relation to ourselves" (faith, temperance, and meekness), he does not intend to limit the gifts to these categories. Moody does not allow the threefold division to control the way he describes the various gifts throughout the rest of the chapter.

Consider, for instance, love. Love is "all to God" (Deut. 6:5; Matt. 22:37) but it is also "toward man" (Lev. 19:18, 34; Matt. 22:29). Peace certainly comes from God (Phil. 4:7), with whom we have peace (Rom. 5:1) through Jesus Christ, but it is also the orientation we take toward

Secret Power

others (Eph. 2:14–15; 1 Thess. 5:13; Heb. 12:14; 1 Tim. 2:2) and have within ourselves (2 Pet. 3:14). When treating love, Moody highlights love for God and neighbor. He does not squeeze the biblical text into his own predetermined framework but allows the text to expand beyond his categories as he highlights the various ways the gifts of the Spirit are interrelated.

The spiritual gifts allow Christians to experience and exhibit God's peace. As Moody notes in the section titled "Not Easily Offended," those who are rooted in God's Word will have peace. Those not rooted in the Word will be easily offended. The troubles and persecutions of this life rob them of whatever peace they may have. In Moody's day, troubles of various sorts would have been par for the course, as the Industrial Revolution, racial tensions, ongoing difficulties after the Civil War, and a variety of other factors like the increased availability of alcohol were fundamentally changing the social fabric. Like Moody's world, our world has a way of robbing us of peace and replacing it with anxiety, anger, and frustration. As such, Moody's words are as important today as they were when he first wrote them.

---*---

"Ye are not your own." "Your bodies are the temples of the Holy Ghost." Is that an unmeaning metaphor, or an over-worded expression? When the Holy Spirit enters the soul, heaven enters with Him. The heart is compared to a temple. God never enters without His attendants; repentance cleanses the house; faith provides for the house; watchfulness, like the porter, takes care of it; prayer is a lively messenger, learns what is wanted, and then goes for it; faith tells him where to go, and he never goes in vain; joy is the musician of this temple, tuning to the praises of God and the Lamb; and this terrestrial temple shall be removed to the celestial world, for the trumpet shall sound, and the dead shall be raised.

Rowland Hill

The power we have been considering is the presence of the Holy Spirit. He is omnipotent. Power in operation is the actions of the Spirit or the fruit of the Spirit. This we shall now consider. Paul writes in Galatians 5:16–18, 22–26:

> This I say then, Walk in the Spirit, and ye shall not fulfil the lust of the flesh. For the flesh lusteth against the Spirit, and the Spirit against the flesh: and these are contrary the one to the other: so that ye cannot do the things that ye would. But if ye be led of the Spirit, ye are not under the law. . . . But the fruit of the Spirit is love, joy, peace, longsuffering, gentleness, goodness, faith, meekness, temperance: against such there is no law. And they that are Christ's have crucified the flesh with the affections and lusts. If we live in the Spirit, let us also walk in the Spirit. Let us not be desirous of vain glory, provoking one another, envying one another.

Now there is a life of perfect peace, perfect joy, and perfect love, and that ought to be the aim of every child of God; that ought to be their standard; and they should not rest until having attained to that position. That is God's standard, where He wants all His children.

These nine graces mentioned in this chapter in Galatians can be divided in this way: Love and peace and joy are all to God. God looks for that fruit from each one of His children, and that is the kind of fruit which is acceptable with Him. Without that we cannot please God. He wants, above everything else that we possess, love, peace, and joy. And then the next three—goodness, long-suffering, and gentleness—are toward man. That is our outward life to those we are coming in contact with continually—daily, hourly. The next three—faith, temperance, meekness—are in relation to ourselves; and in that way we can just take the three divisions, and it will be of some help to us.

The first thing that meets us as we enter the kingdom of God, you might say, are these first three graces: love, peace, and joy.

Love, Peace, and Joy

When a man who has been living in sin turns from his sins, and turns to God with all his heart, he is met on the threshold of the divine life by these sister graces. The love of God is shed abroad in his heart by the Holy Ghost. The peace of God comes at the same time, and also the joy of the Lord.

We can all put the test to ourselves, if we have them. It is not anything that we can make. The great trouble with many is that they are trying to make these graces. They are trying to make love; they are trying to make peace; they are trying to make joy. But they are not creatures of human planting. To produce them of ourselves is impossible. That is an act of God. They come from above.

It is God who speaks the Word and gives the love; it is God who gives the peace; it is God who gives the joy, and we possess all by receiving Jesus Christ by faith into the heart. For when Christ comes by faith into the heart, then the Spirit is there, and if we have the Spirit, we will have the fruit.

If the whole Church of God could live as the Lord would have them live, why Christianity would be the mightiest power this world has ever seen. It is the low standard of Christian life that is causing so much trouble. There are a great many stunted Christians in the Church; their lives are stunted; they are like a tree planted in poor soil—the soil is hard and stony, and the roots cannot find the rich loamy soil needed. Such believers have not grown in these sweet graces.

In 2 Peter 1:5–8, the apostle writes:

> And besides this, giving all diligence, add to your faith virtue; and to virtue knowledge; and to knowledge temperance; and to temperance patience; and to patience, godliness; and to godliness, brotherly kindness; and to brotherly kindness, charity. For if these things be in you and abound, they make you that ye shall neither be barren nor unfruitful in the knowledge of our Lord Jesus Christ.

Now, if we have these things in us, I believe that we will be constantly bringing forth fruit that will be acceptable with God. It won't be just a little every now and then, when we spur ourselves up and work ourselves up into a certain state of mind or into an excited condition, and work a little while and then become cold, and discouraged, and disheartened. We shall be neither unfruitful nor barren, bringing forth fruit constantly; we will grow in grace and be filled with the Spirit of God.

What Wins

A great many parents have inquired of me how to win their children. They say they have talked with them, and sometimes they have scolded them and have lectured them, and signally failed.

I think there is no way so sure to win our families and our neighbors, and those about whom we are anxious, to Christ, than just to adorn the doctrine of Jesus Christ in our lives and grow in all these graces. If we have peace and joy and love and gentleness and goodness and temperance; not only being temperate in what we drink but in what we eat, and temperate in our language, guarded in our expressions. If we just live in our homes as the Lord would have us, an even Christian life day by day, we shall have a quiet and silent power proceeding from us that will constrain them to believe on the Lord Jesus Christ.

But an uneven life, hot today and cold tomorrow, will only repel. Many are watching God's people. It is just the very worst thing that can happen to those whom we want to win to Christ, to see us, at any time, in a cold, backslidden state. This is not the normal condition of the Church; it is not God's intention. He would have us growing in all these graces, and the only true, happy, Christian life is to be growing, constantly growing in the love and favor of God, growing in all those delightful graces of the Spirit.

Even the vilest, the most impure, acknowledge the power of goodness; they recognize the fruit of the Spirit. It may condemn their lives and cause them to say bitter things at times, but down deep in their hearts they know that the man or woman who is living that kind of life is superior to them. The world don't satisfy them, and if we can show the world that Jesus Christ does satisfy us in our present life, it will be more powerful than the eloquent words of professional reformers. A man may preach with the eloquence of an angel, but if he doesn't live what he preaches, and act out in his home and his business what he professes, his testimony goes for naught, and the people say it is all hypocrisy after all; it is all a sham. Words are very empty if there is nothing back of them. Your testimony is poor and worthless if there is not a record back of that testimony consistent with what you profess.

What we need is to pray to God to lift us up out of this low, cold, formal state that we have been living in, that we may live in the atmosphere of God continually, and that the Lord may lift upon us the light of His countenance, and that we may shine in this world, reflecting His grace and glory.

The first of the graces spoken of in Galatians, and the last mentioned in Peter, is charity or love. We cannot serve God, we cannot work for God, unless we have love. That is the key which unlocks the human heart. If I can prove to a man that I come to him out of pure love; if a mother shows by her actions that it is pure love that prompts her advising her boy to lead a different life, not a selfish love, but that it is for the glory of God, it won't be long before that mother's influence will be felt by that boy, and he will begin to think about this matter, because true love touches the heart quicker than anything else.

Power of Love

Love is the badge that Christ gave His disciples. Some put on one sort of badge and some another. Some put on a strange kind of dress, that they may be known as Christians, and some put on a crucifix, or something else, that they may be known as Christians.

94

But love is the only badge by which the disciples of our Lord Jesus Christ are known. "By this shall all men know that ye are My disciples, if ye have love one toward another" (John 13:35).

Therefore, though a man stand before an audience and speak with the eloquence of a Demosthenes, or of the greatest living orator, if there is no love back of his words, it is like sounding brass and a tinkling cymbal. I would recommend all Christians read 1 Corinthians 13 constantly, abiding in it day and night, not spending a night or a day there, but just go in there and spend all our time—summer and winter, twelve months in the year—then the power of Christ and Christianity would be felt as it never has been in the history of the world. See what this chapter says:

> Though I speak with the tongues of men and of angels, and have not charity, I am become as sounding brass, or a tinkling cymbal. And though I have the gift of prophecy, and understand all mysteries, and all knowledge; and though I have all faith, so that I could remove mountains, and have not charity, I am nothing. (1 Cor. 13:1–2)

A great many are praying for faith; they want extraordinary faith; they want remarkable faith. They forget that love exceeds faith. The *charity* spoken of in the above verses is *love*, the fruit of the Spirit, the great motive-power of life. What the Church of God needs today is love—more love to God and more love to our fellowmen. If we love God more, we will love our fellow men more. There is no doubt about that. I used to think that I should like to have lived in the days of the prophets; that I should like to have been one of the prophets, to prophesy, and to see the beauties of heaven and describe them to men; but, as I understand the Scriptures now, I would a good deal rather live in 1 Corinthians 13 and have this love that Paul is speaking of, the love of God burning in my soul like an unquenchable flame, so that I may reach men and win them for heaven.

A man may have wonderful knowledge that may unravel the mysteries of the Bible, and yet be as cold as an icicle. He may glisten like the snow in the sun. Sometimes you have wondered why it was that certain ministers who have had such wonderful magnetism, who have such a marvelous command of language, and who preach with such mental strength haven't had more conversions. I believe, if the truth was known, you would find no divine love back of their words, no pure love in their sermons.

You may preach like an angel, Paul says, "with the tongues of men and of angels," but if you have not love, it amounts to nothing. "And though I bestow all my goods to feed the poor" (v. 3)—a man may be very charitable, and give away all his goods; a man may give all he has, but if it is not the love of God which prompts the gift, it will not be acceptable with God.

"And though I give my body to be burned, and have not charity"—have not love—"it profiteth me nothing" (v. 3). A man may go to the stake for his principles; he may go to the stake for what he believes, but if it is not love to God which actuates him, it will not be acceptable to God.

Love's Wonderful Effects

"Charity suffereth long, and is kind; charity envieth not; charity vaunteth not itself, is not puffed up, doth not behave itself unseemly, seeketh not her own, is not easily provoked, thinketh no evil" (vv. 4–5).

That's the work of love. It is not easily provoked. Now if a man has no love of God in his heart, how easy it is to become offended. Perhaps with the church because some members of the church don't treat him just right, or some men of the church don't bow to him on the street, he takes offense, and that is the last you see of him.

Love is longsuffering. If I love the Lord Jesus Christ, these little things are not going to separate me from His people. They are like the dust in the balance. Nor will the cold, formal treatment of hypocrites in the church quench that love I have in my heart for Him. If this love is in the heart, and the fire is burning on the altar, we will not be all the time finding fault with other people and criticizing what they have done.

Critics Beware

Love will rebuke evil but will not rejoice in it. Love will be impatient of sin but patient with the sinner. To form the habit of finding fault constantly is very damaging to spiritual life; it is about the lowest and meanest position that a man can take. I never saw a man who was aiming to do the best work, but there could have been some improvement; I never did anything in my life, I never addressed an audience, that I didn't think I could have done better, and I have often upbraided myself that I had not done better; but to sit down and find fault with other people when we are doing nothing ourselves, not lifting our hands to save someone, is all wrong, and is the opposite of holy, patient, divine love.

Love is forbearance; and what we want is to get this spirit of criticism and faultfinding out of the Church and out of our hearts and let each one of us live as if we had to answer for ourselves, and not for the community, at the last day. If we are living according to 1 Corinthians 13, we will not be all the time finding fault with other people. "Love suffereth long, and is kind." Love forgets itself and doesn't dwell upon itself. The woman who came to Christ with that alabaster box, I venture to say, never thought of herself. Little did she know what an act she was performing. It was just her love for the Master. She forgot the surroundings, she forgot everything else that was there; she broke that box and poured the ointment upon Him, and filled the house with its odor.

The act, as a memorial, has come down these 1,800 years. It is right here—the perfume of that box is in the world today. That ointment was worth $40 or $50; no small sum of those days for a poor woman. Judas sold the Son of God for about $15 or $20. What this woman gave to Christ was everything that she had, and she became so occupied with Jesus Christ that she didn't think what people were going to say.

So when we act with a single eye for the glory of our Lord, not finding fault with everything about us but doing what we can in the power of this love, then will our deeds for God speak, and the world will acknowledge that we have been with Jesus, and that this glorious love has been shed abroad in our hearts.

If we don't love the Church of God, I am afraid it won't do us much good; if we don't love the blessed Bible, it will not do us much good. What we want, then, is to have love for Christ, to have love for His Word, and to have love for the Church of God, and when we have love, and are living in that spirit, we will not be in the spirit of finding fault and working mischief.

After Love, What?

After love comes peace. I have before remarked a great many people are trying to make peace. But that has already been done. God has not left it for us to do; all that we have to do is to enter into it. It is a condition, and instead of our trying to make peace and to work for peace, we want to cease all that and sweetly enter into peace.

If I discover a man in the cellar complaining because there is no light there, and because it is cold and damp, I say: "My friend, come up out of the cellar. There is a good warm sun up here, a beautiful spring day, and it is warm, it is cheerful and light; come up and enjoy it." Would he reply, "Oh, no, sir; I am trying to see if I can make light down here; I am trying to work myself into a warm feeling." And there he is working away, and he has been at it for a whole week.

I can imagine my reader smile, but you may be smiling at your own picture; for this is the condition of many whom I daily meet who are trying to do this very thing—they are trying to work themselves into peace and joyful feelings.

Peace is a condition into which we enter; it is a state; and instead of our trying to make peace, let us believe what God's Word declares, that peace has already been made by the blood of the cross. Christ has made peace for us, and now what He desires is that we believe it and enter into it.

Now, the only thing that can keep us from peace is sin. God turns the way of the wicked upside down. There is no peace for the wicked, says my God. They are like the troubled sea that cannot rest, casting up filth and mire all the while; but peace with God by faith in Jesus Christ—peace through the knowledge of forgiven sin—is like a rock; the waters go dashing and surging past it, but it abides. When we find peace, we shall not find it on the ground of innate goodness; it comes from without ourselves, but into us. In John 16:33 we read: "These things have I spoken unto you, that in Me ye might have peace." In Me ye might have peace. Jesus Christ is the author of peace. He procured peace. His gospel is the gospel of peace. "Behold I bring you good tidings of great joy which shall be unto all people; for unto you is born this day in the city of David a Savior" (Luke 2:10–11), and then came that chorus from heaven, "Glory to God in the highest; peace on earth" (v. 14). He brought peace. "In the world ye shall have tribulation, but be of good cheer, I have overcome the world" (John 16:33).

How true that in the world we have tribulation. Are you in tribulation? Are you in trouble? Are you in sorrow? Remember this is our lot. Paul had tribulation, and others shared in grief. Nor shall we be exempt from trial. But within, peace may reign undisturbed. If sorrow is our lot, peace is our legacy. Jesus gives peace, and do you know there is a good deal of difference between His peace and our peace? Anyone can disturb our peace, but they can't disturb His peace. That is the kind of peace He has left us. Nothing can offend those who trust in Christ.

Not Easily Offended

In Psalm 119:165, we find "Great peace have they who love Thy law; and nothing shall offend them." The study of God's Word will secure peace. You take those Christians who are rooted and grounded in the Word of God, and you find they have great peace; it is these who don't study their Bible, and don't know their Bible, who are easily offended when some little trouble comes, or some little persecution, and their peace is all disturbed; just a little breath of opposition, and their peace is all gone.

Sometimes I am amazed to see how little it takes to drive all peace and comfort from some people. Some slandering tongue will readily blast it. But if we have the peace of God, the world cannot take that from us. It cannot give it; it cannot destroy it. We have to get it from above the world; it is peace which Christ gives. "Great peace have they which love Thy law, and nothing shall offend them."

Christ says "Blessed is he, whosoever shall not be offended in Me" (Matt. 11:6). Now, if you will notice, wherever there is a Bible-taught Christian, one who has the Bible well marked and daily feeds upon the Word by prayerful meditation, he will not be easily offended.

Such are the people who are growing and working all the while. But it is these people who never open their Bibles, these people who never study the Scriptures, who become offended, and are wondering why they are having such a hard time. They are the persons who tell you that Christianity is not what it has been recommended to them; they have found it was not all that we claim it to be. The real trouble is, they have not done as the Lord has told them to do. They have neglected the Word of God. If they had been studying the Word of God, they would not be in that condition. If they had been studying the Word of God, they would not have wandered these years away from God, living on the husks of the world. But the trouble is, they have neglected to care for the new life; they haven't fed it, and the poor soul, being starved, sinks into weakness and decay, and is easily stumbled or offended.

I met a man who confessed his soul had fed on nothing for forty years. "Well," said I, "that is pretty hard for the soul—giving it nothing to feed on!" And that man is but a type of thousands and tens of thousands today; their poor souls are starving. This body that we inhabit for a day, and then leave, we take good care of; we feed it three times a day, and we clothe it, and take care of it, and deck it, and by and by it is going into the grave to be eaten up by the worms; but the inner man, that is to live on and on, and on forever, is lean and starved.

Sweet Words

In Numbers 6:22 we read:

> And the LORD spake unto Moses, saying: Speak unto Aaron and unto his sons, saying, on this wise ye shall bless the children of Israel, saying unto them: The LORD bless thee and keep thee. The LORD make His face shine upon thee, and be gracious unto thee. The LORD lift up His countenance upon thee, and give thee peace.

I think these are about as sweet verses as we find in the Old Testament. I marked them years ago in my Bible, and many times I have turned over and read them. "The LORD lift up His countenance upon thee, and give thee peace." They remind us of the loving words of Jesus to His troubled disciples, "Peace, be still." The Jewish salutation used to be, as a man went into a house, "Peace be upon this house," and as he left the house the host would say, "Go in peace."

Then again, in John 14:27, Jesus said: "Peace I leave with you, My peace I give unto you; not as the world giveth give I unto you. Let not your heart be troubled, neither let it be afraid." This is the precious legacy of Jesus to all His followers. Every man, every woman, every child who believes in Him may share in this portion. Christ has willed it to them, and His peace is theirs.

This then is our Lord's purpose and promise: My peace I give unto you. I give it, and I am not going to take it away again; I am going to leave it to you. "Not as the world giveth, give I unto you. Let not your heart be troubled, neither let it be afraid." But you know, when some men make their wills and deed away their property, there are some sharp, shrewd lawyers who will get hold of that will and break it all to pieces; they will go into court and break the will, and the jury will set the will aside, and the money goes into another channel.

Now this will that Christ has made, neither devil nor man can break it. He has promised to give us peace, and there are thousands of witnesses who can say, "I have my part of that legacy. I have peace; I came to Him for peace, and I got it; I came to Him in darkness; I came to Him in trouble and sorrow; I was passing under a deep cloud of affliction, and I came to Him and He said, 'Peace, be still.' And from that hour peace reigned in my soul."

Yes, many have proved the invitation true, "Come unto Me all ye that labor and are heavy laden, and I will give you rest" (Matt. 11:28). They found rest when they came. He is the author of rest, He is the author of peace, and no power can break that will; yea, unbelief may question it, but Jesus Christ rose to execute His own will, and it is in vain for man to contest it. Infidels and skeptics may tell us that it is all a myth, and that there isn't anything in it, and yet the glorious tidings are ever repeated, "Peace on earth, good will to man," and the poor and needy, the sad and sorrowful, are made partakers of it.

So, my reader, you need not wait for peace any longer. All you have to do is to enter into it today. You need not try to make peace. It is a false idea; you cannot make it. Peace is already made by Jesus Christ, and is now declared unto you.

Peace Declared

When France and England were at war, a French vessel had gone off on a long voyage, a whaling voyage; when they came back, the crew were short of water, and being now near an English port, they wanted to get water. But they were afraid that they would be taken if they went into that port; and some people in the port saw them, saw their signal of distress, and sent word to them that they need not be afraid, that the war was over and peace had been declared. But they couldn't make those sailors believe it, and they didn't dare to go into port, although they were out of water.

But at last they made up their minds that they had better go in and surrender up their cargo and surrender up their lives to their enemies than to perish at sea without water. When they got in, they found out that peace had been declared, and that what had been told them was true.

So there are a great many people who don't believe the glad tidings that peace has been made. Jesus Christ made peace on the cross. He satisfied the claims of the law, and this law which condemns you and me has been fulfilled by Jesus Christ. He has made peace, and now He wants us just to enjoy it, just to believe it. Nor is there a thing to hinder us from doing it if we will.

We can enter into that blessing now and have perfect peace. The promise is: "Thou wilt keep him in perfect peace, whose mind is stayed on Thee: because he trusteth in Thee. Trust ye in the LORD for ever: for in the LORD Jehovah is everlasting strength" (Isa. 26:3–4). Now, as long as our minds are stayed on our dear selves, we will never have peace. Some people think more of themselves than of all the rest of the world. It is self in the morning, self at noon, and self at night. It is self when they wake up and self when they go to bed; and they are all the time looking at themselves and thinking about themselves instead of looking to Jesus. Faith is an outward look. Faith does not look within; it looks without. It is not what I think, nor what I feel, nor what I have done, but it is what Jesus

Christ is and has done; and so we should trust in Him who is our strength, and whose strength will never fail. After Christ rose from the grave, three times, John tells us, He met His disciples and said unto them, "Peace be unto you." There is peace for the conscience through His blood, and peace for the heart in His love.

Secret of Joy

Remember, then, that love is power, and peace is power; but now I will call attention to another fruit of the Spirit, and this too is power—the grace of *joy*.

It is the privilege, I believe, of every Christian to walk in the light, as God is in the light, and to have that peace which will be flowing unceasingly as we keep busy about His work. And it is our privilege to be full of the joy of the Lord.

We read that when Philip went down to Samaria and preached, there was great joy in the city. Why? Because they believed the glad tidings. And that is the natural order, joy in believing. When we believe the glad tidings, there comes a joy into our souls.

Also we are told in Luke 10 that our Lord sent the seventy out, and that they went forth preaching salvation in the name of Jesus Christ, and the result was that there were a great many who were blessed; the seventy returned, it says, with great joy, and when they came back they said that the very devils were subject to them, through His name.

The Lord seemed to just correct them in this one thing when He said, "Rejoice not that the devils are subject to you, but rejoice that your names are written in heaven" (Luke 10:20). There is assurance for you. They had something to rejoice in now. God doesn't ask us to rejoice over nothing, but He gives us some ground for our joy.

What would you think of a man or woman who seemed very happy today and full of joy, and couldn't tell you what made them so? Suppose I should meet a man on the street, and he was so full of joy that he should get hold of both my hands and say, "Bless the Lord, I am so full of joy!" "What makes you so full of joy?"

"Well, I don't know."

"You don't know?"

"No, I don't; but I am so joyful that I just want to get out of the flesh."

"What makes you feel so joyful?"

"Well, I don't know."

Would we not think such a person unreasonable? But there are a great many people who feel—who want to feel—that they are Christians before they are Christians; they want the Christian's experience before they become Christians; they want to have the joy of the Lord before they receive Jesus Christ. But this is not the gospel order. He brings joy when He comes, and we cannot have joy apart from Him. There is no joy away from Him; He is the author of it, and we find our joy in Him.

Joy Is Unselfish

Now, there are three kinds of joy. There is the joy of one's own salvation. I thought, when I first tasted that, it was the most delicious joy I had ever known, and that I could never get beyond it. But I found afterward there was something more joyful than that; namely, the joy of the salvation of others.

Oh, the privilege, the blessed privilege, to be used of God to win a soul to Christ, and to see a man or woman being led out of bondage by some act of ours toward them. To think that God should condescend to allow us to be coworkers with Him. It is the highest honor we can wear. It surpasses the joy of our own salvation, this joy of seeing others saved.

And then John said he had "no greater joy" than to see his disciples walking in the truth (3 John 4). Every man who has been the means of leading souls to Christ understands what that means.

Young disciples, walk in the truth and you will have joy all the while.

I think there is a difference between happiness and joy. Happiness is caused by things which happen around me, and circumstances will mar it, but joy flows right on through trouble; joy flows on through the dark; joy flows in the night as well as in the day; joy flows all through persecution and opposition; it flows right along, for it is an unceasing fountain bubbling up in the heart, a secret spring which the world can't see and doesn't know anything about; but the Lord gives His people perpetual joy when they walk in obedience to Him.

This joy is fed by the divine Word. Jeremiah 15:16 says: "Thy words were found, and I did eat them; and Thy word was unto me the joy and rejoicing of mine heart: for I am called by Thy name, O LORD God of hosts." He ate the words, and what was the result? He said they were the joy and rejoicing (delight) of his heart. Now people should look for joy in the Word, and not in the world; they should look for the joy which the Scriptures furnish, and then go work in the vineyard. Because a joy that doesn't send me out to someone else, a joy that doesn't impel me to go and help the poor drunkard, a joy that doesn't prompt me to visit the widow and the fatherless, a joy that doesn't cause me to go into the Mission Sunday school or other Christian work is not worth having and is not from above. A joy that does not constrain me to go and work for the Master is purely sentiment and not real joy.

Joy in Persecution

Then it says in Luke 6:22–23:

> Blessed are ye, when men shall hate you, and when they shall separate you from their company, and shall reproach you, and cast out your name as evil, for the Son of man's sake. Rejoice ye in that day,

and leap for joy: for, behold, your reward is great in heaven: for in the like manner did their fathers unto the prophets.

Christians do not receive our reward down here. We have to go right against the current of the world. We may be unpopular, and we may go right against many of our personal friends if we live godly in Christ Jesus. And at the same time, if we are persecuted for the Master's sake, we will have this joy bubbling up; it just comes right up in our hearts all the while—a joy that is unceasing—that flows right on. The world cannot choke that fountain. If we have Christ in the heart, by and by the reward will come.

The longer I live, the more I am convinced that godly men and women are not appreciated in our day. But their work will live after them, and there will be a greater work done after they are gone, by the influence of their lives, than when they were living.

Daniel is doing a thousand times more than when he was living in Babylon. Abraham is doing more today than he did on the plain with his tent and altar. All these centuries he has been living, and so we read, "Blessed are the dead that die in the Lord, from henceforth; yea saith the Spirit, that they may rest from their labors, and their works do follow them" (Rev. 14:13).

Let us set the streams running that shall flow on after we have gone. If we have today persecution and opposition, let us press forward, and our reward will be great by and by. Oh! Think of this; the Lord Jesus, the Maker of heaven and earth, who created the world, says, "Your reward is great."

He calls it great. If some friend should say it is great, it might be very small; but when the Lord, the great and mighty God, says it is great, what must it be? Oh! The reward that is in store for those who serve Him! We have this joy, if we serve Him. A man or woman is not fit to work for God who is cast down, because they go about their work with a telltale face. "The joy of the LORD is your strength" (Neh. 8:10).

What we need today is a joyful church. A joyful church will make inroads upon the works of Satan, and we will see the gospel going down into dark lanes and dark alleys, and into dark garrets and cellars, and we will see the drunkards reached and the gamblers and the harlots come pressing into the kingdom of God.

It is this carrying a sad countenance, with so many wrinkles on our brows, that retards Christianity. Oh, may there come great joy upon believers everywhere, that we may shout for joy and rejoice in God day and night. A joyful church—let us pray for that, that the Lord may make us joyful, and when we have joy, then we will have success; and if we don't have the reward we think we should have here, let us constantly remember the rewarding time will come hereafter.

Someone has said, if you had asked men in Abraham's day who their great man was, they would have said Enoch, and not Abraham. If you had asked in Moses's day who their great man was, they would not have said it was Moses; he was nothing, but it would have been Abraham. If you had asked in the days of Elijah or Daniel, it wouldn't have been Daniel or Elijah; they were nothing, but it would have been Moses. And in the days of Jesus Christ—if you had asked in the days of Jesus Christ about John the Baptist or the apostles, you would hear they were mean and contemptible in the sight of the world and were looked upon with scorn and reproach. But see how mighty they have become.

And so we will not be appreciated in our day, but we are to toil on and work on, possessing this joy all the while. And if we lack it, let us cry: "Restore unto me the joy of Thy salvation, and uphold me with Thy free Spirit; then will I teach transgressors Thy ways, and sinners shall be converted unto Thee" (Ps. 51:12–13).

Again, John 15:11 reads: "These things have I spoken unto you, that my joy might remain in you, and that your joy might be full." And in John 16:22: "And ye now therefore have sorrow: but I will see you again, and your heart shall rejoice, and your joy no man taketh from you."

I am so thankful that I have a joy that the world cannot rob me of. I have a treasure that the world cannot take from me. I have something that it is not in the power of man or devil to deprive me of, and that is the joy of the Lord. "No one will take your joy from you."

In the second century, they brought a martyr before a king, and the king wanted him to recant and give up Christ and Christianity, but the man spurned the proposition. But the king said, "If you don't do it, I will banish you." The man smiled and answered, "You can't banish me from Christ, for He says He will never leave me nor forsake me." The king got angry, and said, "Well, I will confiscate your property and take it all from you." And the man replied, "My treasures are laid up on high; you cannot get them." The king became still more angry, and said, "I will kill you." "Why," the man answered, "I have been dead forty years. I have been dead with Christ; dead to the world, and my life is hid with Christ in God, and you cannot touch it."

And so we can rejoice, because we are on resurrection ground, having risen with Christ. Let persecution and opposition come; we can rejoice continually and remember that our reward is great, reserved for us unto the day when He who is our Life shall appear, and we shall appear with Him in glory.

> The Spirit, oh, sinner,
> In mercy doth move
> Thy heart, so long hardened,
> Of sin to reprove;
>
> *Resist* not the Spirit,
> Nor longer delay;
> God's gracious entreaties may end with today.
>
> Oh, child of the kingdom,
> From sin service cease;
> Be filled with the Spirit,
> With comfort and peace.

Oh, *grieve* not the Spirit,
Thy Teacher is He,
That Jesus, thy Savior, may glorified be.

Defiled is the temple,
Its beauty laid low,
On God's holy altar
The embers faint glow,
By love yet rekindled,
A flame may be fanned;
Oh, *quench* not the Spirit, *the Lord is at hand*!

P. P. Bliss

5

Power Hindered

As is evident from the previous chapters, D. L. Moody did not believe the Holy Spirit's power was a given. In other words, people can operate apart from the Holy Spirit. In this chapter, Moody addresses the various ways we can hinder the power of the Holy Spirit in our lives. While the topics of resisting and grieving the Holy Spirit are important, Moody's analysis can raise some theological questions. In part, these questions arise from Moody's attempt to address the unpardonable sin, which he identifies as blaspheming the Holy Spirit. In speaking about resisting the Holy Spirit, Moody notes the possibility of resisting the Spirit of God until He departs. At first glance, this may seem to suggest that the Holy Spirit, having indwelt a believer, would depart with enough resistance. His comments regarding ministers and other believers who have resisted the Holy Spirit create some ambiguity. However, Moody's reference to Acts 7:51 in the section titled "The Faithful Friend" suggests that the resistance he had in mind (a) is separate from "grieving" the Holy Spirit and (b) likely occurs prior to salvation.

Overall, this section of Moody's work is challenged at the technical level. In part, that may be because the words on which the sections are focused are seldom used in the New Testament. For instance, the Greek word translated "resist" in Acts 7:51 is only found in Acts 7:51 in the New Testament. "Resist" is also used to translate a different Greek word in only seven other passages. These other passages do not refer to the Holy Spirit, though God is in view in Romans 9:19 and 13:2. Overall, resistance appears to be the act of refusing to be moved or influenced by someone or something. "Grieve" is a more common word, used in twenty-one New Testament verses; however, it is only associated with the Holy Spirit in Ephesians 4:30. Given the other New Testament uses, it seems that grieving implies the expression of disappointment and sorrow concerning some state, person, or action. This broad understanding fits well with the context in Ephesians 4:17–32, in which Paul is exhorting the Ephesians to set aside their previous way of life and "to be renewed in the spirit of your minds" (v. 23). Despite the relatively small number of instances, it seems clear that the resistance Stephen notes in Acts 7:51 is quite different than the grieving Paul highlights in Ephesians 4:30.

Moody's treatment here should be viewed as more observational than technical, which is typical of Moody's interpretive and writing styles. In the end, I don't believe Moody was suggesting that resisting the Holy Spirit might result in the Spirit departing from a believer who has been "sealed" (Eph. 4:23). The references to Christian ministers and other believers who have resisted the Spirit are a separate case from his more general statement about the potential for the Spirit's departure at the beginning of the section titled "What It Is Not." Given his concern with blaspheming the Holy Spirit (i.e., claiming that the Holy Spirit is a demon), which he identifies as the unpardonable sin, it seems that when he suggests that one could resist "till the Spirit of God has departed" it is not a *permanent* departure, as would seem more likely with the unpardonable sin. Instead, the departure prompted by resistance is part of an ongoing dynamic involving the Spirit's conviction and, at times, absence. It would seem that the absence Moody had in mind could be for a time, to allow an individual to begin feeling the depth and emptiness of a sinful life.

———————— ✳ ————————

> Every vain thought and idle word, and every wicked deed, is like so many drops to quench the Spirit of God. Some quench Him with the lust of the flesh; some quench Him with cares of the mind; some quench Him with long delays, that is, not plying the motion when it cometh, but crossing the good thoughts with bad thoughts, and doing a thing when the Spirit saith not. The Spirit is often grieved before He be quenched.
>
> H. Smith

Israel, we are told, limited the Holy One of Israel. They vexed and grieved the Holy Spirit, and rebelled against His authority, but there is a special sin against Him, which we may profitably consider.

The Unpardonable Sin

The first description of it is in Matthew 12:22–32:

> Then was brought unto Him one possessed with a devil, blind and dumb; and He healed him, insomuch that the blind and dumb both spake and saw. And all the people were amazed, and said, Is not this the son of David? But when the Pharisees heard it, they said, This fellow doth not cast out devils, but by Beelzebub the prince of the devils. And Jesus knew their thoughts, and said unto them, Every kingdom divided against itself is brought to desolation; and every city or house divided against itself shall not stand:
>
> And if Satan cast out Satan, he is divided against himself; how shall then his kingdom stand? And if I by Beelzebub cast out devils,

by whom do your children cast them out? therefore they shall be your judges. But if I cast out devils by the Spirit of God, then the kingdom of God is come unto you.

Or else how can one enter into a strong man's house, and spoil his goods, except he first bind the strong man? and then he will spoil his house. He that is not with Me is against Me; and he that gathereth not with Me, scattereth abroad. Wherefore I say unto you, All manner of sin and blasphemy shall be forgiven unto men: but the blasphemy against the Holy Ghost shall not be forgiven unto men. And whosoever speaketh a word against the Son of man, it shall be forgiven him: but whosoever speaketh against the Holy Ghost, it shall not be forgiven him, neither in this world, neither in the world to come.

That is Matthew's account. Now let us read Mark's account in 3:21–22:

And when His friends heard of it, they went out to lay hold on Him: for they said, He (that is Christ) is beside Himself. And the scribes which came down from Jerusalem said, He hath Beelzebub, and by the prince of the devils casteth He out devils.

The word *Beelzebub* means the Lord of Filth. They charged the Lord Jesus with being possessed not only with an evil spirit but with a filthy spirit.

And He called them unto Him, and said unto them in parables, How can Satan cast out Satan? And if a kingdom be divided against itself, that kingdom cannot stand. And if a house be divided against itself, that house cannot stand.

And if Satan rise up against himself, and be divided, he cannot stand, but hath an end. No man can enter into a strong man's house, and spoil his goods, except he will first bind the strong man; and then he will spoil his house.

Verily I say unto you, All sins shall be forgiven unto the sons of men, and blasphemies wherewith soever they shall blaspheme: but he that shall blaspheme against the Holy Ghost hath never forgiveness but is in danger of eternal damnation. (vv. 23–29)

Now, if it stopped there, we would be left perhaps in darkness, and we would not exactly understand what the sin against the Holy Ghost is; but the next verse of this same chapter of Mark just throws light upon the whole matter, and we need not be in darkness another minute if we really want light. For observe, the verse reads: "Because they said, He hath an unclean spirit" (v. 30).

Now, I have met a good many atheists and skeptics and deists and infidels, both in this country and abroad, but I never in my life met a man or woman who ever said that Jesus Christ was possessed of an unclean devil. Did you? I don't think you ever met such a person.

I have heard men say bitter things against Christ, but I never heard any man stand up and say that he thought Jesus Christ was possessed with the devil, and that He cast out devils by the power of the devil; and I don't believe any man or woman has any right to say they have committed the unpardonable sin, unless they have maliciously, willfully, and deliberately said that they believe that Jesus Christ had a devil in Him, and that He was under the power of the devil, and that He cast out devils by the power of the devil. Because you perhaps have heard someone say that there is such a thing as grieving the Spirit of God, and resisting the Spirit of God until He has taken His flight and left you, then you have said "That is the unpardonable sin."

What It Is Not

I admit there is such a thing as resisting the Spirit of God, and resisting till the Spirit of God has departed; but if the Spirit of God has left any, they will not be troubled about their sins. The very fact that they are troubled shows that the Spirit of God has not left them. If a man is troubled about his sins, it is the work of the Spirit; for Satan never yet told him he was a sinner. Satan makes us believe that we are pretty good; that we are good enough without God, safe without Christ, and don't need salvation. But when a man wakes up to the fact that he is lost, that he is a sinner, this is the work of the Spirit; if the Spirit of God had left him, he would not be in that state; and just because men and women want to be Christians is a sign that the Spirit of God is drawing them.

If resisting the Spirit of God is an unpardonable sin, then we have all committed it, and there is no hope for any of us; for I do not believe there is a minister, or a worker in Christ's vineyard, who has not, sometime in his life, resisted the Holy Ghost; who has not sometime in his life rejected the Spirit of God. To resist the Holy Ghost is one thing, and to commit that awful sin of blasphemy against the Holy Ghost is another thing; and we want to take the Scripture and just compare them. Now, some people say, "I have such blasphemous thoughts; there are some awful thoughts that come into my mind against God," and they think that is the unpardonable sin.

We are not to blame for having bad thoughts come into our minds. If we harbor them, then we are to blame. But if the devil comes and darts an evil thought into my mind, and I say, "Lord help me," sin is not reckoned to me. Who has not had evil thoughts come into his mind, flash into his heart, and been called to fight them!

One old divine says, "You are not to blame for the birds that fly over your head, but if you allow them to come down and make a nest in your hair, then you are to blame. You are to blame if you don't fight them off."

And so with these evil thoughts that come flashing into our minds, we have to fight them; we are not to harbor them, we are not to entertain them. If I have evil thoughts come into my mind, and evil desires, it is no sign that I have committed the unpardonable sin. If I love these thoughts and harbor them, and think evil of God, and think Jesus Christ a blasphemer, I am responsible for

116

such gross iniquity; but if I charge Him with being the prince of devils, then I am committing the unpardonable sin.

The Faithful Friend

Let us now consider the sin of grieving the Spirit. *Resisting* the Holy Ghost is one thing, *grieving* Him is another. Stephen charged the unbelieving Jews in Acts 7:51, "Ye do always resist the Holy Ghost as your fathers did, so do ye." The world has always been resisting the Spirit of God in all ages. That is the history of the world. The world is today resisting the Holy Spirit.

"Faithful are the wounds of a friend" (Prov. 27:6). The divine Spirit as a friend reveals to this poor world its faults, and the world only hates Him for it. He shows them the plague of their hearts. He convinces or convicts them of sin; therefore they fight the Spirit of God. I believe there is many a man resisting the Holy Ghost; I believe there is many a man today fighting against the Spirit of God.

In Ephesians 4:30–32, we read:

> And grieve not the Holy Spirit of God, whereby ye are sealed unto the day of redemption. Let all bitterness, and wrath, and anger, and clamor, and evil speaking be put away from you, with all malice. And be ye kind, one to another, tender-hearted, forgiving one another, even as God for Christ's sake hath forgiven you.

Now, mark you, that was written to the church at Ephesus. "Grieve not the Holy Spirit, whereby ye are sealed unto the day of redemption." I believe today the Church all over Christendom is guilty of grieving the Holy Spirit. There are a good many believers in different churches wondering why the work of God is not revived.

The Church Grieves the Spirit

I think that if we search, we will find something in the Church grieving the Spirit of God; it may be a mere schism in a church;

it may be some unsound doctrine; it may be some division in a church.

There is one thing I have noticed as I have traveled in different countries; I never yet have known the Spirit of God to work where the Lord's people were divided.

There is one thing that we must have if we are to have the Holy Spirit of God to work in our midst, and that is unity. If a church is divided, the members should immediately seek unity. Let the believers come together and get the difficulty out of the way. If the minister of a church cannot unite the people, if those that were dissatisfied will not fall in, it would be better for that minister to retire.

I think there are a good many ministers in this country who are losing their time; they have lost, some of them, months and years; they have not seen any fruit, and they will not see any fruit because they have a divided church. Such a church cannot grow in divine things. The Spirit of God does not work where there is division, and what we want today is the spirit of unity among God's children, so that the Lord may work.

Worldly Amusements

Then, another thing, I think, that grieves the Spirit, is the miserable policy of introducing questionable entertainments. There are the lotteries, for instance, that we have in many churches. If a man wants to gamble, he doesn't have to go to some gambling den; he can stay in the church. And there are fairs—bazaars, as they call them—where they have rafflings and grab bags. And if he wants to see a drama, he does not need to go to the theater, for many of our churches are turned into theaters; he may stay right in the church and witness the acting. I believe all these things grieve the Spirit of God. I believe when we bring the church down to the level of the world to reach the world, we are losing all the while and grieving the Spirit of God.

But some say, if we take that standard and lift it up high, it will drive away a great many members from our churches. I believe it, and I think the quicker they are gone the better. The world has come into the church like a flood, and how often you find an ungodly choir employed to do the singing for the whole congregation; the idea that we need an ungodly man to sing praises to God! It was not long ago I heard of a church where they had an unconverted choir, and the minister saw something about the choir that he didn't like, and he spoke to the chorister, but the chorister replied: "You attend to your end of the church, and I will attend to mine." You cannot expect the Spirit of God to work in a church in such a state as that.

Unconverted Choirs

Paul tells us not to speak in an unknown tongue, and if we have choirs who are singing in an unknown tongue, why is not that just as great an abomination? I have been in churches where they have had a choir who would rise and sing, and sing, and it seemed as if they sung five or ten minutes, and I could not understand one solitary word they sung, and all the while the people were looking around carelessly. There are, perhaps, a select few very fond of fine music, and they want to bring the opera right into the church, and so they have opera music in the church, and the people, who are drowsy and sleepy, don't take part in the singing.

They hire ungodly men, unconverted men, and these men will sometimes get the Sunday paper, and get back in the organ loft, and the moment the minister begins his sermon, they will take out their papers and read them all the while that the minister is preaching. The organist, provided he does not go out for a walk—if he happens to keep awake, will read his paper, or, perhaps, a novel, while the minister is preaching; and the minister wonders why God doesn't revive his work; he wonders why he is losing his hold on the congregation; he wonders why people don't come crowding into the church, why people are running after the world instead of coming into the church.

The trouble is that we have let down the standard; we have grieved the Spirit of God. One movement of God's power is worth more than all our artificial power, and what the Church of God wants today is to get down in the dust of humiliation and confession of sin, and go out and be separated from the world; then see if we do not have power with God and with man.

What Is Success?

The gospel has not lost its power; it is just as powerful today as it ever has been. We don't want any new doctrine. It is still the old gospel with the old power, the Holy Ghost power; if the churches will but confess their sins and put them away, and lift the standard instead of pulling it down, and pray to God to lift us all up into a higher and holier life, then the fear of the Lord will come upon the people around us.

It was when Jacob put away strange gods and set his face toward Bethel that the fear of God fell upon the nations around. And when the churches turn toward God, and we cease grieving the Spirit, so that He may work through us, we will then have conversions all the while. Believers will be added to the Church daily.

It is sad when you look over Christendom and see how desolate it is, and see how little spiritual life, spiritual power, there is in the Church of God today, many of the church members not even wanting this Holy Ghost power. They don't desire it; they want intellectual power; they want to get some man who will just draw, and a choir that will draw, not caring whether any one is saved. With them that is not the question. Only fill the pews; have good society, fashionable people, and dancing; such persons are found one night at the theater and the next night at the opera. They don't like the prayer meetings, they abominate them; if the minister will only lecture and entertain, that would suit them.

I said to a man some time ago, "How are you getting on at your church?"

"Oh, splendid."

"Many conversions?"

"Well—well, on that side we are not getting on so well. But," he said, "we rented all our pews and are able to pay all our running expenses; we are getting on splendidly."

That is what the godless call "getting on splendidly"; because they rent the pews, pay the minister, and pay all the running expenses. Conversions! That is a strange thing.

There was a man being shown through one of the cathedrals of Europe; he had come in from the country, and one of the men belonging to the cathedral was showing him around, when he inquired, "Do you have many conversions here?"

"Many what?"

"Many conversions here?"

"Ah, man, this is not a Wesleyan chapel."

The idea of there being conversions there! And you can go into a good many churches in this country and ask if they have many conversions there, and they would not know what it meant, they are so far away from the Lord; they are not looking for conversions and don't expect them.

Shipwrecks

Alas! How many young converts have made shipwreck against such churches? Instead of being a harbor of delight to them, they have proved false lights, alluring them to destruction. Isn't it time for us to get down on our faces before God and cry mightily to Him to forgive us our sins? The quicker we own it, the better.

You may be invited to a party, and it may be made up of church members, and what will be the conversation? Oh, I got so sick of such parties that I left years ago; I would not think of spending a night that way. It is a waste of time; there is hardly a chance to say a word for the Master. If you talk of a personal Christ, your company becomes offensive; they don't like it. They want you to talk about the world, a popular minister, a popular church, a good organ, a good choir, and they say, "Oh, we have a grand organ, and a superb choir," and all that, and it suits them; but that doesn't warm the Christian heart. When you speak of a risen Christ and a personal Savior, they don't like it; the fact is, the world has come into the church and taken possession of it, and what we want to do is to wake up and ask God to forgive us for grieving the Spirit.

Dear reader, search your heart and inquire, *Have I done anything to grieve the Spirit of God?* If you have, may God show it to you today; if you have done anything to grieve the Spirit of God, you want to know it today, and get down on your face before God and ask Him to forgive you and help you to put it away. I have lived long enough to know that if I cannot have the power of the Spirit of God on me to help me work for Him, I would rather die than live just for the sake of living. How many are there in the church today who have been members for fifteen or twenty years but have never done a solitary thing for Jesus Christ? They cannot lay their hands upon one solitary soul who has been blessed through their influence; they cannot point today to one single person who has ever been lifted up by them.

Quench Not

In 1 Thessalonians 5:19, we are told not to quench the Spirit. Now, I am confident the cares of the world are coming in and quenching the Spirit with a great many. They say: "I don't care for the world"; perhaps not the *pleasures* of the world so much after all as the *cares* of this life, but they have just let the cares come in and quench the Spirit of God.

Anything that comes between me and God—between my soul and God—quenches the Spirit. It may be my family. You may say, "Is there any danger of my loving my family too much?" Not if we love God more; but God must have the first place. If I love my family more than God, then I am quenching the Spirit of God within me; if I love wealth, if I love fame, if I love honor, if I love position, if I love pleasure, if I love self, more than I love God who created and saved me, then I am committing a sin. I am not only grieving the Spirit of God but quenching Him and robbing my soul of His power.

Emblems of the Spirit

But I would further call attention to the emblems of the Holy Spirit. An emblem is something that represents an object; the same as a balance is an emblem of justice, and a crown an emblem of royalty, and a scepter is an emblem of power; so we find in Exodus that water is an emblem of the Holy Spirit. You find in the smitten rock, in the wilderness, the work of the Trinity illustrated.

"Behold, I will stand before thee there upon the rock in Horeb; and thou shall smite the rock, and there shall come water out of it, that the people may drink. And Moses did so, in the sight of the elders of Israel" (Exod. 17:6).

Paul declares, in 1 Corinthians 10:4, that the rock was Christ; it represented Christ. God says, "I will stand upon the rock," and as Moses smote the rock the water came out, which was an emblem of the Holy Spirit; and it flowed out along through the camp, and they drank of the water. Now water is cleansing; it is fertilizing, it is refreshing, it is abundant, and it is freely given. And so the Spirit of God is the same: cleansing, fertilizing, refreshing, and reviving; and He was freely given when the smitten Christ was glorified.

Then, too, fire is an emblem of the Spirit; it is purifying, illuminating, searching. We talk about searching our hearts. We cannot do it. What we want is to have God search them. Oh, that God may search us and bring out the hidden things, the secret things that cluster there, and bring them to light.

The wind is another emblem. It is independent, powerful, sensible in its effects, and reviving. How the Spirit of God revives when He comes to all the drooping members of the Church.

Then the rain and the dew—fertilizing, refreshing, abundant; and the dove, gentle—what more gentle than the dove; and the lamb—gentle, meek, innocent, a sacrifice. We read of the wrath of God; we read of the wrath of the Lamb, but nowhere do we read of the wrath of the Holy Spirit—gentle, innocent, meek, loving; and that Spirit wants to take possession of our hearts.

And He comes as a voice, another emblem—speaking, guiding, warning, teaching; and as the seal—impressing, securing, and making us as His own.

May we know Him in all His wealth of blessing. This is my prayer for myself—for you. May we heed the words of the grand apostle: "My speech and my preaching was not with enticing words of man's wisdom, but in demonstration of the Spirit, and of power: that your faith should not stand in the wisdom of men, but in the power of God" (1 Cor. 2:4–5).

The Overcoming Life

And Other Sermons

This is the victory that overcometh the world, even our faith.

1 John 5:4

CONTENTS

PART 1

The Christian's Warfare

Dwight Moody was never known to pull his punches. In *The Overcoming Life*, he reminds believers that they are in the midst of a battle. While our salvation is not in jeopardy, Moody is clear that we are not out of danger. This set of sermons from D. L. Moody have a certain natural progression and order. "The Christian's Warfare" frames the broad context in which the overcoming life can be realized or lost. As Moody argues, if we are not overcoming the world, we are being overcome by it. Christianity is to be lived out in "our homes and everyday lives." Christianity must change our lives. Moody's concern in "The Christian's Warfare" is challenging believers to recognize the dangers and trials they face in their day-to-day lives. These dangers manifest in two sorts of foes: internal and external. Internal foes emerge due to the ongoing influence of the flesh. As believers seek to live for Christ, they battle against their own sinful state, which does not go away at the moment of salvation. We are sinners who continually seek to "walk in newness of life" (Rom. 6:4). Among the internal foes, Moody lists (1) appetite, (2) temper, (3) covetousness, (4) jealousy, and (5) pride. Of these, the first two (appetite and temper) were quite personal for him. His feelings about alcohol were no secret. He believed it was detrimental to society, and he was generally supportive of the temperance movement.

Moody was also prone to outbursts of anger. At one of his meetings, he got mad at a man who confronted him in the hall and pushed him. While Moody apologized from the pulpit, the incident showcased Moody's occasional struggles with anger. These internal foes often join forces with external foes, making the overcoming life that much more difficult to sustain. External foes include (1) worldly habits and fashions, (2) pleasure, (3) business, and (4) persecution. Moody's discussion of the third foe, business, is particularly interesting given Moody's context (and our own!). As noted in the introduction, Moody's world was rapidly changing. Industrialization was altering the social fabric in innumerable ways. Business was becoming a bigger part of life, but, for Christians, Moody believed business could become a distraction if given too much of our lives. These first three sermons set the stage for the rest. They serve as Moody's wakeup call. Christians are at war. We face internal and external foes. We must be diligent as we navigate this fallen world, and careful to avoid the trappings of our own desires and limitations.

I would like to have you open your Bible at 1 John 5:4–5: "Whatsoever is born of God overcometh the world: and this is the victory that overcometh the world, even our faith. Who is he that overcometh the world, but he that believeth that Jesus is the Son of God?"

When a battle is fought, all are anxious to know who are the victors. In these verses we are told who is to gain the victory in life. When I was converted, I made this mistake: I thought the battle was already mine, the victory already won, the crown already in my grasp. I thought that old things had passed away, that all things had become new; that my old corrupt nature, the Adam life, was gone. But I found out, after serving Christ for a few months, that conversion was only like enlisting in the army, that there was a battle on hand, and that if I was to get a crown, I had to work for it and fight for it.

Salvation is a gift, as free as the air we breathe. It is to be obtained, like any other gift, without money and without price: there are no other terms. "To him that worketh not, but believeth." But on the other hand, if we are to gain a crown, we must work for it. Let me quote a few verses in 1 Corinthians:

> For other foundation can no man lay than that is laid, which is Jesus Christ.
>
> Now if any man build upon this foundation gold, silver, costly stones, wood, hay, stubble; every man's work shall be made manifest: for the day shall declare it, because it is revealed by fire; and the fire itself shall prove each man's work, of what sort it is.
>
> If any man's work abide which he hath built thereupon, he shall receive a reward. If any man's work shall be burned, he shall suffer loss: but he himself shall be saved; yet so as by fire. (3:11–15)

We see clearly from this that we may be saved, but all our works burned up. I may have a wretched, miserable voyage through life, with no victory, and no reward at the end; saved, yet so as by fire, or as Job puts it, "with the skin of my teeth" (Job 19:20). I believe that a great many men will barely get to heaven as Lot got out of Sodom, burned out, nothing left, works and everything else destroyed.

It is like this: when a man enters the army, he is a member of the army the moment he enlists; he is just as much a member as a man who has been in the army ten or twenty years. But enlisting is one thing, and participating in a battle another. Young converts are like those just enlisted.

It is folly for any man to attempt to fight in his own strength. The world, the flesh, and the devil are too much for any man. But if we are linked to Christ by faith, and He is formed in us the hope of glory, then we shall get the victory over every enemy. It is believers who are the overcomers. "Thanks be unto God, which always causeth us to triumph in Christ" (2 Cor. 2:14). Through Him we shall be more than conquerors.

I wouldn't think of talking to unconverted men about overcoming the world, for it is utterly impossible. They might as well try to cut down the American forest with their penknives. But a good many Christian people make this mistake: they think the battle is already fought and won. They have an idea that all they have to do is to put the oars down in the bottom of the boat, and the current will drift them into the ocean of God's eternal love. But we have to cross the current. We have to learn how to watch and fight, and how to overcome. The battle is only just commenced. The Christian life is a conflict and a warfare, and the quicker we find it out the better. There is not a blessing in this world that God has not linked Himself to. All the great and higher blessings God associates with Himself. When God and man work together, then it is that there is going to be victory. We are coworkers with Him. You might take a mill, and put it forty feet above a river, and there isn't capital enough in the States to make that river turn the mill; but get it down about forty feet, and away it works. We want to keep in mind that if we are going to overcome the world, we have got to work with God. It is His power that makes all the means of grace effectual.

The story is told that Frederick Douglass, the great slave orator, once said in a mournful speech when things looked dark for his race: "The white man is against us, governments are against us, the spirit of the times is against us. I see no hope for the colored race. I am full of sadness."

Just then a poor old colored woman rose in the audience, and said: "Frederick, is God dead?"*

* The source of this anecdote is almost certainly one of many widely circulating versions of a meeting between Frederick Douglass and abolitionist and women's rights advocate Sojourner Truth. For example, see *The Liberator*, May 6,

My friend, it makes a difference when you count God in.

Now many a young believer is discouraged and disheartened when he realizes this warfare. He begins to think that God has forsaken him, that Christianity is not all that it professes to be. But he should rather regard it as an encouraging sign. No sooner has a soul escaped from his snare than the great adversary takes steps to ensnare it again. He puts forth all his power to recapture his lost prey. The fiercest attacks are made on the strongest forts, and the fiercer the battle the young believer is called on to wage, the surer evidence it is of the work of the Holy Spirit in his heart. God will not desert him in his time of need, any more than He deserted His people of old when they were hard pressed by their foes.

The Only Complete Victor

This brings me to another verse of the same epistle: "Ye are of God, little children, and have overcome them: because greater is He that is in you, than he that is in the world" (1 John 4:4). The only man that ever conquered this world—was complete victor—was Jesus Christ. When He shouted on the cross, "It is finished!" it was the shout of a conqueror. He had overcome every enemy. He had met sin and death. He had met every foe that you and I have got to meet, and had come off victor. Now if I have got the Spirit of Christ, if I have got that same life in me, then I have got a power that is greater than any power in the world, and with that same power I overcome the world.

Notice that everything human in this world fails. Every man, the moment he takes his eye off God, has failed. Every man has been a failure at some period of his life. Abraham failed. Moses failed. Elijah failed. Take the men that have become so famous and

---

1862 (Boston, MA), 2, https://www.newspapers.com/article/the-liberator-excerpt-from-1862-account/69807407/; Alex Schwartz, ed., "'Is God Dead?': Frederick Douglass's Recollection of a Contentious Moment in Antislavery History," *New North Star* vol. 3 (2021): 64–66, https://journals.iupui.edu/index.php/NNS/article/view/25879/24024.

that were so mighty—the moment they got their eye off God, they were weak like other men; and it is a very singular thing that those men failed on the strongest point in their character. I suppose it was because they were not on the watch. Abraham was noted for his faith, and he failed right there—he denied his wife. Moses was noted for his meekness and humility, and he failed right there—he got angry. God kept him out of the promised land because he lost his temper. I know he was called "the servant of God," and that he was a mighty man and had power with God, but humanly speaking, he failed, and was kept out of the promised land.

Elijah was noted for his power in prayer and for his courage, yet he became a coward. He was the boldest man of his day and stood before Ahab, and the royal court, and all the prophets of Baal; yet when he heard that Jezebel had threatened his life, he ran away to the desert, and under a juniper tree prayed that he might die. Peter was noted for his boldness, and a little maid scared him nearly out of his wits. As soon as she spoke to him, he began to tremble, and he swore that he didn't know Christ. I have often said to myself that I'd like to have been there on the day of Pentecost alongside of that maid when she saw Peter preaching.

"Why," I suppose she said, "what has come over that man? He was afraid of *me* only a few weeks ago, and now he stands up before all Jerusalem and charges these very Jews with the murder of Jesus."

The moment he got his eye off the Master, he failed; and every man, I don't care who he is—even the strongest—every man that hasn't Christ in him is a failure. John, the beloved disciple, was noted for his meekness; and yet we hear of him wanting to call fire down from heaven on a little town because it had refused the common hospitalities.

Triumphs of Faith

Now, how are we to get the victory over all our enemies? Turn to Galatians 2:20: "I am crucified with Christ; nevertheless I live;

yet not I, but Christ liveth in me: and the life which I now live in the flesh, I live by the faith of the Son of God, who loved me and gave Himself for me." We live by faith. We get this life by faith, and become linked to Immanuel—"God with us." If I have God for me, I am going to overcome. How do we gain this mighty power? By faith.

The next passage I want to call your attention to is Romans 11:20: "Because of unbelief they were broken off; and thou standest by faith." The Jews were cut off on account of their unbelief: We were grafted in on account of our belief. So notice: We live by faith, and we stand by faith.

Next: We walk by faith. Second Corinthians 5:7: "For we walk by faith, not by sight." The most faulty Christians I know are those who want to walk by sight. They want to see the end—how a thing is going to come out. That isn't walking by faith at all— that is walking by sight.

I think the characters that best represent this difference are Joseph and Jacob. Jacob was a man who walked with God by sight. You remember his vow at Bethel: "If God will be with me, and will keep me in this way that I go, and will give me bread to eat, and raiment to put on, so that I come again to my father's house in peace; then shall the LORD be my God" (Gen. 28:20–21). And you remember how his heart revived when he saw the wagons Joseph sent him from Egypt. He sought after signs. He never could have gone through the temptations and trials that his son Joseph did. Joseph represents a higher type of Christian. He could walk in the dark. He could survive thirteen years of misfortune, in spite of his dreams, and then ascribe it all to the goodness and providence of God.

Lot and Abraham are a good illustration. Lot turned away from Abraham and tented on the plains of Sodom. He got a good stretch of pasture land, but he had bad neighbors. He was a weak character, and he should have kept with Abraham in order to get strong. A good many men are just like that. As long as their mothers are living, or they are bolstered up by some godly person, they get along very well; but they can't stand alone. Lot walked by sight, but Abraham walked by faith; he went out in the footsteps of God.

> By faith Abraham, when he was called to go out into a place which he should after receive for an inheritance, obeyed; and he went out, not knowing whither he went. By faith he sojourned in the land of promise, as in a strange country, dwelling in tabernacles with Isaac and Jacob, the heirs with him of the same promise: for he looked for a city which hath foundations, whose builder and maker is God. (Heb. 11:8–10)

And again: we fight by faith. Ephesians 6:16: "Above all, taking the shield of faith, wherewith ye shall be able to quench all the fiery darts of the wicked." Every dart Satan can fire at us we can quench by faith. By faith we can overcome the evil one. To fear is to have more faith in your antagonist than in Christ.

Some of the older people can remember when our war broke out. Secretary Seward, who was Lincoln's secretary of state—a long-headed and shrewd politician—prophesied that the war would be over in ninety days, and young men in thousands and hundreds of thousands came forward and volunteered to go down to Dixie and whip the South. They thought they would be back in ninety days, but the war lasted four years and cost about half a million lives. What was the matter? Why, the South was a good deal stronger than the North supposed. Its strength was underestimated.

Jesus Christ makes no mistake of that kind. When He enlists a man in His service, He shows him the dark side; He lets him know that he must live a life of self-denial. If a man is not willing to go to heaven by way of Calvary, he cannot go at all. Many men want a religion in which there is no cross, but they cannot enter heaven that way. If we are to be disciples of Jesus Christ, we must deny ourselves and take up our cross and follow Him. So let us sit down and count the cost. Do not think that you will have no battles if you follow the Nazarene, because many battles are before you. Yet if I had ten thousand lives, Jesus Christ should have every one of them. Men do not object to a battle if they are confident that they will have victory, and, thank God, every one of us may have the victory if we will.

The reason why so many Christians fail all through life is just this: they underestimate the strength of the enemy. My dear friend, you and I have got a terrible enemy to contend with. Don't let Satan deceive you. Unless you are spiritually dead, it means warfare. Nearly everything around tends to draw us away from God. We do not step clear out of Egypt on to the throne of God. There is the wilderness journey, and there are enemies in the land.

Don't let any man or woman think all he or she has to do is to join the church. That will not save you. The question is, are you overcoming the world, or is the world overcoming you? Are you more patient than you were five years ago? Are you more amiable? If you are not, the world is overcoming you, even if you are a church member. That epistle Paul wrote to Titus says that we are to be sound in patience, faith, and charity. We have got Christians, a good many of them, that are good in spots but mighty poor in other spots. Just a little bit of them seems to be saved, you know. They are not rounded out in their characters. It is just because they haven't been taught that they have a terrible foe to overcome.

If I wanted to find out whether a man was a Christian, I wouldn't go to his minister. I would go and ask his wife. I tell you, we want more *home piety* just now. If a man doesn't treat his wife right, I don't want to hear him talk about Christianity. What is the use of his talking about salvation for the next life, if he has no salvation for this? We want a Christianity that goes into our homes and everyday lives. Some men's religion just repels me. They put on a whining voice and a sort of a religious tone, and talk so sanctimoniously on Sunday that you would think they were wonderful saints. But on Monday they are quite different. They put their religion away with their clothes, and you don't see any more of it until the next Sunday. You laugh, but let us look out that we don't belong to that class. My friend, we have got to have a higher type of Christianity, or the Church is gone. It is wrong for a man or woman to profess what they don't possess. If you are not overcoming temptations, the world is overcoming you. Just get on your knees and ask God to help you. My dear friends, let us go to God and ask Him to search us. Let us ask Him to wake us up, and let us not think that just because we are church members we are all right. We are all wrong if we are not getting victory over sin.

PART 2

Internal Foes

Now if we are going to overcome, we must begin inside. God always begins there. An enemy inside the fort is far more dangerous than one outside.

Scripture teaches that in every believer there are two natures warring against each other. Paul says, in his epistle to the Romans:

> For we know that the law is spiritual: but I am carnal, sold under sin. For that which I do I allow not: for what I would, that do I not; but what I hate, that do I. If then I do that which I would not, I consent unto the law that it is good.
>
> Now then it is no more I that do it, but sin that dwelleth in me. For I know that in me (that is, in my flesh,) dwelleth no good thing: for to will is present with me; but how to perform that which is good I find not. For the good that I would I do not: but the evil which I would not, that I do.
>
> Now if I do that I would not, it is no more I that do it, but sin that dwelleth in me. I find then a law, that when I would do good, evil is present with me. For I delight in the law of God after the inward man: but I see another law in my members, warring against the law of my mind, and bringing me into captivity to the law of sin which is in my members. (7:14–23)

Again, in the epistle to the Galatians, he says: "For the flesh lusteth against the Spirit, and the Spirit against the flesh: and these are contrary the one to the other: so that ye cannot do the things that ye would" (5:17).

When we are born of God, we get His nature, but He does not immediately take away all the old nature. Each species of animal and bird is true to its nature. You can tell the nature of the dove or canary-bird. The horse is true to his nature, the cow is true to hers. But a man has two natures, and do not let the world or Satan make you think that the old nature is extinct, because it is not. "Reckon ye yourselves dead"; but if you were dead, you wouldn't need to reckon yourselves dead, would you? The dead self would be dropped out of the reckoning. "I keep my body under"; if it were dead, Paul wouldn't have needed to keep it under. I am judicially dead, but the old nature is alive, and therefore if I don't keep my body under and crucify the flesh with its affections, this lower nature will gain the advantage, and I shall be in bondage. Many men live all their lives in bondage to the old nature, when they might have liberty if they would only live this overcoming life. The old Adam never dies. It remains corrupt. "From the sole of the foot even unto the head there is no soundness in it; but wounds, and bruises, and putrefying sores: they have not been closed, neither bound up, neither mollified with ointment."

A gentleman in India once got a tiger cub, and tamed it so that it became a pet. One day when it had grown up, it tasted blood, and the old tiger-nature flashed out, and it had to be killed. So with the old nature in the believer. It never dies, though it is subdued; unless he is watchful and prayerful, it will gain the upper hand and rush him into sin. Someone has pointed out that "I" is the center of S-I-N. It is the medium through which Satan acts.

And so the worst enemy you have to overcome, after all, is *yourself*. When Capt. T— became converted in London, he was a great society man. After he had been a Christian some months, he was asked: "What have you found to be your greatest enemy since you began to be a Christian?"

After a few minutes of deep thought he said, "Well, I think it is myself."

"Ah!" said the lady, "the King has taken you into His presence, for it is only in His presence that we are taught these truths."

I have had more trouble with D. L. Moody than with any other man who has crossed my path. If I can only keep him right, I don't have any trouble with other people. A good many have trouble with servants. Did you ever think that the trouble lies with you instead of the servants? If one member of the family is constantly snapping, he will have the whole family snapping. It is true whether you believe it or not. You speak quickly and snappishly to people, and they will do the same to you.

Appetite

Now take *appetite*. That is an enemy inside. How many young men are ruined by the appetite for strong drink! Many a young man has grown up to be a curse to his father and mother, instead of a blessing. Not long ago the body of a young suicide was discovered in one of our large cities. In his pocket was found a paper on which he had written: "I have done this myself. Don't tell anyone. It is all through drink." An intimation of these facts in the public press drew 246 letters from 246 families, each of whom had a prodigal son who, it was feared, might be the suicide.

Strong drink is an enemy, both to body and soul. It is reported that Sir Andrew Clarke, the celebrated London physician, once made the following statement:

Now let me say that I am speaking solemnly and carefully when I tell you that I am considerably within the mark in saying that within the rounds of my hospital wards today, seven out of every ten that lie there in their beds owe their ill health to alcohol. I do not say that seventy in every hundred are drunkards; I do not know that one of them is; but they use alcohol. So soon as a man begins to take one drop, then the desire begotten in him becomes a part of his nature, and that nature, formed by his acts, inflicts curses inexpressible when handed down to the generations that are to follow him as part and parcel of their being. When I think of this I am disposed to give up my profession—to give up everything—and to go forth upon a holy crusade to preach to all men, "Beware of this enemy of the race!"

It is the most destructive agency in the world today. It kills more than the bloodiest wars. It is the fruitful parent of crime and idleness and poverty and disease. It spoils a man for this world, and damns him for the next. The Word of God has declared it: "Be not deceived: neither fornicators, nor idolaters, nor adulterers . . . nor *drunkards* . . . shall inherit the kingdom of God" (1 Cor. 6:9).

How can we overcome this enemy? Bitter experience proves that man is not powerful enough in his own strength. The only cure for the accused appetite is regeneration—a new life—the power of the risen Christ within us. Let a man that is given to strong drink look to God for help, and He will give him victory over his appetite. Jesus Christ came to destroy the works of the devil, and He will take away that appetite if you will let Him.

Temper

Then there is *temper*. I wouldn't give much for a man that hasn't temper. Steel isn't good for anything if it hasn't got temper. But when temper gets the mastery over me, I am its slave, and it is a source of weakness. It may be made a great power for good all through my life, and help me; or it may become my greatest enemy from within, and rob me of power. The current in some rivers is so strong as to make them useless for navigation.

Someone has said that a preacher will never miss the people when he speaks of temper. It is astonishing how little mastery even professing Christians have over it. A friend of mine in England was out visiting, and while sitting in the parlor, heard an awful noise in the hall. He asked what it meant, and was told that it was only the doctor throwing his boots downstairs because they were not properly blacked. "Many Christians," said an old divine, "who bore the loss of a child or of all their property with the most heroic Christian fortitude, are entirely vanquished by the breaking of a dish or the blunders of a servant."

I have had people say to me, "Mr. Moody, how can I get control of my temper?"

If you really want to get control, I will tell you how, but you won't like the medicine. Treat it as a sin and confess it. People look upon it as a sort of misfortune, and one lady told me she inherited it from her father and mother. Supposing she did. That is no excuse for her.

When you get angry again and speak unkindly to a person, and when you realize it, go and ask that person to forgive you. You won't get mad with that person for the next twenty-four hours. You might do it in about forty-eight hours, but go the second time, and after you have done it about half a dozen times, you will get out of the business, because it makes the old flesh burn.

A lady said to me once, "I have got so in the habit of exaggerating that my friends accuse me of exaggerating so that they don't understand me."

She said, "Can you help me? What can I do to overcome it?"

"Well," I said, "the next time you catch yourself lying, go right to that party and say you have lied, and tell him you are sorry. Say it is a lie; stamp it out, root and branch; that is what you want to do."

"Oh," she said, "I wouldn't like to call it *lying*." But that is what it was.

Christianity isn't worth a snap of your finger if it doesn't straighten out your character. I have got tired of all mere gush and sentiment. If people can't tell when you are telling the truth, there is something radically wrong, and you had better straighten it out right away. Now, are you ready to do it? Bring yourself to it whether you want to or not. Do you find someone who has been offended by something you have done? Go right to them and tell them you are sorry. You say you are not to blame. Never mind, go right to them, and tell them you are sorry. I have had to do it a good many times. An impulsive man like myself has to do it often, but I sleep all the sweeter at night when I get things straightened out. Confession never fails to bring a blessing. I have sometimes had to get off the platform and go down and ask a man's forgiveness before I could go on preaching. A Christian man ought to be a gentleman every time; but if he is not, and he finds he has wounded or hurt someone, he ought to go and straighten it out at once. You know there are a great many people who want just Christianity enough to make them respectable. They don't think about this overcoming life that gets the victory all the time. They have their blue days and their cross days, and the children say, "Mother is cross today, and you will have to be very careful."

We don't want any of these touchy blue days, these ups and downs. If we are overcoming, that is the effect our lives are going to have on others; they will have confidence in our Christianity. The reason that many a man has no power is that there is some cursed sin covered up. There will not be a drop of dew until that sin is brought to light. Get right inside. Then we can go out like giants and conquer the world if everything is right within.

Paul says that we are to be sound in faith, in patience, and in love. If a man is unsound in his faith, the clergy take the ecclesiastical sword and cut him off at once. But he may be ever so unsound in charity, in patience, and nothing is said about that. We must be sound in faith, in love, and in patience if we are to be true to God.

How delightful it is to meet a man who can control his temper! It is said of Wilberforce that a friend once found him in the greatest agitation, looking for a dispatch he had mislaid, for which one of the royal family was waiting. Just then, as if to make it still more trying, a disturbance was heard in the nursery.

Now, thought the friend, *surely his temper will give way.*

The thought had hardly passed through his mind when Wilberforce turned to him and said: "What a blessing it is to hear those dear children! Only think what a relief, among other hurries, to hear their voices and know they are well."

Covetousness

Take the sin of *covetousness*. There is more said in the Bible against it than against drunkenness. I must get it out of me—destroy it, root and branch—and not let it have dominion over me. We think that a man who gets drunk is a horrid monster, but a covetous man will often be received into the church, and put into office, who is as vile and black in the sight of God as any drunkard.

The most dangerous thing about this sin is that it is not generally regarded as very heinous. Of course we all have a contempt for misers, but all covetous men are not misers. Another thing to be noted about it is that it fastens upon the old rather than upon the young.

Let us see what the Bible says about covetousness:

"Mortify therefore your members . . . covetousness, which is idolatry."

"No covetous man hath any inheritance in the kingdom of God."

"They that will be (that is, desire to be) rich fall into temptation and a snare, and into many foolish and hurtful lusts, which drown men in destruction and perdition."

"For the love of money is the root of all evil: which while some coveted after, they have erred from the faith, and pierced themselves through with many sorrows."

"The wicked blesseth the covetous, whom the Lord abhorreth."

Covetousness enticed Lot into Sodom. It caused the destruction of Achan and all his house. It was the iniquity of Balaam. It was the sin of Samuel's sons. It left Gehazi a leper. It sent the rich young ruler away sorrowful. It led Judas to sell his Master and Lord. It brought about the death of Ananias and Sapphira. It was the blot in the character of Felix. What victims it has had in all ages!

Do you say: "How am I going to check covetousness?"

Well, I don't think there is any difficulty about that. If you find yourself getting very covetous—very miserly—wanting to get everything you can into your possession, just begin to scatter. Just say to covetousness that you will strangle it, and rid it out of your disposition.

A wealthy farmer in New York state, who had been a noted miser, a very selfish man, was converted. Soon after his conversion a poor man came to him one day to ask for help. He had been burned out, and had no provisions. This young convert thought he would be liberal and give him a ham from his smokehouse. He started toward the smokehouse, and on the way the tempter said, "Give him the smallest one you have."

He struggled all the way as to whether he would give a large or a small one. In order to overcome his selfishness, he took down the biggest ham and gave it to the man.

The tempter said, "You are a fool."

But he replied, "If you don't keep still, I will give him every ham I have in the smokehouse."

If you find that you are selfish, give something. Determine to overcome that spirit of selfishness, and to keep your body under, no matter what it may cost.

Mr. Durant told me he was engaged by Goodyear to defend the rubber patent, and he was to have half of the money that came from the patent if he succeeded. One day he woke up to find that he was a rich man, and he said that the greatest struggle of his life then took place as to whether he would let money be his master, or he be master of money; whether he would be its slave, or make it a slave to him. At last he got the victory, and that is how Wellesley College was built.

Are You Jealous, Envious?

Go and do a good turn for that person of whom you are jealous. That is the way to cure jealousy; it will kill it. Jealousy is a devil, it is a horrid monster. The poets imagined that Envy dwelt in a dark cave, being pale and thin, looking asquint, never rejoicing except in the misfortune of others, and hurting himself continually.

There is a fable of an eagle which could outfly another, and the other didn't like it. The latter saw a sportsman one day, and said to him, "I wish you would bring down that eagle."

The sportsman replied that he would if he only had some feathers to put into the arrow. So the eagle pulled one out of his wing. The arrow was shot, but didn't quite reach the rival eagle; it was flying too high. The envious eagle pulled out more feathers, and kept pulling them out until he lost so many that he couldn't fly, and then the sportsman turned around and killed him. My friend, if you are jealous, the only man you can hurt is yourself.

There were two businessmen—merchants—and there was great rivalry between them, a great deal of bitter feeling. One of them was converted. He went to his minister and said, "I am still jealous of that man, and I do not know how to overcome it."

"Well," he said, "if a man comes into your store to buy goods, and you cannot supply him, just send him over to your neighbor."

He said he wouldn't like to do that.

"Well," the minister said, "you do it and you will kill jealousy."

He said he would, and when a customer came into his store for goods which he did not have, he would tell him to go across the street to his neighbor's. By and by the other began to send his customers over to this man's store, and the breach was healed.

Pride

Then there is *pride*. This is another of those sins which the Bible so strongly condemns, but which the world hardly reckons as a sin at all. "An high look and a proud heart is sin." "Every one that is proud in heart is an abomination to the LORD; though hand join in hand, he shall not be unpunished." Christ included pride among those evil things which, proceeding out of the heart of a man, defile him.

People have an idea that it is just the wealthy who are proud. But go down on some of the back streets, and you will find that some of the very poorest are as proud as the richest. It is the heart, you know. People that haven't any money are just as proud as those that have. We have got to crush it out. It is an enemy. You needn't be proud of your face, for there is not one but that after ten days in the grave the worms would be eating your body. There is nothing to be proud of—is there? Let us ask God to deliver us from pride.

You can't fold your arms and say, "Lord, take it out of me"; but just go and work with Him.

Mortify your pride by cultivating humility. "Put on, therefore," says Paul, "as the elect of God, holy and beloved . . . humbleness of mind." "Be clothed with humility," says Peter. "Blessed are the poor in spirit."

PART 3

External Foes

What are our enemies without? What does James say? "Know ye not that the friendship of the world is enmity with God? Whosoever therefore will be a friend of the world is the enemy of God." And John? "Love not the world, neither the things that are in the world. If any man love the world, the love of the Father is not in him."

Now, people want to know what is *the world*. When you talk with them they say: "Well, when you say 'the world,' what do you mean?"

Here we have the answer in the next verse: "For all that is in the world, the lust of the flesh, and the lust of the eyes, and the pride of life, is not of the Father, but is of the world. And the world passeth away, and the lust thereof: but he that doeth the will of God abideth forever."

"The world" does not mean nature around us. God nowhere tells us that the material world is an enemy to be overcome. On the contrary, we read: "The earth is the LORD's, and the fullness thereof; the world, and they that dwell therein." "The heavens declare the glory of God; and the firmament sheweth His handywork."

It means "human life and society as far as alienated from God, through being centered on material aims and objects, and thus opposed to God's Spirit and kingdom." Christ said: "If the world hate you, ye know that it hated Me before it hated you . . . the world hath hated them because they are not of the world, even as I am not of the world." Love of the world means the forgetfulness of the eternal future by reason of love for passing things.

How can the world be overcome? Not by education, not by experience; only by faith. "This is the victory that overcometh the world, even our faith. Who is he that overcometh the world, but he that believeth that Jesus is the Son of God?"

Worldly Habits and Fashions

For one thing, we must fight *worldly habits and fashions*. We must often go against the customs of the world. I have great respect for a man who can stand up for what he believes is right against all the world. He who can stand alone is a hero.

Suppose it is the custom for young men to do certain things you wouldn't like your mother to know of—things that your mother taught you are wrong. You may have to stand up alone among all your companions.

They will say: "You can't get away from your mother, eh? Tied to your mother's apron-strings!"

But just you say: "Yes! I have some respect for my mother. She taught me what is right, and she is the best friend I have. I believe that is wrong, and I am going to stand for the right." If you have to stand alone, *stand*. Enoch did it, and Joseph, and Elisha, and Paul. God has kept such men in all ages.

Someone says: "I move in society where they have wine parties. I know it is rather a dangerous thing because my son is apt to follow me. But I can stop just where I want to; perhaps my son hasn't got the same power as I have, and he may go over the dam. But it is the custom in the society where I move."

Once I got into a place where I had to get up and leave. I was invited into a home, and they had a late supper, and there were seven kinds of liquor on the table. I am ashamed to say they were Christian people. A deacon urged a young lady to drink until her face flushed. I rose from the table and went out; I felt that it was no place for me. They considered me very rude. That was going against custom; that was entering a protest against such an infernal thing. Let us go against custom, when it leads astray.

I was told in a southern college, some years ago, that no man was considered a first-class gentleman who did not drink. Of course it is not so now.

Pleasure

Another enemy is *worldly pleasure*. A great many people are just drowned in pleasure. They have no time for any meditation at all. Many a man has been lost to society, and lost to his family, by giving himself up to the god of pleasure. God wants His children to be happy, but in a way that will help and not hinder them.

A lady came to me once and said: "Mr. Moody, I wish you would tell me how I can become a Christian." The tears were rolling down her cheeks, and she was in a very favorable mood; "But," she said, "I don't want to be one of your kind."

"Well," I asked, "have I got any peculiar kind? What is the matter with my Christianity?"

"Well," she said, "my father was a doctor, and had a large practice, and he used to get so tired that he used to take us to the theater. There was a large family of girls, and we had tickets for the theaters three or four times a week. I suppose we were there a good deal oftener than we were in church. I am married to a lawyer, and he has a large practice. He gets so tired that he takes us out to the theater." And she said, "I am far better acquainted with the theater and theater people than with the church and church people, and I don't want to give up the theater."

"Well," I said, "did you ever hear me say anything about theaters? There have been reporters here every day for all the different papers, and they are giving my sermons verbatim in one paper. Have you ever seen anything in the sermons against the theaters?"

She said, "No."

"Well," I said, "I have seen you in the audience every afternoon for several weeks and have you heard me say anything against theaters?"

No, she hadn't.

"Well," I said, "what made you bring them up?"

"Why, I supposed you didn't believe in theaters."

"What made you think that?"

"Why," she said. "Do you ever go?"

"No."

"Why don't you go?"

"Because I have got something better. I would sooner go out into the street and eat dirt than do some of the things I used to do before I became a Christian."

"Why!" she said, "I don't understand."

"Never mind," I said. "When Jesus Christ has the preeminence, you will understand it all. He didn't come down here and say we shouldn't go here and we shouldn't go there, and lay down a lot of rules; but He laid down great principles. Now, He says if you love Him you will take delight in pleasing Him." And I began to preach Christ to her. The tears started again.

She said: "I tell you, Mr. Moody, that sermon on the indwelling Christ yesterday afternoon just broke my heart. I admire Him, and I want to be a Christian, but I don't want to give up the theaters."

I said, "Please don't mention them again. I don't want to talk about theaters. I want to talk to you about Christ." So I took my Bible, and I read to her about Christ.

But she said again, "Mr. Moody, can I go to the theater if I become a Christian?"

"Yes," I said, "you can go to the theater just as much as you like if you are a real, true Christian, and can go with His blessing."

"Well," she said, "I am glad you are not so narrow-minded as some."

She felt quite relieved to think that she could go to the theaters and be a Christian. But I said, "If you can go to the theater for the glory of God, keep on going; only be sure that you go for the glory of God. If you are a Christian you will be glad to do whatever will please Him."

I really think she became a Christian that day. The burden had gone, there was joy; but just as she was leaving me at the door, she said, "I am not going to give up the theater."

In a few days she came back to me and said, "Mr. Moody, I understand all about that theater business now. I went the other night. There was a large party at our house, and my husband wanted us to go, and we went; but when the curtain lifted, everything looked so different. I said to my husband, 'This is no place for me; this is horrible. I am not going to stay here, I am going home.' He said, 'Don't make a fool of yourself. Everyone has heard that you have been converted in the Moody meetings, and if you go out, it will be all through fashionable society. I beg of you don't make a fool of yourself by getting up and going out.' But I said, 'I have been making a fool of myself all of my life.'"

Now, the theater hadn't changed, but she had got something better and she was going to overcome the world. "They that are after the flesh do mind the things of the flesh; but they that are after the Spirit the things of the Spirit." When Christ has the first place in your heart, you are going to get victory. Just do whatever you know will please Him. The great objection I have to these things is that they get the mastery, and become a hindrance to spiritual growth.

Business

It may be that we have got to overcome in *business*. Perhaps it is business morning, noon, and night, and Sundays too. When a man will drive like Jehu all the week and like a snail on Sunday, isn't there something wrong with him? Now, business is legitimate; and a man is not, I think, a good citizen that will not go out and earn his bread by the sweat of his brow; and he ought to be a good businessman, and whatever he does, do thoroughly. At the same time, if he lays his whole heart on his business, and makes a god of it, and thinks more of it than anything else, then the world has come in. It may be very legitimate in its place—like fire, which, in its place, is one of the best friends of man; out of place, is one of the worst enemies of man—or like water, which we cannot live without; and yet, when not in place, it becomes an enemy.

So, my friends, that is the question for you and me to settle. Now look at yourself. Are you getting the victory? Are you growing more even in your disposition? Are you getting mastery over the world and the flesh?

And bear this in mind: Every temptation you overcome makes you stronger to overcome others, while every temptation that defeats you makes you weaker. You can become weaker and weaker, or you can become stronger and stronger. Sin takes the pith out of your sinews, but virtue makes you stronger. How many men have been overcome by some little thing! Turn a moment to the Song of Solomon 2:15: "Take us the foxes, the little foxes that spoil the vines: for our vines have tender grapes." A great many people seem to think these little things—getting out of patience, using little deceits, telling white lies (as they call them), and when somebody calls on you sending word by the servant you are not at home—all these are little things. Sometimes you can brace yourself up against a great temptation; and almost before you know it you fall before some little thing. A great many men are overcome by a little *persecution*.

Persecution

Do you know, I don't think we have enough persecution nowadays. Some people say we have persecution that is just as hard to bear as in the Dark Ages. Anyway, I think it would be a good thing if we had a little of the old-fashioned kind just now. It would bring out the strongest characters and make us all healthier. I have heard men get up in prayer meeting and say they were going to make a few remarks, and then keep on till you would think they were going to talk all week. If we had a little persecution, people of that kind wouldn't talk so much. Charles Spurgeon used to say some Christians would make good martyrs; they would burn well, they are so dry. If there were a few stakes for burning Christians, I think it would take all the piety out of some men. I admit they haven't got much; but then if they are not willing to suffer a little persecution for Christ, they are not fit to be His disciples. We are told: "All that will live godly in Christ Jesus shall suffer persecution." Make up your mind to this: If the world has nothing to say against you, Jesus Christ will have nothing to say for you.

The most glorious triumphs of the Church have been won in times of persecution. The early church was persecuted for about three hundred years after the crucifixion, and they were years of growth and progress. But then, as Saint Augustine has said, the cross passed from the scene of public executions to the diadem of the Caesars, and the downgrade movement began. When the Church has joined hands with the State, it has invariably retrograded in spirituality and effectiveness; but the opposition of the State has only served to purify it of all dross. It was persecution that gave Scotland to Presbyterianism. It was persecution that gave this country to civil and religious freedom.

How are we to overcome in time of persecution? Hear the words of Christ: "In the world ye shall have tribulation: but be of good cheer: I have overcome the world." Paul could testify that though persecuted, he was never forsaken; that the Lord stood by him, and strengthened him, and delivered him out of all his persecutions and afflictions.

A great many shrink from the Christian life because they will be *sneered at*. And then, sometimes when persecution won't bring a man down, *flattery* will. Foolish persons often come up to a man after he has preached and flatter him. Sometimes ladies do that. Perhaps they will say to some worker in the church: "You talk a great deal better than so-and-so," and he becomes proud and begins to strut around as if he was the most important person in the town. I tell you, we have a wily devil to contend with. If he can't overcome you with opposition, he will try flattery or ambition; and if that doesn't serve his purpose, perhaps there will come some affliction or disappointment, and he will overcome in that way. But remember that anyone that has got Christ to help him can overcome every foe, and overcome them singly or collectively. Let them come. If we have got Christ within us, we will overthrow them all. Remember what Christ is able to do. In all the ages men have stood in greater temptations than you and I will ever have to meet.

Now, there is one more thing on this line: I have either got to overcome the world, or the world is going to overcome me. I have either got to conquer sin in me—or sin about me—and get it under my feet, or it is going to conquer me. A good many people are satisfied with one or two victories, and think that is all. I tell you, my dear friends, we have got to do sometimes more than that. It is a battle all the time. We have this to encourage us: we are assured of victory at the end. We are promised a glorious triumph.

Eight "Overcomes"

Let me give you the eight "overcomes" of Revelation.

The first is: "*To him that overcometh will I give to eat of the tree of life.*" He shall have a right to the tree of life. When Adam fell, he lost that right. God turned him out of Eden lest he should eat of the tree of life and live as he was forever. Perhaps He just took that tree and transplanted it to the garden above; and through the second Adam we are to have the right to eat of it.

Second: "*He that overcometh shall not be hurt of the second death.*" Death has no terrors for him, it cannot touch him. Why?

Because Christ tasted death for every man. Hence he is on resurrection ground. Death may take this body, but that is all. This is only the house I live in. We need have no fear of death if we overcome.

Third: "*To him that overcometh will I give to eat of the hidden manna, and will give him a white stone and in the stone a new name written, which no man knoweth saving he that receiveth it.*" If I overcome, God will feed me with bread that the world knows nothing about, and give me a new name.

Fourth: "*He that overcometh, and keepeth My works unto the end, to him will I give power over the nations.*" Think of it! What a thing to have; power over the nations! A man that is able to rule himself is the man that God can trust with power. Only a man who can govern himself is fit to govern other men. I have an idea that we are down here in training, that God is just polishing us for some higher service. I don't know where the kingdoms are, but if we are to be kings and priests we must have kingdoms to reign over.

Fifth: "*He that overcometh, the same shall be clothed in white raiment; and I will not blot out his name out of the book of life, but I will confess his name before My Father, and before His angels.*" He shall present us to the Father in white garments, without spot or wrinkle. Every fault and stain shall be taken out, and we will be made perfect. He that overcomes will not be a stranger in heaven.

Sixth: "*Him that overcometh will I make a pillar in the temple of My God; and he shall go no more out; and I will write upon him the name of My God and the name of the city of My God, which is New Jerusalem, which cometh down out of heaven from My God: and I will write upon him My new name.*" Think of it! No more backsliding, no more wandering over the dark mountains of sin, but forever with the King, and He says, "I will write upon him the name of My God." He is going to put His name upon us. Isn't it grand? Isn't it worth fighting for? It is said when Mahomet came in sight of Damascus and found that they had all left the city, he said: "If they won't fight for this city, what will they fight for?" If men won't fight here for all this reward, what will they fight for?

Seventh: "*To him that overcometh will I grant to sit with Me in My throne, even as I also overcame, and am set down with My Father in His throne.*" My heart has often melted as I have looked at that. The Lord of Glory coming down and saying: "I will grant to you to set on My throne, even as I sit on My Father's throne, if you will just overcome." Isn't it worth a struggle? How many will fight for a crown that is going to fade away! Yet we are to be placed above the angels, above the archangels, above the seraphim, above the cherubim, away up, upon the throne with Himself, and there we shall be forever with Him. May God put strength into every one of us to fight the battle of life, so that we may sit with Him on His throne. When Frederick of Germany was dying, his own son would not have been allowed to sit with him on the throne, nor to have let anyone else sit there with him. Yet we are told that we are joint heirs with Jesus Christ, and that we are to sit with Him in glory!

And now, the last I like best of all: "*He that overcometh shall inherit all things; and I will be his God, and he shall be My son.*" My dear friends, isn't that a high calling? I used to have my Sabbath school children sing "I want to be an angel," but I have not done so for years. We shall be above angels: we shall be sons of God. Just see what a kingdom we shall come into; we shall inherit all things! Do you ask me how much I am worth? I don't know. The Rothschilds cannot compute their wealth. They don't know how many millions they own. That is my condition—I haven't the slightest idea how much I am worth. God has no poor children. If we overcome we shall inherit all things.

Oh, my dear friends, what an inheritance! Let us then get the victory, through Jesus Christ our Lord and Master.

1

Results of True Repentance

Moody notes five signs of true repentance: (1) conviction, (2) contrition, (3) confession of sin, (4) conversion, and (5) confession of Jesus Christ before the world. Repentance is the solution to the problem Dwight Moody saw in the church of his day. Too many Christians had a "low standard of Christian living." Many accepted Christ without recognizing the depth of their sin. Repentance, then, is crucial if we are to move beyond "weak Christianity."

———※———

I want to call your attention to what true repentance leads to. I am not addressing the unconverted only, because I am one of those who believe that there is a good deal of repentance to be done by the Church before much good will be accomplished in the world. I firmly believe that the low standard of Christian living is keeping a good many in the world and in their sins. When the ungodly see that Christian people do not repent, you cannot expect them to repent and turn away from their sins. I have repented ten thousand times more since I knew Christ than ever before, and I think most Christians have some things to repent of.

So now I want to preach to Christians as well as to the unconverted; to myself as well as to one who has never accepted Christ as his Savior.

There are five things that flow out of true repentance:

1. Conviction
2. Contrition
3. Confession of sin
4. Conversion
5. Confession of Jesus Christ before the world

1. Conviction

When a man is not deeply convicted of sin, it is a pretty sure sign that he has not truly repented. Experience has taught me that men who have very slight conviction of sin sooner or later lapse back into their old life. For the last few years, I have been a good deal more anxious for a deep and true work in professing converts than I have for great numbers. If a man professes to be converted without realizing the heinousness of his sins, he is likely to be one of those stony-ground hearers who don't amount to anything. The first breath of opposition, the first wave of persecution or ridicule, will suck them back into the world again.

I believe we are making a woeful mistake in taking so many people into the Church who have never been truly convicted of sin. Sin is just as black in a man's heart today as it ever was. I sometimes think it is blacker. For the more light a man has, the greater his responsibility, and therefore the greater need of deep conviction.

William Dawson once told this story to illustrate how humble the soul must be before it can find peace. He said that at a revival meeting, a little lad who was used to Methodist ways went home to his mother and said, "Mother, John So-and-So is under conviction and seeking for peace, but he will not find it tonight, Mother."

"Why, William?" said she.

"Because he is only down on one knee, Mother, and he will never get peace until he is down on both knees."

Until conviction of sin brings us down on both knees, until we are completely humbled, until we have no hope in ourselves left, we cannot find the Savior.

There are three things that lead to conviction: (1) conscience, (2) the Word of God, (3) the Holy Spirit. All three are used by God.

Long before we had any Word, God dealt with men through the conscience. That is what made Adam and Eve hide themselves from the presence of the Lord God among the trees of the garden of Eden. That is what convicted Joseph's brethren when they said: "We are verily guilty concerning our brother in that we saw the anguish of his soul when he besought us and we would not hear. Therefore," said they (and remember, over twenty years had passed away since they had sold him into captivity), "therefore is this distress come upon us." That is what we must use with our children before they are old enough to understand about the Word and the Spirit of God. This is what accuses or excuses the heathen.

Conscience is "a divinely implanted faculty in man, telling him that he ought to do right." Someone has said that it was born when Adam and Eve ate of the forbidden fruit, when their eyes were opened and they "knew good and evil." It passes judgment, without being invited, upon our thoughts, words, and actions, approving or condemning according as it judges them to be right or wrong. A man cannot violate his conscience without being self-condemned.

But conscience is not a safe guide, because very often it will not tell you a thing is wrong until you have done it. It needs illuminating by God because it partakes of our fallen nature. Many a person does things that are wrong without being condemned by conscience. Paul said: "I verily thought with myself that I ought to do many things contrary to the name of Jesus of Nazareth." Conscience itself needs to be educated.

Again, conscience is too often like an alarm clock, which awakens and arouses at first, but after a time the man becomes used to it, and it loses its effect. Conscience can be smothered. I think we make a mistake in not preaching more to the conscience.

Hence, in due time, conscience was superseded by the law of God, which in time was fulfilled in Christ.

In this Christian land, where men have Bibles, these are the agency by which God produces conviction. The old Book tells you what is right and wrong before you commit sin, and what you need is to learn and appropriate its teachings, under the guidance of the Holy Spirit. Conscience compared with the Bible is as a rushlight compared with the sun in the heavens.

See how the truth convicted those Jews on the day of Pentecost. Peter, filled with the Holy Ghost, preached that "God hath made this same Jesus, whom we have crucified, both Lord and Christ." "Now when they heard this, they were *pricked in their heart*, and said unto Peter and to the rest of the apostles, 'Men and brethren, what shall we do?'"

Then, thirdly, the Holy Ghost convicts. I once heard the late Dr. A. J. Gordon expound that passage—"And when He (the Comforter) is come, He will reprove the world of sin, of righteousness, and of judgment; of sin because they believe not on Me"—as follows:

Some commentators say there was no real conviction of sin in the world until the Holy Ghost came. I think that foreign missionaries will say that that is not true, that a heathen who never heard of Christ may have a tremendous conviction of sin. For notice that God gave conscience first, and gave the Comforter afterward. Conscience bears witness to the law, the Comforter bears witness to Christ. Conscience brings legal conviction, the

Comforter brings evangelical conviction. Conscience brings conviction unto condemnation, and the Comforter brings conviction unto justification. "He shall convince the world of sin, because they believe not on Me." That is the sin about which He convinces. It does not say that He convinces men of sin, because they have stolen or lied or committed adultery; but the Holy Ghost is to convince men of sin because they have not believed on Jesus Christ. The coming of Jesus Christ into the world made a sin possible that was not possible before. Light reveals darkness . . . and there are a great many people in this world that never knew they were sinful until they saw the face of Jesus Christ in all its purity.

Jesus Christ now stands between us and the law. He has fulfilled the law for us. He has settled all claims of the law, and now whatever claim it had upon us has been transferred to Him, so that it is no longer the *sin* question, but the *Son* question, that confronts us. And, therefore, you notice that the first thing Peter does when he begins to preach after the Holy Ghost has been sent down is about Christ: "Him being delivered by the determinate counsel of God, ye have taken and by wicked hands have crucified and slain." It doesn't say a word about any other kind of sin. That is the sin that runs all through Peter's teaching, and as he preached, the Holy Ghost came down and convicted them, and they cried out, "What shall we do to be saved?"

Well, but we had no part in crucifying Christ; therefore, what is our sin? It is the same sin in another form. They were convicted of crucifying Christ; we are convicted because we have not believed on Christ crucified. They were convicted because they had despised and rejected God's Son. The Holy Ghost convicts us because we have not believed in the Despised and Rejected One. It is really the same sin in both cases—the sin of unbelief in Christ.

Some of the most powerful meetings I have ever been in were those in which there came a sort of hush over the people, and it seemed as if an unseen power gripped their consciences. I remember a man coming to one meeting, and the moment he entered, he felt that God was there. There came an awe upon him, and that very hour he was convicted and converted.

2. Contrition

The next thing is contrition, deep godly sorrow and humiliation of heart because of sin. If there is not true contrition, a man will turn right back into the old sin. That is the trouble with many Christians.

A man may get angry, and if there is not much contrition, the next day he will get angry again. A daughter may say mean, cutting things to her mother, and then her conscience troubles her, and she says: "Mother, I am sorry: forgive me."

But soon there is another outburst of temper, because the contrition is not deep and real. A husband speaks sharp words to his wife, and then to ease his conscience, he goes and buys her a bouquet of flowers. He will not go like a man and say he has done wrong.

What God wants is contrition, and if there is not contrition, there is not full repentance. "The Lord is nigh to the broken of heart, and saveth such as be contrite of spirit." "A broken and a contrite heart, O God, Thou wilt not despise." Many sinners are sorry for their sins, sorry that they cannot continue in sin; but they repent only with hearts that are not broken. I don't think we know how to repent nowadays. We need some John the Baptist, wandering through the land, crying: "Repent! Repent!"

3. Confession of Sin

If we have true contrition, that will lead us to confess our sins. I believe that nine-tenths of the trouble in our Christian life comes from failing to do this. We try to hide and cover up our sins; there is very little confession of them. Someone has said: "Unconfessed sin in the soul is like a bullet in the body."

If you have no power, it may be there is some sin that needs to be confessed, something in your life that needs straightening out. There is no amount of psalm-singing, no amount of attending religious meetings, no amount of praying or reading your Bible that is going to cover up anything of that kind. It must be confessed, and if I am too proud to confess, I need expect no mercy from God and no answers to my prayers. The Bible says: "He that covereth his sins shall not prosper." He may be a man in the pulpit, a priest behind the altar, a king on the throne; I don't care who he is. Man has been trying it for six thousand years. Adam tried it, and failed. Moses tried it when he buried the Egyptian whom he killed, but he failed. "Be sure your sin will find you out." You cannot bury your sin so deep but it will have a resurrection by and by, if it has not been blotted out by the Son of God. What man has failed to do for six thousand years, you and I had better give up trying to do.

There are three ways of confessing sin. All sin is against God, and must be confessed to Him. There are some sins I need never confess to anyone on earth. If the sin has been between myself and God, I may confess it alone in my closet: I need not whisper it in the ear of any mortal. "Father, I have sinned against heaven, and before Thee." "Against Thee, Thee only, have I sinned, and done this evil in Thy sight."

But if I have done some man a wrong, and he knows that I have wronged him, I must confess that sin not only to God but also to that man. If I have too much pride to confess it to him, I need not come to God. I may pray, and I may weep, but it will do no good. First confess to that man, and then go to God and see how quickly He will hear you, and send peace. "If thou bring thy gift to the altar, and there rememberest that thy brother hath aught against thee; leave there thy gift before the altar, and go thy ways. First be reconciled to thy brother, and then come and offer thy gift." That is the Scripture way.

Then there is another class of sins that must be confessed publicly. Suppose I have been known as a blasphemer, a drunkard, or a reprobate. If I repent of my sins, I owe the public a confession. The confession should be as public as the transgression. Many a person will say some mean thing about another in the presence of others, and then try to patch it up by going to that person alone. The confession should be made so that all who heard the transgression can hear it.

We are good at confessing other people's sins, but if it is true repentance, we shall have as much as we can do to look after our own. When a man or woman gets a good look into God's looking-glass, he is not finding fault with other people; he has as much as he can do at home.

"If we confess our sins, He is faithful and just to forgive us our sins, and to cleanse us from all unrighteousness." Thank God for the gospel! Church member, if there is any sin in your life, make up your mind that you will confess it, and be forgiven. Do not have any cloud between you and God. Be able to read your title clear to the mansion Christ has gone to prepare for you.

4. Conversion

Confession leads to true conversion, and there is no conversion at all until these three steps have been taken.

Now, the word *conversion* means two things. We say a man is *converted* when he is born again. But it also has a different meaning in the Bible. Peter said: "Repent ye therefore, and be converted." The Revised Version reads: "Repent therefore, and *turn*" (Acts 3:19 RSV). Paul said that he was not disobedient unto the heavenly vision, but began to preach to Jews and Gentiles that they should repent and *turn* to God. Some old divine has said: "Every man is born with his back to God. Repentance is a change of one's course. It is right about face."

Sin is a turning away from God. As someone has said, it is *aversion* from God and *conversion* to the world: and true repentance means conversion to God and aversion from the world. When there is true contrition, the heart is broken *for* sin; when there is true conversion, the heart is broken *from* sin. We leave the old life, we are translated out of the kingdom of darkness into the kingdom of light. Wonderful, isn't it?

Unless our repentance includes this conversion, it is not worth much. If a man continues in sin, it is proof of an idle profession. It is like pumping away continually at the ship's pumps, without stopping the leaks. Solomon said: "If they pray, and confess Thy name, and turn from their sin." Prayer and confession would be of no avail while they continued in sin. Let us heed God's call; let us forsake the old wicked way; let us return unto the Lord, and He will have mercy upon us; and to our God, for He will abundantly pardon.

If you have never turned to God, turn now. I have no sympathy with the idea that it takes six months, or six weeks, or six hours to be converted. It doesn't take you very long to turn around, does it? If you know you are wrong, then turn right about.

5. Confession of Christ

If you are converted, the next step is to confess it openly. Listen: "If thou shalt confess with thy mouth the Lord Jesus Christ, and shalt believe in thine heart that God hath raised Him from the dead, thou shalt be saved. For with the heart man believeth unto righteousness, and with the mouth confession is made unto salvation."

Confession of Christ is the culmination of the work of true repentance. We owe it to the world, to our fellow Christians, to ourselves. He died to redeem us, and shall we be ashamed or afraid to confess Him? Religion as an abstraction, as a doctrine, has little interest for the world, but what people can say from personal experience always has weight.

I remember some meetings being held in a locality where the tide did not rise very quickly, and bitter and reproachful things were being said about the work. But one day, one of the most prominent men in the place rose and said: "I want it to be known that I am a disciple of Jesus Christ; and if there is any odium to be cast on His cause, I am prepared to take my share of it."

It went through the meeting like an electric current, and a blessing came at once to his own soul and to the souls of others.

Men come to me and say: "Do you mean to affirm, Mr. Moody, that I've got to make a public confession when I accept Christ; do you mean to say I've got to confess Him in my place of business, and in my family? Am I to let the whole world know that I am on His side?"

That is precisely what I mean. A great many are willing to accept Christ, but they are not willing to publish it, to confess it. A great many are looking at the lions and the bears in the way. Now, my friends, the devil's mountains are only made of smoke. He can throw a straw into your path and make a mountain of it. He says to you: "You cannot confess and pray to your family; why, you'll break down! You cannot tell it to your shopmate; he will laugh at you." But when you accept Christ, you will have power to confess Him.

There was a young man in the West—it was the West in those days—who had been more or less interested about his soul's salvation. One afternoon, in his office, he said: "I will accept Jesus Christ as my Lord and Savior."

He went home and told his wife (who was a nominal professor of religion) that he had made up his mind to serve Christ, and he added: "After supper tonight I am going to take the company into the drawing room and erect the family altar."

"Well," said his wife, "you know some of the gentlemen who are coming to tea are skeptics, and they are older than you are, and don't you think you had better wait until after they have gone, or else go out in the kitchen and have your first prayer with the servants?"

The young man thought for a few moments, and then he said: "I have asked Jesus Christ into my house for the first time, and I shall take Him into the best room, not into the kitchen."

So he called his friends into the drawing room. There was a little sneering, but he read and prayed. That man afterwards became Chief Justice of the United States Court. Never be ashamed of the gospel of Christ: it is the power of God unto salvation.

A young man enlisted and was sent to his regiment. The first night he was in the barracks with about fifteen other young men who passed the time playing cards and gambling. Before retiring, he fell on his knees and prayed, and they began to curse him and jeer at him and throw boots at him.

So it went on the next night and the next, and finally the young man went and told the chaplain what had taken place, and asked what he should do.

"Well," said the chaplain, "you are not at home now, and the other men have just as much right in the barracks as you have. It makes them mad to hear you pray, and the Lord will hear you just as well if you say your prayers in bed and don't provoke them."

For weeks after the chaplain did not see the young man again, but one day he met him, and asked—"By the way, did you take my advice?"

"I did, for two or three nights."

"How did it work?"

"Well," said the young man, "I felt like a whipped hound, and the third night I got out of bed, knelt down, and prayed."

"Well," asked the chaplain, "how did that work?"

The young soldier answered: "We have a prayer meeting there now every night, and three have been converted, and we are praying for the rest."

Oh, friends, I am so tired of weak Christianity. Let us be out and out for Christ; let us give no uncertain sound. If the world wants to call us fools, let them do it. It is only a little while; the crowning day is coming. Thank God for the privilege we have of confessing Christ.

2

True Wisdom

This sermon might have been called "How to Shine." The central point of the sermon involves three assertions: (1) everyone wants to outshine their neighbor, (2) in human endeavors there are limited opportunities to outshine others, and (3) there are no limits to shining in the kingdom of God. Moody highlights the enduring influence of various Old and New Testament figures. In each case, Moody emphasizes the faithfulness these men of God exhibited despite the difficulties they faced. They showed true wisdom by looking past their situation and continuing to follow God.

True wisdom is exhibited when we live according to God's instruction. In both repentance and true wisdom, obedience is key. It is through obedience that we reflect Christ and win souls. Living according to what the world considers wisdom is not only limiting but wrongheaded. Moody demonstrates that if we want to shine, our best option (the only one that truly matters) is to shine in the kingdom of heaven.

———— ✳ ————

They that be wise shall shine as the brightness of the firmament; and they that turn many to righteousness as the stars for ever and ever.

Daniel 12:3

This verse is the testimony of an old man, and one who had the richest and deepest experience of any man living on the face of the earth at the time. He was taken down to Babylon when a young man; some Bible students think he was not more than twenty years of age. If anyone had said, when this young Hebrew was carried away into captivity, that he would outrank all the mighty men of that day—that all the generals who had been victorious in almost every nation at that time were to be eclipsed by this young slave— probably no one would have believed it. Yet for five hundred years no man whose life is recorded in history shone as did this man. He outshone Nebuchadnezzar, Belshazzar, Cyrus, Darius, and all the princes and mighty monarchs of his day.

We are not told when he was converted to a knowledge of the true God, but I think we have good reason to believe he had been brought under the influence of Jeremiah the prophet. Evidently some earnest, godly man, and no worldly professor, had made a deep impression upon him. Someone had at any rate taught him how he was to serve God.

We hear people nowadays talking about the hardness of the field where they labor; they say their position is a very peculiar one. Think of the field in which Daniel had to work. He was not only a slave but was held captive by a nation that detested the Hebrews. The language was unknown to him. There he was among idolaters; yet he commenced at once to shine. He took his stand for God from the very first, and so he went on through his whole life. He gave the dew of his youth to God, and he continued faithful right on till his pilgrimage was ended.

Notice that all those who have made a deep impression on the world, and have shone most brightly, have been men who lived in a dark day. Look at Joseph; he was sold as a slave into Egypt by the Ishmaelites, yet he took his God with him into captivity, as Daniel afterwards did. And he remained true to the last; he did not give up his faith because he had been taken away from home and placed among idolaters. He stood firm, and God stood by him.

Look at Moses, who turned his back upon the gilded palaces of Egypt and identified himself with his despised and downtrodden nation. If a man ever had a hard field it was Moses; yet he shone brightly and never proved unfaithful to his God.

Elijah lived in a far darker day than we do. The whole nation was going over to idolatry. Ahab and his queen and all the royal court were throwing their influence against worship of the true God. Yet Elijah stood firm, and shone brightly in that dark and evil day. How his name stands out on the page of history!

Look at John the Baptist. I used to think I would like to live in the days of the prophets, but I have given up that idea. You may be sure that when a prophet appears on the scene, everything is dark, and the professing Church of God has gone over to the service of the god of this world. So it was when John the Baptist made his appearance. See how his name shines out today! Eighteen centuries have rolled away, and yet the fame of that wilderness preacher shines brighter than ever. He was looked down upon in his day and generation, but he has outlived all his enemies; his name will be revered and his work remembered as long as the Church is on the earth.

Talk about your field being a hard one! See how Paul shone for God as he went out, the first missionary to the heathen, telling them of the God whom he served, and who had sent His Son to die a cruel death in order to save the world. Men reviled him and his teachings; they laughed him to scorn when he spoke of the crucified One. But he went on preaching the gospel of the Son of God. He was regarded as a poor tent-maker by the great and mighty ones of his day; but no one can now tell the name of any of his persecutors, or of those who lived at that time, unless their names happen to be associated with his and they were brought into contact with him.

Now, the fact is, all men like to shine. We may as well acknowledge it at once. Go into business circles, and see how men struggle to get into the front rank. Everyone wants to outshine his neighbor and to stand at the head of his profession. Go into the political world and see how there is a struggle going on as to who shall be the greatest. If you go into a school, you find that there is a rivalry among the boys and girls. They all want to stand at the top of the class. When a boy does reach this position and outranks all the rest, the mother is very proud of it. She will manage to tell all the neighbors how Johnnie has got on, and what a number of prizes he has gained.

Go into the army and you find the same thing—one trying to outstrip the other; everyone is very anxious to shine and rise above his comrades. Go among the young men in their games, and see how anxious the one is to outdo the other. So we have all that desire in us; we like to shine above our fellows.

And yet there are very few who can really shine in the world. Once in a while one man will outstrip all his competitors. Every four years what a struggle goes on throughout our country as to who shall be the president of the United States, the battle raging for six months or a year. Yet only one man can get the prize. There are a good many struggling to get the place, but many are disappointed, because only one can attain the coveted prize. But in the kingdom of God the very least and the very weakest may shine if they will. Not only can *one* obtain the prize, but *all* may have it if they will.

It does not say in this passage that the statesmen are going to shine as the brightness of the firmament. The statesmen of Babylon are gone; their very names are forgotten.

It does not say that the nobility are going to shine. Earth's nobility are soon forgotten. John Bunyan, the Bedford tinker, has outlived the whole crowd of those who were the nobility in his day. They lived for self, and their memory is blotted out. He lived for God and for souls, and his name is as fragrant as ever it was.

We are not told that the merchants are going to shine. Who can tell the name of any of the millionaires of Daniel's day? They were all buried in oblivion a few years after their death. Who were the mighty conquerors of that day? But few can tell. It is true that we hear of Nebuchadnezzar, but probably we should not have known very much about him but of his relations to the prophet Daniel.

How different with this faithful prophet of the Lord! Twenty-five centuries have passed away, and his name shines on and on and on, brighter and brighter. And it is going to shine while the Church of God exists. "They that be wise shall shine as the brightness of the firmament; and they that turn many to righteousness as the stars forever and ever."

How quickly the glory of this world fades away! Eighty years ago the great Napoleon almost made the earth to tremble. How he blazed and shone as an earthly warrior for a little while! A few years passed and a little island held that once proud and mighty conqueror; he died a poor brokenhearted prisoner. Where is he today? Almost forgotten. Who in all the world will say that Napoleon lives in their heart's affections?

But look at this despised and hated Hebrew prophet. They wanted to put him into the lions' den because he was too sanctimonious and too religious. Yet see how green his memory is today! How his name is loved and honored for his faithfulness to his God.

Many years ago I was in Paris, at the time of the Great Exhibition. Napoleon the Third was then in his glory. Cheer after cheer would rise as he drove along the streets of the city. A few short years, and he fell from his lofty estate. He died an exile from his country and his throne, and where is his name today? Very few think about him at all, and if his name is mentioned it is not with love and esteem. How empty and short-lived are the glory and the pride of this world! If we are wise, we will live for God and eternity; we will get outside of ourselves, and will care nothing for the honor and glory of this world. In Proverbs we read: "He that winneth souls is wise." If any man, woman, or child by a godly life and example can win one soul to God, their life will not have been a failure. They will have outshone all the mighty men of their day, because they will have set a stream in motion that will flow on and on forever and ever.

God has left us down here to shine. We are not here to buy and sell and get gain, to accumulate wealth, to acquire worldly position. This earth, if we are Christians, is not our home; it is up yonder. God has sent us into the world to shine for Him—to light up this dark world. Christ came to be the Light of the world, but men put out that light. They took it to Calvary and blew it out. Before Christ went up on high, He said to His disciples: "You are the light of the world. You are My witnesses. Go forth and carry the gospel to the perishing nations of the earth."

So God has called us to shine, just as much as Daniel was sent into Babylon to shine. Let no man or woman say that they cannot shine because they have not so much influence as some others may have. What God wants you to do is to use the influence you have. Daniel probably did not have much influence down in Babylon at first, but God soon gave him more, because he was faithful and used what he had.

Remember a small light will do a good deal when it is in a very dark place. Put one little tallow candle in the middle of a large hall, and it will give a good deal of light.

Away out in the prairie regions, when meetings are held at night in the log schoolhouses, the announcement of the meeting is given out in this way: "A meeting will be held by early candlelight."

The first man who comes brings a tallow dip with him. It is perhaps all he has, but he brings it and sets it on the desk. It does not light the building much, but it is better than nothing at all. The next man brings his candle, and the next family bring theirs. By the time the house is full, there is plenty of light. So if we all shine a little, there will be a good deal of light. That is what God wants us to do. If we cannot all be lighthouses, any one of us can at any rate be a tallow candle.

A little light will sometimes do a great deal. The city of Chicago was set on fire by a cow kicking over a lamp, and a hundred thousand people were burnt out of house and home. Do not let Satan get the advantage of you and make you think that because you cannot do any great thing you cannot do anything at all.

Then we must remember that we are to *let* our light shine. It does not say, "*Make* your light shine." You do not have to *make* light to shine; all you have to do is to *let* it shine.

I remember hearing of a man at sea who was very seasick. If there is a time when a man feels that he cannot do any work for the Lord it is then—in my opinion. While this man was sick, he heard that someone had fallen overboard. He was wondering if he could do anything to help to save the man. He laid hold of a light, and held it up to the porthole. The drowning man was saved. When this man got over his attack of sickness, he went on deck one day and was talking with the man who was rescued. The saved man gave this testimony. He said he had gone down the second time, and was just going down again for the last time, when he put out his hand. Just then, he said, someone held a light at the porthole, and the light fell on him. A sailor caught him by the hand and pulled him into the lifeboat.

It seemed a small thing to do to hold up the light, yet it saved the man's life. If you cannot do some great thing you can hold the light for some poor, perishing drunkard, who may be won to Christ and delivered from destruction. Let us take the torch of salvation and go into the dark homes, and hold up Christ to the people as the Savior of the world. If the perishing masses are to be reached, we must lay our lives right alongside theirs, and pray with them and labor for them. I would not give much for a man's Christianity if he is saved himself and is not willing to try to save others. It seems to me the basest ingratitude if we do not reach out the hand to others who are down in the same pit from which we were delivered. Who is able to reach and help drinking men like those who have themselves been slaves to the intoxicating cup? Will you not go out this very day and seek to rescue these men? If we were all to do what we can, we should soon empty the drinking-saloons.

I remember reading of a blind man who was found sitting at the corner of a street in a great city with a lantern beside him. Someone went up to him and asked what he had the lantern there for, seeing that he was blind, and the light was the same to him as the darkness. The blind man replied: "I have it so that no one may stumble over me."

Dear friends, let us think of that. Where one man reads the Bible, a hundred read you and me. That is what Paul meant when he said we were to be living epistles of Christ, known and read of all men. I would not give much for all that can be done by sermons, if we do not preach Christ by our lives. If we do not commend the gospel to people by our holy walk and conversation, we shall not win them to Christ. Some little act of kindness will perhaps do more to influence them than any number of long sermons.

A vessel was caught in a storm on Lake Erie, and they were trying to make for the harbor of Cleveland. At the entrance of that port they had what are called the upper lights and the lower lights. Away back on the bluffs were the upper lights burning brightly enough; but when they came near the harbor they could not see the lights showing the entrance to it. The pilot said he thought they had better get back on the lake again. The captain said he was sure they would go down if they went back, and he urged the pilot to do what he could to gain the harbor. The pilot said there was very little hope of making the harbor, as he had nothing to guide him as to how he should steer the ship. They tried all they could to get her in. She rode on the top of the waves, and then into the trough of the sea, and at last they found themselves stranded on the beach, where the vessel was dashed to pieces. Someone had neglected the lower lights, and they had gone out.

Let us take warning. God keeps the upper lights burning as brightly as ever, but He has left us down here to keep the lower lights burning. We are to represent Him here, as Christ represents us up yonder. I sometimes think if we had as poor a representative in the courts above as God has down here on earth, we would have a pretty poor chance of heaven. Let us have our loins girt and our lights brightly burning, so that others may see the way and not walk in darkness.

Speaking of a lighthouse reminds me of what I heard about a man in the state of Minnesota, who, some years ago, was caught in a fearful storm. That state is cursed with storms which come sweeping down so suddenly in the wintertime that escape is difficult. The snow will fall and the wind will beat it into the face of the traveler so that he cannot see two feet ahead. Many a man has been lost on the prairies when he has got caught in one of those storms.

This man was caught and was almost on the point of giving up when he saw a little light in a log house. He managed to get there and found a shelter from the fury of the tempest. He is now a wealthy man. As soon as he was able, he bought the farm and built a beautiful house on the spot where the log building stood. On the top of a tower he put a revolving light, and every night when there comes a storm he lights it up in the hope that it may be the means of saving someone else.

That is true gratitude, and that is what God wants us to do. If He has rescued us and brought us up out of the horrible pit, let us be always looking to see if there is not someone else whom we can help to save.

I remember hearing of two men who had charge of a revolving light in a lighthouse on a rock-bound and stormy coast. Somehow the machinery went wrong, and the light did not revolve. They were so afraid that those at sea should mistake it for some other light that they worked all the night through to keep the light moving round.

Let us keep our lights in the proper place, so that the world may see that the religion of Christ is not a sham but a reality. It is said that in the Grecian sports they had one game where the men ran with lights. They lit a torch at the altar and ran a certain distance; sometimes they were on horseback. If a man came in with his light still burning, he received a prize; if his light had gone out, he lost the prize.

How many there are who, in their old age, have lost their light and their joy! They were once burning and shining lights in the family, in the Sunday school, and in the church. But something has come in between them and God—the world or self—and their light has gone out. Reader, if you are one who has had this experience, may God help you to come back to the altar of the Savior's love and light up your torch anew, so that you can go out into the lanes and alleys and let the light of the gospel shine in these dark homes.

As I have already said, if we only lead one soul to Jesus Christ we may set a stream in motion that will flow on when we are dead and gone. Away up the mountainside there is a little spring; it seems so small that an ox might drink it up at a draught. By and by it becomes a rivulet; other rivulets run into it. Before long it is a large brook, and then it becomes a broad river sweeping onward to the sea. On its banks are cities, towns, and villages where many thousands live. Vegetation flourishes on every side, and commerce is carried down its stately bosom to distant lands.

So if you turn one to Christ, that one may turn a hundred; they may turn a thousand, and so the stream, small at first, goes on broadening and deepening as it rolls toward eternity.

In the book of Revelation we read: "I heard a voice from heaven saying unto me, Write, Blessed are the dead which die in the Lord from henceforth: Yea, saith the Spirit, that they may rest from their labors; and their works do follow them" (14:13).

There are many mentioned in the Scriptures of whom we read that they lived so many years and then they died. The cradle and the grave are brought close together; they lived and they died, and that is all we know about them. So in these days you could write on the tombstone of a great many professing Christians that they were born on such a day and they died on such a day; there is nothing whatever between.

But there is one thing you cannot bury with a good man; his influence still lives. They have not buried Daniel yet; his influence is as great today as it ever was. Do you tell me that Joseph is dead? His influence still lives and will continue to live on and on. You may bury the frail tenement of clay that a good man lives in, but you cannot get rid of his influence and example. Paul was never more powerful than he is today.

Do you tell me that John Howard, who went into so many of the dark prisons in Europe, is dead? Is Henry Martyn, or William Wilberforce, or John Bunyan dead? Go into the Southern states, and there you will find millions of men and women who once were slaves. Mention to any of them the name of Wilberforce, and see how quickly the eye will light up. He lived for something else besides himself, and his memory will never die out of the hearts of those for whom he lived and labored.

Is Wesley or Whitefield dead? The names of those great evangelists were never more honored than they are now. Is John Knox dead? You can go to any part of Scotland today and feel the power of his influence.

I will tell you who are dead. The enemies of these servants of God—those who persecuted them and told lies about them. But the men themselves have outlived all the lies that were uttered concerning them. Not only that; they will shine in another world. How true are the words of the old Book: "They that be wise shall shine as the brightness of the firmament; and they that turn many to righteousness as the stars forever and ever."

Let us go on turning as many as we can to righteousness. Let us be dead to the world, to its lies, its pleasures, and its ambitions. Let us live for God, continually going forth to win souls for Him.

Let me quote a few words by Dr. Chalmers:

Thousands of men breathe, move and live, pass off the stage of life, and are heard no more—Why? They do not partake of good in the world, and none were blessed by them; none could point to them as the means of their redemption; not a line they wrote, not a word they spoke could be recalled; and so they perished; their light went out in darkness, and they were not remembered more than insects of yesterday. Will you thus live and die, O man immortal? Live for something. Do good, and leave behind you a monument of virtue that the storms of time can never destroy. Write your name in kindness, love and mercy, on the hearts of the thousands you come in contact with year by year; you will never be forgotten. No, your name, your deeds will be as legible on the hearts you leave behind as the stars on the brow of evening. Good deeds will shine as the stars of heaven.

3

"Come Thou and All Thy House into the Ark"

Calling this sermon an exposition of Genesis 7 would be a stretch. In "Come Thou and All Thy House into the Ark," Moody uses the flood narrative in Genesis as a jumping-off point to reflect on the various sorts of opposition that often come with following God's Word. As he seeks to identify with Noah, Moody paints a picture of the pre-flood world that looks suspiciously like the world of his day. He assumes that there must have been atheists and agnostics ridiculing Noah. He references those who didn't believe God would destroy the world and those who thought Noah was wrong. He even posits that there must have been "saloons" because where there is violence there is also alcohol. Despite some creative retelling of Noah's experience while building the ark, Moody's sermon highlights the dangers of denying God and ignoring those who know Him. Noah, and the experience Dwight Moody imagines him to have had, become something of a cautionary tale. Just as there were people who were left outside the ark to be engulfed by the flood, so there will be those who refuse to accept Christ and suffer eternal judgment.

———*———

I want to call your attention to a text that you will find in Genesis 7:1. When God speaks, you and I can afford to listen. It is not man speaking now, but it is God. "The Lord said unto Noah, Come thou and all thy house into the ark."

Perhaps some skeptic is reading this, and perhaps some church member will join with him and say, "I hope Mr. Moody is not going to preach about the ark. I thought that was given up by all intelligent people."

But I want to say that I haven't given it up. When I do, I am going to give up the whole Bible. There is hardly any portion of the Old Testament Scripture but that the Son of God set His seal to it when He was down here in the world.

Men say, "I don't believe in the story of the flood."

Christ connected His own return to this world with that flood: "And as it was in the days of Noah, so shall it be also in the days of the Son of man. They did eat, they drank, they married wives, they were given in marriage, until the day that Noah entered into the ark, and the flood came, and destroyed them all."

I believe the story of the flood just as much as I do the third chapter of John. I pity any man that is picking the old Book to pieces. The moment that we give up any one of these things, we touch the deity of the Son of God. I have noticed that when a man does begin to pick the Bible to pieces, it doesn't take him long to tear it all to pieces. What is the use of being five years about what you can do in five minutes?

A Solemn Message

One hundred and twenty years before God spoke the words of my text, Noah had received the most awful communication that ever came from heaven to earth. No man up to that time, and I think no man since, has ever received such a communication. God said that on account of the wickedness of the world, He was going to destroy the world by water. We can have no idea of the extent and character of that antediluvian wickedness. The Bible piles one expression on another, in its effort to emphasize it. "God saw that the wickedness of man was great in the earth, and that every imagination of the thoughts of his heart was only evil continually. And it repented the LORD that He had made man on the earth, and it grieved Him at His heart. . . . The earth also was corrupt before God, and the earth was filled with violence. And God looked upon the earth, and, behold, it was corrupt; for all flesh had corrupted his way upon the earth." Men lived five hundred years and more then, and they had time to mature in their sins.

How the Message Was Received

For one hundred and twenty years, God strove with those antediluvians. He never smites without warning, and they had their warning. Every time Noah drove a nail into the ark it was a warning to them. Every sound of the hammer echoed, "I believe in God." If they had repented and cried as they did at Nineveh, I believe God would have heard their cry and spared them. But there was no cry for mercy. I have no doubt but that they ridiculed the idea that God was going to destroy the world. I have no doubt but that there were atheists who said there was not any God anyhow. I got hold of one of them some time ago. I said, "How do you account for the formation of the world?"

"Oh! Force and matter work together, and by chance the world was created."

I said, "It is a singular thing that your tongue isn't on the top of your head if force and matter just threw it together in that manner."

If I should take out my watch and say that force and matter worked together, and out came the watch, you would say I was a lunatic of the first order. Wouldn't you? And yet they say that this old world was made by chance! "It threw itself together!"

I met a man in Scotland, and he took the ground that there was no God. I asked him, "How do you account for creation, for all these rocks?" (They have a great many rocks in Scotland.)

"Why!" he said, "any school boy could account for that."

"Well, how was the first rock made?"

"Out of sand."

"How was the first sand made?"

"Out of rock."

You see he had it all arranged so nicely. Sand and rock, rock and sand. I have no doubt but that Noah had these men to contend with.

Then there was a class called agnostics, and there are a good many of their grandchildren alive today. Then there was another class who said they believed there was a God; they couldn't make themselves believe the world happened by chance, but God was too merciful to punish sin. He was so full of compassion and love that He couldn't punish sin. The drunkard, the harlot, the gambler, the murderer, the thief, and the libertine would all share alike with the saints at the end. Supposing the governor of your state was so tenderhearted that he could not bear to have a man suffer, could not bear to see a man put in jail, and he should go and set all the prisoners free. How long would he be governor? You would have him out of office before the sun set. These very men that talk about God's mercy would be the first to raise a cry against a governor who would not have a man put in prison when he had done wrong.

Then another class took the ground that God could not destroy the world anyway. They might have a great flood which would rise up to the meadowlands and lowlands, but all it would be necessary to do would be to go up on the hills and mountains. That would be a hundred times better than Noah's ark. Or if it should come to that, they could build rafts which would be a good deal better than that ark. They had never seen such an ugly looking thing. It was about five hundred feet long, and about eighty feet wide, and fifty feet high. It had three stories, and only one small window.

And then, I suppose there was a large class who took the ground that Noah must be wrong because he was in such a minority. That is a great argument now, you know. Noah was greatly in the minority. But he went on working.

If they had saloons then, and I don't doubt but that they had, for we read that there was "violence in the land," and wherever you have alcohol you have violence. We read also that Noah planted a vineyard and fell into the sin of intemperance. He was a righteous man, and if he did that, what must the others have done? Well, if they had saloons, no doubt they sang ribald songs about Noah and his ark, and if they had theaters they likely acted it out, and mothers took their children to see it.

And if they had the press in those days, every now and then there would appear a skit about "Noah and his folly." Reporters would come and interview him, and if they had an Associated Press, every few days a dispatch would be sent out telling how the work on the ark was progressing.

And perhaps they had excursions, and offered as an inducement that people could go through the ark. And if Noah happened to be around they would nudge each other and say: "That's Noah. Don't you think there is a strange look in his eye?"

As a Scotsman would say, they thought him a little daft. Thank God a man can afford to be mad. A mad man thinks everyone else mad but himself. A drunkard does not call himself mad when he is drinking up all his means. Those men who stand and deal out death and damnation to men are not called mad; but a man is called mad when he gets into the ark and is saved for time and eternity. And I expect if the word *crank* was in use, they called Noah "an old crank."

And so all manner of sport was made of Noah and his ark. And the businessmen went on buying and selling, while Noah went on preaching and toiling. They perhaps had some astronomers,

185

and they were gazing up at the stars and saying, "Don't you be concerned. There is no sign of a coming storm in the heavens. We are very wise men, and if there was a storm coming, we should read it in the heavens." And they had geologists digging away, and they said, "There is no sign in the earth." Even the carpenters who helped build the ark might have made fun of him, but they were like lots of people at the present day, who will help build a church, and perhaps give money for its support, but will never enter it themselves.

Well, things went on as usual. Little lambs skipped on the hillsides each spring. Men sought after wealth, and if they had leases, I expect they ran for longer periods than ours do. We think ninety-nine years a long time, but I don't doubt but that theirs ran for nine hundred and ninety-nine years. And when they came to sign a lease they would say with a twinkle in their eyes: "Why, this old Noah says the world is coming to an end in one hundred and twenty years, and it's twenty years since he started the story. But I guess I will sign the lease and risk it."

Someone has said that Noah must have been deaf, or he could not have stood the jeers and sneers of his countrymen. But if he was deaf to the voice of men, he heard the voice of God when He told him to build the ark.

I can imagine one hundred years have rolled away, and the work on the ark ceases. Men say, "What has he stopped work for?" He has gone on a preaching tour, to tell the people of the coming storm—that God is going to sweep every man from the face of the earth unless he is in the ark. But he cannot get a man to believe him except his own family. Some of the old men have passed away, and they died saying: "Noah is wrong." Poor Noah! He must have had a hard time of it. I don't think I should have had the grace to work for one hundred and twenty years without a convert. But he just toiled on, believing the Word of God.

And now the hundred and twenty years are up. In the spring of the year Noah did not plant anything, for he knew the flood was coming, and the people say: "Every year before he has planted, but this year he thinks the world is going to be destroyed, and he hasn't planted anything."

Moving In

But I can imagine one beautiful morning, not a cloud to be seen, Noah has got his communication. He has heard the voice that he heard one hundred and twenty years before—the same old voice. Perhaps there had been silence for one hundred and twenty years. But the voice rang through his soul once again: "Noah, come thou and all thy house into the ark."

The word *come* occurs about nineteen hundred times in the Bible, it is said, and this is the first time it meant salvation. You can see Noah and all his family moving into the ark. They are bringing the household furniture.

Some of his neighbors say, "Noah, what is your hurry? You will have plenty of time to get into that old ark. What is your hurry? There are no windows and you cannot look out to see when the storm is coming." But he heard the voice and obeyed.

Some of his relatives might have said, "What are you going to do with the old homestead?"

Noah says, "I don't want it. The storm is coming." He tells them the day of grace is closing, that worldly wealth is of no value, and that the ark is the only place of safety. We must bear in mind that these railroads that we think so much of will soon go down; they only run for time, not for eternity. The heavens will be on fire, and then what will property, honor, and position in society be worth?

The first thing that alarms them is, they rise one morning, and lo! The heavens are filled with the fowls of the air. They are flying into the ark, two by two. They come from the desert; they come from the mountain; they come from all parts of the world. They are going into the ark. It must have been a strange sight. I can hear the people cry, "Great God! What is the meaning of this?" And they look down on the earth; and, with great alarm and surprise, they see little insects creeping up two by two, coming from all parts of the world. Then behold! There come cattle and beasts, two by two. The neighbors cry out, "What does this mean?" They run to their statesmen and wise men, who have told them there was no sign of a coming storm, and ask them why it is that those birds, animals, and creeping things go toward the ark, as if guided by some unseen hand.

"Well," the statesmen and wise men say, "we cannot explain it; but give yourselves no trouble; God is not going to destroy the world. Business was never better than it is now. Do you think if God was going to destroy the world, He would let us go on so prosperously as He has? There is no sign of a coming storm. What has made these creeping insects and these wild beasts of the forest go into the ark, we do not know. We cannot understand it; it is very strange. But there is no sign of anything going to happen. The stars are bright, and the sun shines as bright as ever it did. Everything moves on as it has been moving for all time past. You can hear the children playing in the street. You can hear the voice of the bride and bridegroom in the land, and all is merry as ever."

I imagine the alarm passed away, and they fell into their regular courses. Noah comes out and says: "The door is going to be shut. Come in. God is going to destroy the world. See the animals, how they have come up. The communication has come to them direct from heaven." But the people only mocked on.

Do you know, when the hundred and twenty years were up, God gave the world seven days' grace? Did you ever notice that? If there had been a cry during those seven days, I believe it would have been heard. But there was none.

At length the last day had come, the last hour, the last minute, ay! The last second. God Almighty came down and shut the door of the ark. No angel, no man, but God Himself shut that door, and when once the master of the house has risen and shut the door, the doom of the world is sealed; and the doom of that old world was forever sealed. The sun had gone down upon the glory of that old world for the last time. You can hear away off in the distance the mutterings of the storm. You can hear the thunder rolling. The lightning begins to flash, and the old world reels. The storm bursts upon them, and that old ark of Noah's would have been worth more than the whole world to them.

I want to say to any scoffer who reads this, that you can laugh at the Bible, you can scoff at your mother's God, you can laugh at ministers and Christians, but the hour is coming when one promise in that old Book will be worth more to you than ten thousands of worlds like this.

The windows of heaven are opened and the fountains of the great deep are broken up. The waters come bubbling up, and the sea bursts its bounds and leaps over its walls. The rivers begin to swell. The people living in the lowlands flee to the mountains and highlands. They flee up the hillsides. And there is a wail going up: "Noah! Noah! Noah! Let us in."

They leave their homes and come to the ark now. They pound on the ark. Hear them cry: "Noah! Let us in. Noah! Have mercy on us."

"I am your nephew."

"I am your niece."

"I am your uncle."

Ah, there is a voice inside, saying: "I would like to let you in; but God has shut the door, and I cannot open it!"

God shut that door! When the door is shut, there is no hope. Their cry for mercy was too late; their day of grace was closed. Their last hour had come. God had pled with them; God had invited them to come in, but they had mocked at the invitation. They scoffed and ridiculed the idea of a deluge. Now it was too late.

God did not permit anyone to survive to tell us how they perished. When Job lost his family, there came a messenger to him, but there came no messenger from the antediluvians; not even Noah himself could see the world perish. If he could, he would have seen men and women and children dashing against that ark; the waves rising higher and higher, while those outside are perishing, dying in unbelief. Some think to escape by climbing the trees, and think the storm will soon go down; but it rains on, day and night, for forty days and forty nights, and they are swept away as the waves dash against them. The statesmen and astronomers and great men call for mercy, but it is too late. They had disobeyed the God of mercy. He had called, and they refused. He had pled with them, but they had laughed and mocked. But now the time is come for judgment instead of mercy.

Judgment

The time is coming again when God will deal in judgment with the world. It is but a little while; we know not when, but it is sure to come. God's Word has gone forth that this world shall be rolled together like a scroll, and shall be on fire. What then will become of your soul? It is a loving call: "Now come, thou and all thy house, into the ark." Twenty-four hours before the rain began to fall, Noah's ark, if it had been sold at auction, would not have brought as much as it would be worth for kindling wood. But twenty-four hours after the rain began to fall, Noah's ark was worth more than all the world. There was not then a man living but would have given all he was worth for a seat in the ark. You may turn away and laugh.

"I believe in Christ!" you say; "I would rather be without Him than have Him."

But bear in mind, the time is coming when Christ will be worth more to you than ten thousand worlds like this. Bear in mind that He is offered to you now. This is a day of grace; it is a day of mercy. You will find, if you read your Bible carefully, that God always precedes judgment with grace. Grace is a forerunner of judgment. He called these men in the days of Noah in love. They would have been saved if they had repented in those one hundred and twenty years. When Christ came to plead with the people in Jerusalem, it was their day of grace, but they mocked and laughed at Him. He said: "O Jerusalem, Jerusalem, thou that killest the prophets, and stonest them which are sent unto thee, how often would I have gathered thy children together, even as a hen gathereth her chickens under her wings, and ye would not!" Forty years afterward, thousands of the people begged that their lives might be spared; and eleven hundred thousand perished in that city.

In 1857 a revival swept over this country in the east and on to the western cities, clear over to the Pacific coast. It was God calling the nation to Himself. Half a million people united with the Church at that time. Then the war broke out. We were baptized with the Holy Ghost in 1857, and in 1861 we were baptized in blood. It was a call of mercy, preceding judgment.

Are Your Children Safe?

The text which I have selected has a special application to Christian people and to parents. This command of the Scripture was given to Noah not only for his own safety but that of his household, and the question which I put to each father and mother is this: "Are your children in the ark of God?" You may scoff at it, but it is a very important question. Are all your children in? Are all your grandchildren in? Don't rest day or night until you get your children in. I believe my children have fifty temptations where I had one. I am one of those who believe that in the great cities there is a snare set upon the corner of every street for our sons and daughters; and I don't believe it is our business to spend our time in accumulating bonds and stocks. Have I done all I can to get my children in? That is it.

Now, let me ask another question: What would have been Noah's feelings if, when God called him into the ark, his children would not have gone with him? If he had lived such a false life that his children had no faith in his word, what would have been

191

his feelings? He would have said: "There is my poor boy on the mountain. Would to God I had died in his place! I would rather have perished than had him perish." David cried over his son: "O my son Absalom, my son, my son Absalom! Would God I had died for thee!" Noah loved his children, and they had confidence in him.

Someone sent me a paper a number of years ago, containing an article that was marked. Its title was: "Are All the Children In?" An old wife lay dying. She was nearly one hundred years of age, and the husband who had taken the journey with her sat by her side. She was just breathing faintly, but suddenly she revived, opened her eyes, and said: "Why! It is dark."

"Yes, Janet, it is dark."

"Is it night?"

"Oh, yes! It is midnight."

"Are all the children in?"

There was that old mother living life over again. Her youngest child had been in the grave twenty years, but she was traveling back into the old days, and she fell asleep in Christ asking, "Are all the children in?"

Dear friend, are they all in? Put the question to yourself now. Is John in? Is James in? Or is he immersed in business and pleasure? Is he living a double and dishonest life? Say! Where is your boy, mother? Where is your son, your daughter? Is it well with your children? Can you say it is?

After being superintendent of a Sunday school in Chicago for a number of years, a school of over a thousand members, children that came from godless homes, having mothers and fathers working against me, taking the children off on excursions on Sunday, and doing all they could to break up the work I was trying to do, I used to think that if I should ever stand before an audience I would speak to no one but parents; they would be my chief business. It is an old saying—"Get the lamb, and you will get the sheep." I gave up on that years ago. Give me the sheep, and then I will have someone to nurse the lamb; but get a lamb and convert him, and if he has a godless father and mother, you will have little chance with that child. What we want is godly homes. The home was established long before the Church.

I have no sympathy with the idea that our children have to grow up before they are converted. Once I saw a lady with three daughters at her side, and I stepped up to her and asked her if she was a Christian.

"Yes, sir."

Then I asked the oldest daughter if she was a Christian. The chin began to quiver, and the tears came into her eyes, and she said, "I wish I was."

The mother looked very angrily at me and said, "I don't want you to speak to my children on that subject. They don't understand." And in great rage she took them all away from me. One daughter was fourteen years old, one twelve, and the other ten, but they were not old enough to be talked to about religion. Let them drift into the world and plunge into worldly amusements, and then see how hard it is to reach them. Many a mother is mourning today because her boy has gone beyond her reach and will not allow her to pray with him. She may pray *for* him, but he will not let her pray or talk *with* him. In those early days when his mind was tender and young, she might have led him to Christ. Bring them in. "Suffer the little children to come unto Me." Is there a prayerless father reading this? May God let the arrow go down into your soul! Make up your mind that, God helping you, you will get the children in. God's order is to the father first, but if he isn't true to his duty, then the mother should be true, and save the children from the wreck. Now is the time to do it while you have them under your roof. Exert your parental influence over them.

I never speak to parents but I think of two fathers, one of whom lived on the banks of the Mississippi, the other in New York. The first one devoted all his time to amassing wealth. He had a son to whom he was much attached, and one day the boy was brought home badly injured. The father was informed that the boy could live but a short time, and he broke the news to his son as gently as possible.

"You say I cannot live, father? Oh! Then pray for my soul," said the boy.

In all those years that father had never said a prayer for that boy, and he told him he couldn't. Shortly after, the boy died. That father has said since that he would give all that he possessed if he could call that boy back only to offer one short prayer for him.

The other father had a boy who had been sick some time, and he came home one day and found his wife weeping. She said: "I cannot help but believe that this is going to prove fatal."

The man started, and said: "If you think so, I wish you would tell him."

But the mother could not tell her boy. The father went to the sick room, and he saw that death was feeling for the cords of life, and he said: "My son, do you know you are not going to live?"

The little fellow looked up and said: "No; is this death that I feel stealing over me? Will I die today?"

"Yes, my son, you cannot live the day out."

And the little fellow smiled and said: "Well father, I shall be with Jesus tonight, shan't I?"

"Yes, you will spend the night with the Lord," and the father broke down and wept.

The little fellow saw the tears, and said: "Don't weep for me. I will go to Jesus and tell Him that ever since I can remember you have prayed for me."

I have three children, and if God should take them from me, I would rather have them take such a message home to Him than to have the wealth of the whole world. Oh! Would to God I could say something to stir you, fathers and mothers, to get your children into the ark.

4

Humility

Using Matthew 11:29 as his jumping-off point, Moody highlights the importance of humility in the Christian life. He does not focus on any particular text but points to Jesus, Moses, David, and John the Baptist to illustrate what it means to be humble and how humility benefits God's people. While one might expect to find a critique of pride and boasting, Moody doesn't provide one. Instead, he focuses on smaller actions that too often keep us in the limelight. For instance, he notes that if Luke were written today, it would have been signed by "Dr. Luke." Surely Moody would not encourage pride, but his sermon reminds us of the little ways we seek to draw honor to ourselves.

Learn of Me; for I am meek and lowly in heart.

Matthew 11:29

There is no harder lesson to learn than the lesson of humility. It is not taught in the schools of men, only in the school of Christ. It is the rarest of all the gifts. Very rarely do we find a man or woman who is following closely the footsteps of the Master in meekness and in humility. I believe that it is the hardest lesson which Jesus Christ had to teach His disciples while He was here upon earth. It almost looked at first as though He had failed to teach it to the twelve men who had been with Him almost constantly for three years.

I believe that if we are humble enough we shall be sure to get a great blessing. After all, I think that more depends upon us than upon the Lord, because He is always ready to give a blessing and give it freely, but we are not always in a position to receive it. He always blesses the humble, and, if we can get down in the dust before Him, no one will go away disappointed. It was Mary, at the feet of Jesus, who had chosen the "better part."

Did you ever notice the reason Christ gave for learning of Him? He might have said: "Learn of Me, because I am the most advanced thinker of the age. I have performed miracles that no man else has performed. I have shown My supernatural power in a thousand ways." But no: the reason He gave was that He was "meek and lowly in heart."

We read of the three men in Scripture whose faces shone, and all three were noted for their meekness and humility. We are told that the face of Christ shone at His transfiguration; Moses, after he had been in the mount for forty days, came down from his communion with God with a shining face; and when Stephen stood before the Sanhedrin on the day of his death, his face was lighted up with glory. If our faces are to shine, we must get into the valley of humility; we must go down in the dust before God.

Bunyan says that it is hard to get down into the valley of humiliation; the descent into it is steep and rugged, but it is very fruitful and fertile and beautiful when once we get there. I think that no one will dispute that; almost every man, even the ungodly, admire meekness.

Someone asked Augustine what was the first of the religious graces, and he said, "Humility." They asked him what was the second, and he replied, "Humility." They asked him the third, and he said, "Humility." I think that if we are humble, we have all the graces.

Some years ago I saw what is called a sensitive plant. I happened to breathe on it, and suddenly it drooped its head; I touched it, and it withered away. Humility is as sensitive as that; it cannot safely be brought out on exhibition. A man who is flattering himself that he is humble and is walking close to the Master is self-deceived. It consists not in thinking meanly of ourselves, but in not thinking of ourselves at all. "Moses wist not that the skin of his face shone" (Exod. 34:29). If humility speaks of itself, it is gone.

Someone has said that the grass is an illustration of this lowly grace. It was created for the lowliest service. Cut it, and it springs up again. The cattle feed upon it, and yet how beautiful it is.

The showers fall upon the mountain peaks, and very often leave them barren because they rush down into the meadows and valleys and make the lowly places fertile. If a man is proud and lifted up, rivers of grace may flow over him and yet leave him barren and unfruitful, while they bring blessing to the man who has been brought low by the grace of God.

A man can counterfeit love, he can counterfeit faith, he can counterfeit hope and all the other graces, but it is very difficult to counterfeit humility. You soon detect mock humility. They have a saying in the East among the Arabs, that as the tares and the wheat grow they show which God has blessed. The ears that God has blessed bow their heads and acknowledge every grain, and the more fruitful they are the lower their heads are bowed. The tares which God has sent as a curse lift up their heads erect, high above the wheat, but they are only fruitful of evil. I have a pear tree on my farm which is very beautiful; it appears to be one of the most beautiful trees on my place. Every branch seems to be reaching up to the light and stands almost like a wax candle, but I never get any fruit from it. I have another tree, which was so full of fruit last year that the branches almost touched the ground. If we only get down low enough, my friends, God will use every one of us to His glory.

> As the lark that soars the highest builds her nest the lowest; as the nightingale that sings so sweetly, sings in the shade when all things rest; as the branches that are most laden with fruit, bend lowest; as the ship most laden, sinks deepest in the water;—so the holiest Christians are the humblest.

The *London Times* some years ago told the story of a petition that was being circulated for signatures. It was a time of great excitement, and this petition was intended to have great influence in the House of Lords; but there was one word left out. Instead of reading, "We humbly beseech thee," it read, "We beseech thee." So it was ruled out. My friends, if we want to make an appeal to the God of heaven, we must humble ourselves; and if we do humble ourselves before the Lord, we shall not be disappointed.

As I have been studying some Bible characters that illustrate humility, I have been ashamed of myself. If you have any regard for me, pray that I may have humility. When I put my life beside the life of some of these men, I say, shame on the Christianity of the present day. If you want to get a good idea of yourself, look at some of the Bible characters that have been clothed with meekness and humility, and see what a contrast is your position before God and man.

One of the meekest characters in history was John the Baptist. You remember when they sent a deputation to him and asked if he was Elias, or this prophet, or that prophet, he said, "No." Now he might have said some very flattering things of himself. He might have said: "I am the son of the old priest Zacharias. Haven't you heard of my fame as a preacher? I have baptized more people, probably, than any man living. The world has never seen a preacher like myself."

I honestly believe that in the present day most men standing in his position would do that. On the railroad train, some time ago, I heard a man talking so loud that all the people in the car could hear him. He said that he had baptized more people than any man in his denomination. He told how many thousand miles he had traveled, how many sermons he had preached, how many open-air services he had held, and this and that, until I was so ashamed that I had to hide my head. This is the age of boasting. It is the day of the great "I."

My attention was recently called to the fact that in all the psalms you cannot find any place where David refers to his victory over the giant, Goliath. If it had been in the present day, there would have been a volume written about it at once; I don't know how many poems there would be telling of the great things that this man had done. He would have been in demand as a lecturer, and would have added a title to his name: G. G. K.—Great Giant Killer. That is how it is today: great evangelists, great preachers, great theologians, great bishops.

"John," they asked, "who are you?"

"I am nobody. I am to be heard, not to be seen. I am only a voice."

He hadn't a word to say about himself. I once heard a little bird faintly singing close by me—at last it got clear out of sight, and then its notes were still sweeter. The higher it flew the sweeter sounded its notes. If we can only get self out of sight and learn of Him who was meek and lowly in heart, we shall be lifted up into heavenly places.

Mark 1:7 tells us that John came and preached, saying, "There cometh one mightier than I after me, the latchet of whose shoes I am not worthy to stoop down and unloose." Think of that, and bear in mind that Christ was looked upon as a deceiver, a village carpenter, and yet here is John, the son of the old priest, who had a much higher position in the sight of men than that of Jesus. Great crowds were coming to hear him, and even Herod attended his meetings.

When his disciples came and told John the Christ was beginning to draw crowds, he nobly answered:

> A man can receive nothing, except it be given him from heaven. Ye yourselves bear me witness, that I said, I am not the Christ, but that I am sent before Him.
>
> He that hath the bride is the bridegroom: but the friend of the bridegroom, which standeth and heareth him, rejoiceth greatly because of the bridegroom's voice: this my joy therefore is fulfilled. He must increase, but I must decrease. (John 3:27–30)

It is easy to read that, but it is hard for us to live in the power of it. It is very hard for us to be ready to decrease, to grow smaller and smaller, that Christ may increase. The morning star fades away when the sun rises.

> He that cometh from above is above all: he that is of the earth is earthly, and speaketh of the earth: he that cometh from heaven is above all. And what he hath seen and heard, that he testifieth; and no man receiveth his testimony.
>
> He that hath received his testimony hath set to his seal that God is true. For he whom God hath sent speaketh the words of God: for God giveth not the Spirit by measure unto him. (vv. 31–34)

Let us now turn the light upon ourselves. Have we been decreasing of late? Do we think less of ourselves and of our position than we did a year ago? Are we seeking to obtain some position of dignity? Are we wanting to hold on to some title, and are we offended because we are not treated with the courtesy that we think is due us? Some time ago I heard a man in the pulpit say that he should take offense if he was not addressed by his title. My dear friend, are you going to take that position that you must have a title, and

that you must have every letter addressed with that title or you will
be offended? John did not want any title, and when we are right
with God, we shall not be caring about titles. In one of his early
epistles Paul calls himself the "least of all the apostles." Later on
he claims to be "less than the least of all saints," and again, just
before his death, humbly declares that he is the "chief of sinners."
Notice how he seems to have grown smaller and smaller in his own
estimation. So it was with John. And I do hope and pray that as
the days go by we may feel like hiding ourselves, and let God have
all the honor and glory.

Says Andrew Murray,

> When I look back upon my own religious experience, or round
> upon the Church of Christ in the world, I stand amazed at the
> thought of how little humility is sought after as the distinguishing
> feature of the discipleship of Jesus. In preaching and living, in the
> daily intercourse of the home and social life, in the more special
> fellowship with Christians, in the direction and performance of
> work for Christ—alas! How much proof there is that humility is
> not esteemed the cardinal virtue, the only root from which the
> graces can grow, the one indispensable condition of true fellow-
> ship with Jesus.

See what Christ says about John. "He was a burning and shining light." Christ gave him the honor that belonged to him. If you
take a humble position, Christ will see it. If you want God to help
you, then take a low position.

I am afraid that if we had been in John's place, many of us
would have said: "What did Christ say—I am a burning and shining light?" Then we would have had that recommendation put in
the newspapers, and would have sent them to our friends, with
that part marked in blue pencil. Sometimes I get a letter just full
of clippings from the newspapers, stating that this man is more
eloquent than Gough, etc. And the man wants me to get him some

church. Do you think that a man who has such eloquence would be looking for a church? No, they would all be looking for him.

My dear friends, isn't it humiliating? Sometimes I think it is a wonder that any man is converted these days. Let another praise you. Don't be around praising yourself. If we want God to lift us up, let us get down. The lower we get, the higher God will lift us. It is Christ's eulogy of John, "Greater than any man born of woman."

There is a story told of Carey, the great missionary, that he was invited by the governor-general of India to go to a dinner party at which were some military officers belonging to the aristocracy, and who looked down upon missionaries with scorn and contempt.

One of these officers said at the table: "I believe that Carey was a shoemaker, wasn't he, before he took up the profession of a missionary?"

Mr. Carey spoke up and said: "Oh no, I was only a cobbler. I could mend shoes, and wasn't ashamed of it."

The one prominent virtue of Christ, next to His obedience, is His humility; and even His obedience grew out of His humility. Being in the form of God, He counted it not a thing to be grasped to be on an equality with God, but He emptied Himself, taking the form of a bond-servant, and was made in the likeness of men. And being found in fashion as a man, He humbled Himself, and became obedient unto death, yea, the death of the cross. In His lowly birth, His submission to His earthly parents, His seclusion during thirty years, His consorting with the poor and despised, His entire submission and dependence upon His Father, this virtue that was consummated in His death on the cross shines out.

One day Jesus was on His way to Capernaum, and was talking about His coming death and suffering, and about His resurrection, and He heard quite a heated discussion going on behind Him. When He came into the house at Capernaum, He turned to His disciples, and said: "What was all that discussion about?"

I see John look at James, and Peter at Andrew—and they all looked ashamed. "Who shall be the greater?" That discussion has wrecked party after party, one society after another—"Who shall be the greatest?"

The way Christ took to teach them humility was by putting a little child in their midst and saying: "If you want to be great, take that little child for an example, and he who wants to be the greatest, let him be servant of all."

To me, one of the saddest things in all the life of Jesus Christ was the fact that just before His crucifixion, His disciples should have been striving to see who should be the greatest, that night He instituted the Supper, and they ate the Passover together. It was His last night on earth, and they never saw Him so sorrowful before. He knew Judas was going to sell Him for thirty pieces of silver. He knew that Peter would deny Him. And yet, in addition to this, when going into the very shadow of the cross, there arose this strife as to who should be the greatest. He took a towel and girded Himself like a slave, and He took a basin of water and stooped and washed their feet. That was another object lesson of humility. He said, "You call me Lord, and you do well. If you want to be great in My kingdom, be servant of all. If you serve, you shall be great."

When the Holy Ghost came, and those men were filled, from that time on mark the difference: Matthew takes up his pen to write, and he keeps Matthew out of sight. He tells us what Peter and Andrew did, but he calls himself Matthew "the publican." He tells how they left all to follow Christ, but does not mention the feast he gave. Jerome says that Mark's Gospel is to be regarded as memoirs of Peter's discourses, and to have been published by his authority. Yet here we constantly find that damaging things are mentioned about Peter, and things to his credit are not referred to. Mark's Gospel omits all allusion to Peter's faith in venturing on the sea but goes into detail about the story of his fall and denial of our Lord. Peter put himself down and lifted others up.

If the Gospel of Luke had been written today, it would be signed by the great Dr. Luke, and you would have his photograph as a frontispiece. But you can't find Luke's name; he keeps out of sight. He wrote two books, and his name is not to be found in either. John covers himself always under the expression "the disciple whom Jesus loved." None of the four men whom history and tradition assert to be the authors of the Gospels lay claim to the authorship in their writings. Dear man of God, I would that I had the same spirit, that I could just get out of sight—hide myself.

My dear friends, I believe our only hope is to be filled with the Spirit of Christ. May God fill us, so that we shall be filled with meekness and humility. Let us take the hymn, "O, to be nothing, nothing," and make it the language of our hearts. It breathes the Spirit of Him who said: "The Son can do *nothing* of Himself!"

5

Rest

After a discussion of promises and the various conditions associated with some of them, Moody turns his attention to the primary focus of his discussion: rest. While Moody was an advocate of Sabbath-keeping, he doesn't address the Sabbath in "Rest." Instead, he considers the sort of people who are likely to experience rest: not the wealthy, the politicians, the wicked, nor anyone who lives according to the world's ways. Sin and unrest are inseparable. As such, rest can only be found among those who follow Jesus.

While Moody seems to suggest that there was no rest prior to Christ, such a claim neglects Old Testament texts such as Psalm 116:7, "Return, O my soul, to your rest; for the Lord has dealt bountifully with you" (ESV), and Proverbs 19:23, "The fear of the Lord leads to life, and whoever has it rests satisfied" (ESV). While there is a fullness of rest that comes in Christ who is the "burden-bearer," God's people were not without comfort and peace in the Old Testament. In the end, Moody's desire is to point people to Christ because coming to Christ is the only way to find rest in this world.

Some years ago a gentleman came to me and asked me which I thought was the most precious promise of all those that Christ left. I took some time to look them over, but I gave it up. I found that I could not answer the question. It is like a man with a large family of children. He cannot tell which he likes best; he loves them all. But if not the best, this is one of the sweetest promises of all:

Come unto Me, all ye that labour and are heavy laden, and I will give you rest. Take My yoke upon you, and learn of Me, for I am meek and lowly in heart: and ye shall find rest unto your souls. For My yoke is easy, and My burden is light. (Matt. 11:28–30)

There are a good many people who think the promises are not going to be fulfilled. There are some that you do see fulfilled, and you cannot help but believe they are true. Now, remember that all the promises are not given without conditions. Some are given with, and others without, conditions attached to them. For instance, it says, "If I regard iniquity in my heart, the Lord will not hear me." Now, I need not pray as long as I am cherishing some known sin. He will not hear me, much less answer me. The Lord says in Psalm 84:11, "No good thing will He withhold from them that walk uprightly." If I am not walking uprightly I have no claims under the promise. Again, some of the promises were made to certain individuals or nations. For instance, God said that He would make Abraham's seed to multiply as the stars of heaven: but that is not a promise for you or me. Some promises were made to the Jews and do not apply to the Gentiles.

Then there are promises without conditions. He promised Adam and Eve that the world should have a Savior, and there was no power in earth or perdition that could keep Christ from coming at the appointed time. When Christ left the world, He said He would send us the Holy Ghost. He had only been gone ten days

when the Holy Ghost came. And so you can run right through
the Scriptures, and you will find that some of the promises are
with, and some without, conditions; if we don't comply with the
conditions, we cannot expect them to be fulfilled.

I believe it will be the experience of every man and woman on the
face of the earth; I believe that everyone will be obliged to testify in
the evening of life that, if they have complied with the condition,
the Lord has filled His work to the letter. Joshua, the old Hebrew
hero, was an illustration. After having tested God forty years in the
Egyptian brick-kilns, forty years in the desert, and thirty years in the
promised land, his dying testimony was: "Not one thing hath failed
of all the good things which the Lord promised." I believe you could
heave the ocean easier than break one of God's promises. So when
we come to a promise like the one we have before us now, I want
you to bear in mind that there is no discount upon it. "Come unto
Me, all ye that labour and are heavy laden, and I will give you rest."

Perhaps you say: "I hope Mr. Moody is not going to preach
on this old text." Yes, I am. When I take up an album, it does not
interest me if all the photographs are new; but if I know any of
the faces, I stop at once. So with these old, well-known texts. They
have quenched our thirst before, but the water is still bubbling
up—we cannot drink it dry.

If you probe the human heart, you will find a want, and that
want is rest. The cry of the world today is, "Where can rest be
found?" Why are theaters and places of amusement crowded at
night? What is the secret of Sunday driving, of the saloons and
brothels? Some think they are going to get it in pleasure, others
think they are going to get it in wealth, and others in literature.
They are seeking and finding no rest.

Where Can Rest Be Found?

If I wanted to find a person who had rest, I would not go among
the very wealthy. The man that we read of in Luke 12 thought he

was going to get rest by multiplying his goods, but he was disappointed. "Soul, take thine ease." I venture to say that there is not a person in this wide world who has tried to find rest in that way and found it.

Money cannot buy it. Many a millionaire would gladly give millions if he could purchase it as he does his stocks and shares. God has made the soul a little too large for this world. Roll the whole world in, and still there is room. There is care in getting wealth, and more care in keeping it.

Nor would I go among the pleasure-seekers. They have a few hours' enjoyment, but the next day there is enough sorrow to counterbalance it. They may drink the cup of pleasure today, but the cup of pain comes on tomorrow.

To find rest I would never go among the politicians, or among the so-called great. Congress is the last place on earth that I would go. In the Lower House they want to go to the Senate; in the Senate they want to go to the Cabinet; and then they want to go to the White House; and rest has never been found there. Nor would I go among the halls of learning. "Much study is a weariness to the flesh." I would not go among the upper ten, the "bon-ton," for they are constantly chasing after fashion. Have you not noticed their troubled faces on our streets? And the face is index to the soul. They have no hopeful look. Their worship of pleasure is slavery. Solomon tried pleasure and found bitter disappointment, and down the ages has come the bitter cry, "All is vanity."

Now, there is no rest in sin. The wicked know nothing about it. The Scriptures tell us the wicked "are like the troubled sea that cannot rest." You have, perhaps, been on the sea when there is a calm, when the water is as clear as crystal, and it seemed as if the sea were at rest. But if you looked you would see that the waves came in, and that the calm was only on the surface. Man, like the sea, has no rest. He has had no rest since Adam fell, and there is none for him until he returns to God again, and the light of Christ shines into his heart.

Rest cannot be found in the world, and thank God the world cannot take it from the believing heart! Sin is the cause of all this unrest. It brought toil and labor and misery into the world.

Now for something positive. I would go successfully to someone who has heard the sweet voice of Jesus, and has laid his burden down at the cross. There is rest, sweet rest. Thousands could certify to this blessed fact. They could say, and truthfully:

> I heard the voice of Jesus say,
>> "Come unto Me and rest.
> Lay down, thou weary one, lay down,
>> Thy head upon My breast."
> I came to Jesus as I was,
>> Weary and worn and sad.
> I found in Him a resting-place,
>> And He hath made me glad.

Among all his writings St. Augustine has nothing sweeter than this: "Thou has made us for Thyself, O God, and our heart is restless till it rests in Thee."

Do you know that for four thousand years no prophet or priest or patriarch ever stood up and uttered a text like this? It would be blasphemy for Moses to have uttered a text like it. Do you think he had rest when he was teasing the Lord to let him go into the promised land? Do you think Elijah could have uttered such a text as this, when, under the juniper tree, he prayed that he might die? And this is one of the strongest proofs that Jesus Christ was not only man but God. He was God-Man, and this is heaven's proclamation: "Come unto Me, and I will give you rest." He brought it down from heaven with Him.

Now, if this text was not true, don't you think it would have been found out by this time? I believe it as much as I believe in my existence. Why? Because I not only find it in the Book but in my own experience. The "I wills" of Christ have never been broken, and never can be.

I thank God for the word *give* in that passage. He doesn't sell it. Some of us are so poor that we could not buy it if it was for sale. Thank God, we can get it for nothing.

I like to have a text like this, because it takes us all in. "Come unto Me *all* ye that labor." That doesn't mean a select few—refined ladies and cultured men. It doesn't mean good people only. It applies to saint and sinner. Hospitals are for the sick, not for healthy people. Do you think that Christ would shut the door in anyone's face and say, "I did not mean *all*; I only meant certain ones"? If you cannot come as a saint, come as a sinner. Only come!

A lady told me once that she was so hardhearted she couldn't come.

"Well," I said, "my good woman, it doesn't say 'all ye softhearted people come.' Black hearts, vile hearts, hard hearts, soft hearts, all hearts come. Who can soften your hard heart but Himself?"

The harder the heart, the more need you have to come. If my watch stops, I don't take it to a drugstore or to a blacksmith's shop but to the watchmaker's to have it repaired. So if the heart gets out of order, take it to its keeper, Christ, to have it set right. If you can prove that you are a sinner, you are entitled to the promise. Get all the benefit you can out of it.

Now, there are a good many believers who think this text applies only to sinners. It is just the thing for them too. What do we see today? The Church, Christian people, all loaded down with cares and troubles. "Come unto Me all ye that labor." All! I believe that includes the Christian whose heart is burdened with some great sorrow. The Lord wants you to come.

Christ the Burden-Bearer

It says in another place, "[Cast] all your care upon Him, for He careth for you." We would have a victorious Church if we could get Christian people to realize that. But they have never made the discovery. They agree that Christ is the sin-bearer, but they do not realize that He is also the burden-bearer. "Surely He hath borne our griefs, and carried our sorrows." It is the privilege of every child of God to walk in unclouded sunlight.

Some people go back into the past and rake up all the troubles they ever had, and then they look into the future and anticipate that they will have still more trouble, and they go reeling and staggering all through life. They give you the cold chills every time they meet you. They put on a whining voice, and tell you what "a hard time they have had." I believe they embalm them, and bring out the mummy on every opportunity. The Lord says, "Cast all your care on Me. I want to carry your burdens and your troubles." What we want is a joyful Church, and we are not going to convert the world until we have it. We want to get this long-faced Christianity off the face of the earth.

Take these people that have some great burden, and let them come into a meeting. If you can get their attention upon the singing or preaching, they will say, "Oh, wasn't it grand! I forgot all my cares." And they just drop their bundle at the end of the pew. But the moment the benediction is pronounced they grab the bundle again. You laugh, but you do it yourself. Cast your care on Him.

Sometimes they go into their closet and close their door, and they get so carried away and lifted up that they forget their trouble; but they just take it up again the moment they get off their knees. Leave your sorrow now; cast all your care upon Him. If you cannot come to Christ as a saint, come as a sinner. But if you are a saint with some trouble or care, bring it to Him. Saint and sinner, come! He wants you all. Don't let Satan deceive you into believing that you cannot come if you will. Christ says, "Ye will not come unto Me." With the command comes the power.

A man in one of our meetings in Europe said he would like to come, but he was chained and couldn't come.

A Scotsman said to him, "Ay, man, why don't you come chain and all?"

He said, "I never thought of that."

Are you cross and peevish, and do you make things unpleasant at home? My friend, come to Christ and ask Him to help you. Whatever the sin is, bring it to Him.

What Does It Mean to Come?

Perhaps you say, "Mr. Moody, I wish you would tell us what it is to come." I have given up trying to explain it. I always feel like the minister who said he was going to *confound*, instead of *expound*, the chapter.

The best definition is just—come. The more you try to explain it, the more you are mystified. About the first thing a mother teaches her child is to look. She takes the baby to the window, and says, "Look, baby, Papa is coming!" Then she teaches the child to come. She props the child up against a chair, and says, "Come!" and by and by the little thing pushes the chair along toward mamma. That's coming. You don't need to go to college to learn how. You don't need any minister to tell you what it is. Now will you come to Christ? He said, "Him that cometh unto Me, I will in no wise cast out."

When we have such a promise as this, let us cling to it, and never give it up. Christ is not mocking us. He wants us to come, with all our sins and backslidings, and throw ourselves upon His bosom. It is our sins God wants, not our tears only. They alone do no good. And we cannot come through resolutions. Action is necessary. How many times at church have we said, "I will turn over a new leaf," but the Monday leaf is worse than the Saturday leaf?

The way to heaven is straight as a rule, but it is the way of the cross. Don't try to get around it. Shall I tell you what the "yoke" referred to in the text is? It is the cross which Christians must bear. The only way by which you can find rest in this dark world is by taking up the yoke of Christ. I do not know what it may include in your case, beyond taking up your Christian duties, acknowledging Christ, and acting as becomes one of His disciples. Perhaps it may be to erect a family altar, or to tell a godless husband that you have made up your mind to serve God, or to tell your parents that you want to be a Christian. Follow the will of God, and happiness and peace and rest will come. The way of obedience is always the way of blessing.

I was preaching in Chicago to a hall full of women one Sunday afternoon, and after the meeting was over a lady came to me and said she wanted to talk to me. She said she would accept Christ, and after some conversations she went home. I looked for her for a whole week but didn't see her until the following Sunday afternoon. She came and sat down right in front of me, and her face had such a sad expression. She seemed to have entered into the misery, instead of the joy, of the Lord.

After the meeting was over I went to her and asked her what the trouble was. She said: "Oh, Mr. Moody, this has been the most miserable week of my life."

I asked her if there was anyone with whom she had had trouble and whom she could not forgive. She said: "No, not that I know of."

"Well, did you tell your friends about having found the Savior?"

"Indeed I didn't. I have been all the week trying to keep it from them."

"Well," I said, "that is the reason why you have no peace."

She wanted to take the crown but did not want the cross. My friends, you must go by the way of Calvary. If you ever get rest, you must get it at the foot of the cross.

"Why," she said, "if I should go home and tell my infidel husband that I had found Christ, I don't know what he would do. I think he would turn me out."

"Well," I said, "go out."

She went away, promising that she would tell him, timid and pale, but she did not want another wretched week. She was bound to have peace.

The next night I gave a lecture for men only, and in the hall there were eight thousand men and one solitary woman. When I got through and went into the inquiry meeting, I found this lady with her husband. She introduced him to me (he was a doctor, and a very influential man) and said: "He wants to become a Christian."

I took my Bible and told him all about Christ, and he accepted Him. I said to her after it was all over: "It turned out quite differently from what you expected, didn't it?"

"Yes," she replied, "I was never so scared in my life. I expected he would do something dreadful, but it has turned out so well."

She took God's way and got rest.

I want to say to young ladies, perhaps you have a godless father or mother, a skeptical brother who is going down through drink, and perhaps there is no one who can reach them but you. How many times a godly, pure young lady has taken the light into some darkened home! Many a home might be lit up with the gospel if the mothers and daughters would only speak the Word.

The last time Mr. Sankey and myself were in Edinburgh, there were a father, two sisters, and a brother, who used every morning to take the morning paper and pick my sermon to pieces. They were indignant to think that the Edinburgh people should be carried away with such preaching. One day one of the sisters was going by the hall, and she thought she would drop in and see what class of people went there. She happened to take a seat by a godly lady, who said to her: "I hope you are interested in this work."

She tossed her head and said: "Indeed I am not. I am disgusted with everything I have seen and heard."

"Well," said the lady, "perhaps you come prejudiced."

"Yes, and the meeting has not removed any of it, but has rather increased it."

"I have received a great deal of good from them."

"There is nothing here for me. I don't see how an intellectual person can be interested."

To make a long story short, the lady got the sister to promise to come back. When the meeting broke up, just a little of the prejudice had worn away. She promised to come back again the next day, and then she attended three or four more meetings, and became quite interested. She said nothing to her family, until finally the burden became too heavy, and she told them. They laughed at her and made her the butt of their ridicule.

One day the two sisters were together, and the other said: "Now what have you got at those meetings that you didn't have in the first place?"

"I have a peace that I never knew of before. I am at peace with God, myself, and all the world." Did you ever have a little war of your own with your neighbors, in your own family? And she said: "I have self-control. You know, sister, if you had said half the mean things before I was converted that you have said since, I would have been angry and answered back, but if you remember correctly, I haven't answered once since I have been converted."

The sister said: "You certainly have something that I have not." The other told her it was for her too, and she brought the sister to the meetings, where she found peace.

Like Martha and Mary, they had a brother, but he was a member of the University of Edinburgh. He be converted? He go to these meetings? It might do for women, but not for him. One night they came home and told him that a chum of his own, a member of the university, had stood up and confessed Christ, and when he sat down his brother got up and confessed; and so with the third one.

When the young man heard it, he said: "Do you mean to tell me that he has been converted?"

"Yes."

"Well," he said, "there must be something in it."

He put on his hat and coat, and went to see his friend Black. Black got him down to the meetings, and he was converted.

We went through to Glasgow, and had not been there six weeks when news came that this young man had been stricken down and died. When he was dying, he called his father to his bedside and said:

"Wasn't it a good thing that my sisters went to those meetings? Won't you meet me in heaven, Father?"

"Yes, my son, I am so glad you are a Christian; that is the only comfort that I have in losing you. I will become a Christian and will meet you again."

I tell this to encourage some sister to go home and carry the message of salvation. It may be that your brother may be taken away in a few months. My dear friends, are we not living in solemn days? Isn't it time for us to get our friends into the kingdom of God? Come, wife, won't you tell your husband? Come, sister, won't you tell your brother? Won't you take up your cross now? The blessing of God will rest on your soul if you will.

I was in Wales once, and a lady told me this little story: an English friend of hers, a mother, had a child that was sick. At first they considered there was no danger, until one day the doctor came in and said that the symptoms were very unfavorable. He took the mother out of the room, and told her that the child could not live. It came like a thunderbolt. After the doctor had gone the mother went into the room where the child lay and began to talk to the child and tried to divert her mind.

"Darling, do you know you will soon hear the music of heaven? You will hear a sweeter song than you have ever heard on earth. You will hear them sing the song of Moses and the Lamb. You are very fond of music. Won't it be sweet, darling?"

And the little tired, sick child turned her head away, and said, "Oh, Mamma, I am so tired and so sick that I think it would make me worse to hear all that music."

"Well," the mother said, "you will soon see Jesus. You will see the seraphim and cherubim and the streets all paved with gold," and she went on picturing heaven as it is described in Revelation.

The little tired child again turned her head away, and said, "Oh, Mamma, I am so tired that I think it would make me worse to see all those beautiful things!"

At last the mother took the child up in her arms, and pressed her to her living heart. And the little sick one whispered: "Oh, Mamma, that is what I want. If Jesus will only take me in His arms and let me rest!"

Dear friend, are you not tired and weary of sin? Are you not weary of the turmoil of life? You can find rest on the bosom of the Son of God.

6

Seven "I Wills" of Christ

Though it is relatively common to consider Christ's "I am" statements in John's Gospel, Moody opts to consider seven "I wills" of Christ. The seven "I wills" are as follows: salvation (John 6:37), cleansing (Luke 5:12–13), confession (Matt. 10:32), service (Matt. 4:19), comfort (John 14:18), resurrection (John 6:40), and glory (John 17:24). Each of these is rooted in a specific statement of Jesus. Moody's point in laying out these "I wills" is to provide assurance. What Christ says He will do, He will do. The treatment of the seven "I wills" serves as a fitting conclusion to the collection of sermons, as it reminds us of what Christ has done, is doing, and will do.

A man, when he says "I will," may not mean much. We often say "I will" when we don't mean to fulfill what we say; but when we come to the "I will" of Christ, He means to fulfill it. Everything He has promised to do, He is able and willing to accomplish; and

He is going to do it. I cannot find any passage in Scripture in which He says "I will" do this, or "I will" do that, but it will be done.

1. The "I Will" of Salvation

The first "I will" to which I want to direct your attention is to be found in John 6:37: "Him that cometh to Me I will in no wise cast out."

I imagine someone will say, "Well, if I was what I ought to be, I would come; but when my mind goes over the past record of my life, it is too dark. I am not fit to come."

You must bear in mind that Jesus Christ came to save not good people, not the upright and just, but sinners like you and me, who have gone astray, sinned, and come short of the glory of God. Listen to this "I will"—it goes right into the heart—"Him that cometh to Me, I will in no wise cast out." Surely that is broad enough—is it not? I don't care who the man or woman is; I don't care what their trials, what their troubles, what their sorrows, or what their sins are, if they will only come straight to the Master, He will not cast them out. Come then, poor sinner; come just as you are, and take Him at His Word.

He is so anxious to save sinners, He will take everyone who comes. He will take those who are so full of sin that they are despised by all who know them, who have been rejected by their fathers and mothers, who have been cast off by the wives of their bosoms. He will take those who have sunk so low that upon them no eye of pity is cast. His occupation is to hear and save. That is what He left heaven and came into the world for; that is what He left the throne of God for—to save sinners. "The Son of Man is come to seek and to save that which was lost." He did not come to condemn the world but that the world through Him might be saved.

A wild and prodigal young man, who was running a headlong career to ruin, came into one of our meetings in Chicago. The

Spirit of God got hold of him. Whilst I was conversing with him, and endeavoring to bring him to Christ, I quoted this verse to him.

I asked him: "Do you believe Christ said that?"

"I suppose He did."

"Suppose He did! Do you believe it?"

"I hope so."

"Hope so! Do you believe it? You do your work, and the Lord will do His. Just come as you are, and throw yourself upon His bosom, and He will not cast you out."

This man thought it was too simple and easy.

At last light seemed to break in upon him, and he seemed to find comfort from it. It was past midnight before he got down on his knees, but down he went, and was converted.

I said: "Now, don't think you are going to get out of the devil's territory without trouble. The devil will come to you tomorrow morning, and say it was all feeling; that you only imagined you were accepted by God. When he does, don't fight him with your own opinions, but fight him with John 6:37: 'Him that cometh to me I will in no wise cast out.' Let that be the 'sword of the Spirit.'"

I don't believe that any man ever starts to go to Christ but the devil strives somehow or other to meet him and trip him up. And even after he has come to Christ, the devil tries to assail him with doubts and make him believe there is something wrong in it.

The struggle came sooner than I thought in this man's case. When he was on his way home the devil assailed him. He used this text, but the devil put this thought into his mind: *How do you know Christ ever said that after all? Perhaps the translators made a mistake.*

Into darkness he went again. He was in trouble till about two in the morning. At last he came to this conclusion. Said he: "I will believe it anyway; and when I get to heaven, if it isn't true, I will just tell the Lord *I* didn't make the mistake—the translators made it."

The kings and princes of this world, when they issue invitations, call round them the rich, the mighty and the powerful, the

221

honorable and the wise; but the Lord, when He was on earth, called round Him the vilest of the vile. That was the principal fault the people found with Him. Those self-righteous Pharisees were not going to associate with harlots and publicans. The principal charge against Him was: "This man receiveth sinners and eateth with them." Who would have such a man around him as John Bunyan in his time? He, a Bedford tinker, couldn't get inside one of the princely castles. I was very much amused when I was over on the other side. They had erected a monument to John Bunyan, and it was unveiled by lords and dukes and great men. While he was on earth, they would not have allowed him inside the walls of their castles. Yet he was made one of the mightiest instruments in the spread of the gospel. No book that has ever been written comes so near the Bible as John Bunyan's *Pilgrim's Progress*. And he was a poor Bedford tinker. So it is with God. He picks up some poor, lost tramp, and makes him an instrument to turn hundreds and thousands to Christ.

George Whitefield, standing in his tabernacle in London, and with a multitude gathered about him, cried out: "The Lord Jesus will save the devil's castaways!"

Two poor abandoned wretches, standing outside in the street, heard him as his silvery voice rang out on the air. Looking into each other's faces, they said: "That must mean you and me." They wept and rejoiced. They drew near and looked in at the door, at the face of the earnest messenger, the tears streaming from his eyes as he pled with the people to give their hearts to God. One of them wrote him a little note and sent it to him.

Later that day, as he sat at the table of Lady Huntington, who was his special friend, someone present said: "Mr. Whitefield, did you not go a little too far today when you said that the Lord would save the devil's castaways?"

Taking the note from his pocket he gave it to the lady, and said: "Will you read that note aloud?"

She read: "Mr. Whitefield: two poor lost women stood outside your tabernacle today, and heard you say that the Lord would save the devil's castaways. We seized upon that as our last hope, and we write you this to tell you that we rejoice now in believing in Him, and from this good hour we shall endeavor to serve Him, who has done so much for us."

2. The "I Will" of Cleansing

The next "I will" is found in Luke 5:12. We read of a leper who came to Christ and said: "Lord, if Thou wilt, Thou canst make me clean." The Lord touched him, saying, "I will: be thou clean"; and immediately the leprosy left him.

Now if any man or woman full of the leprosy of sin reads this, if you will but go to the Master and tell all your case to Him, He will speak to you as He did to that poor leper and say: "I will: be thou clean," and the leprosy of your sins will flee away from you. It is the Lord, and the Lord alone, who can forgive sins. If you say to Him: "Lord, I am full of sin; Thou canst make me clean." "Lord, I have a terrible temper; Thou canst make me clean." "Lord, I have a deceitful heart. Cleanse me, O Lord; give me a new heart. O Lord, give me the power to overcome the flesh, and the snares of the devil!" "Lord, I am full of unclean habits"—if you come to Him with a sincere spirit, you will hear the voice, "I will; be thou clean." It will be done. Do you think that the God who created the world out of nothing, who by a breath put life into the world—do you think that if He says, "Thou shalt be clean," you will not?

Now, you can make a wonderful exchange today. You can have health in the place of sickness; you can get rid of everything that is vile and hateful in the sight of God. The Son of God comes down, and says, "I will take away your leprosy, and give you health in its stead. I will take away that terrible disease that is ruining your body and soul, and give you My righteousness in its stead. I will clothe you with the garments of salvation."

Is it not wonderful? That's what He means when He says—*I will*. Oh, lay hold of this "I will!"

3. The "I Will" of Confession

Now turn to Matthew 10:32: "Whosoever therefore shall confess Me before men, him will I confess also before My Father which is in heaven." There's the "I will" of confession.

Now, that's the next thing that takes place after a man is saved. When we have been washed in the blood of the Lamb, the next thing is to get our mouths opened. We have to confess Christ here in this dark world and tell His love to others. We are not to be ashamed of the Son of God.

A man thinks it a great honor when he has achieved a victory that causes his name to be mentioned in the English Parliament, or in the presence of the queen and her court. How excited we used to be during the war, when some general did something extraordinary, and someone got up in Congress to confess his exploits; how the papers used to talk about it! In China, we read, the highest ambition of the successful soldier is to have his name written in the palace or temple of Confucius. But just think of having your name mentioned in the kingdom of heaven by the Prince of Glory, by the Son of God, because you confess Him here on earth! You confess Him here; He will confess you yonder.

If you wish to be brought into the clear light of liberty, you must take your stand on Christ's side. I have known many Christians go groping about in darkness, and never get into the clear light of the kingdom, because they were ashamed to confess the Son of God. We are living in a day when men want a religion without the cross. They want the crown but not the cross. But if we are to be disciples of Jesus Christ, we have to take up our crosses *daily*—not once a year or on the Sabbath, but daily. And if we take up our crosses and follow Him, we shall be blessed in the very act.

I remember a man in New York who used to come and pray with me. He had his cross. He was afraid to confess Christ. It seemed that down at the bottom of his trunk he had a Bible. He wanted to get it out and read it to the companion with whom he lived, but he was ashamed to do it. For a whole week that was his cross; after he had carried the burden that long, and after a terrible struggle, he made up his mind. He said, "I will take my Bible out tonight and read it." He took it out, and soon he heard the footsteps of his mate coming upstairs.

His first impulse was to put it away again, but then he thought he would not—he would face his companion with it. His mate came in, and seeing him at his Bible, said, "John, are you interested in these things?"

"Yes," he replied.

"How long has this been, then?" asked his companion.

"Exactly a week," he answered. "For a whole week I have tried to get out my Bible to read to you, but I have never done so till now."

"Well," said his friend, "it is a strange thing. *I was converted on the same night*, and I too was ashamed to take my Bible out."

You are ashamed to take your Bible out and say, "I have lived a godless life for all these years, but I will commence now to live a life of righteousness." You are ashamed to open your Bible and read that blessed psalm, "The LORD is my shepherd; I shall not want." You are ashamed to be seen on your knees. No man can be a disciple of Jesus Christ without bearing His cross. A great many people want to know how it is Jesus Christ has so few disciples, whilst Mahomet has so many. The reason is that Mahomet gives no cross to bear. There are so few men who will come out to take their stand.

I was struck during the American war with the fact that there were so many men who could go to the cannon's mouth without trembling but had not courage to take up their Bibles to read them at night. They were ashamed of the gospel of Jesus Christ, which is the power of God unto salvation. "Whosoever therefore shall confess Me before men, him will I confess also before My Father which is in heaven. But whosoever shall deny Me before men, him will I also deny before My Father which is in heaven."

4. The "I Will" of Service

The next *I will* is the "I will" of service.

There are a good many Christians who have been quickened and aroused to say, "I want to do some service for Christ."

Well, Christ says, "Follow Me, and I will make you fishers of men."

There is no Christian who cannot help to bring someone to the Savior. Christ says, "And I, if I be lifted up, will draw all men unto Me," and our business is just to lift up Christ.

Our Lord said, "Follow Me, Peter, and I will make you a fisher of men"; and Peter simply obeyed Him, and there, on that day of Pentecost, we see the result. Peter had a good haul on the day of Pentecost. I doubt if he ever caught so many fish in one day as he did men on that day. It would have broken every net they had on board, if they had had to drag up three thousand fishes.

I read some time ago of a man who took passage in a stagecoach. There were first-, second-, and third-class passengers. But when he looked into the coach, he saw all the passengers sitting together without distinction. He could not understand it till by and by they came to a hill, and the coach stopped, and the driver called out, "First-class passengers keep their seats, second-class passengers get out and walk, third-class passengers get behind and push." Now in the Church we have no room for first-class passengers—people who think that salvation means an easy ride all the way to heaven. We have no room for second-class passengers—people who are carried most of the time, and who, when they must work out their own salvation, go trudging on, giving never a thought to helping their fellows along. All church members ought to be third-class passengers—ready to dismount and push all together, and push with a will. That was John Wesley's definition of a church: "All at it, and always at it." Every Christian ought to be a worker. He need not be a preacher, he need not be an evangelist, to be useful. He may be useful in business. See what power an employer has, if he likes! How he could labor with his employees, and in his business relations!

Often a man can be far more useful in a business sphere than he could in another.

There is one reason, and a great reason, why so many do not succeed. I have been asked by a great many good men, "Why is it we don't have any results? We work hard, pray hard, and preach hard, and yet the success does not come." I will tell you. It is because they spend all their time mending their nets. No wonder they never catch anything.

The great matter is to hold inquiry meetings, and thus pull the net in, and see if you have caught anything. If you are always mending and setting the net, you won't catch many fish. Whoever heard of a man going out to fish and setting his net, and then letting it stop there and never pulling it in? Everybody would laugh at the man's folly.

A minister in England came to me one day, and said, "I wish you would tell me why we ministers don't succeed better than we do."

I brought before him this idea of pulling in the net, and I said, "You ought to pull in your nets. There are many ministers in Manchester who can preach much better than I can, but I pull in the net."

Many people have objections to inquiry meetings, but I urged upon him the importance of them, and the minister said, "I never did pull in my net, but I will try next Sunday."

He did so, and eight persons, anxious inquirers, went into his study. The next Sunday he came down to see me, and said he had never had such a Sunday in his life. He had met with marvelous blessing. The next time he drew the net there were forty, and when he came to see me later, he said to me joyfully,

"Moody, I HAVE HAD EIGHT HUNDRED CONVERSIONS THIS LAST YEAR! It is a great mistake I did not begin earlier to pull in the net."

So, my friends, if you want to catch men, just pull in the net. If you only catch one, it will be something. It may be a little child, but I have known a little child to convert a whole family. You don't know what is in that little dull-headed boy in the inquiry room; he may become a Martin Luther, a reformer that shall make the world tremble—you cannot tell. God uses the weak things of this world to confound the mighty. God's promise is as good as a bank note—"I promise to pay So-and-So," and here is one of Christ's promissory notes—"If you follow Me, I will make you fishers of men." Will you not lay hold of the promise, and trust it, and follow Him now?

If a man preaches the gospel, and preaches it faithfully, he ought to expect results then and there. I believe it is the privilege of God's children to reap the fruit of their labor three hundred and sixty-five days in the year.

"Well, but," say some, "is there not a sowing time as well as harvest?"

Yes, it is true, there is; but then, you can sow with one hand and reap with the other. What would you think of a farmer who went on sowing all the year round, and never thought of reaping? I repeat it: we want to sow with one hand and reap with the other, and if we look for the fruit of our labors, we shall see it. "I, if I be lifted up, will draw all men unto Me." We must lift Christ up, and then seek men out and bring them to Him.

You must use the right kind of bait. A good many don't do this, and then they wonder they are not successful. You see them getting up all kinds of entertainments with which to try and catch men. They go the wrong way to work. This perishing world wants Christ, and Him crucified. There's a void in every man's bosom that wants filling up, and if we only approach him with the right kind of bait, we shall catch him. This poor world needs a Savior; and if we are going to be successful in catching men, we must preach Christ crucified—not His life only, but His death. And if we are only faithful in doing this, we shall succeed. And why? Because there is His promise: "If you follow Me, I will make you fishers of men." That promise holds just as good to you and me as it did to His disciples, and is as true now as it was in their time.

Think of Paul up yonder. People are going up every day and every hour, men and women who have been brought to Christ through his writings. He set streams in motion that have flowed on for more than a thousand years. I can imagine men going up there, and saying, "Paul, I thank you for writing that letter to the Ephesians; I found Christ in that." "Paul, I thank you for writing that epistle to the Corinthians." "Paul, I found Christ in that epistle to the Philippians." "I thank you, Paul, for that epistle to the Galatians; I found Christ in that." And so, I suppose, they are going up still, thanking Paul all the while for what he had done. Ah, when Paul was put in prison he did not fold his hands and sit down in idleness! No, he began to write; his epistles have come down through the long ages of time and brought thousands on thousands to a knowledge of Christ crucified. Yes, Christ said to Paul, "I will make you a fisher of men if you will follow Me," and he has been fishing for souls ever since. The devil thought he had done a very wise thing when he got Paul into prison, but he was very much mistaken; he overdid it for once. I have no doubt Paul has thanked God ever since for that Philippian gaol, and his stripes and imprisonment there. I am sure the world has made more by it than we shall ever know till we get to heaven.

5. The "I Will" of Comfort

The next "I will" is in John 14:18: "I will not leave you comfortless."

To me it is a sweet thought that Christ has not left us alone in this dark wilderness here below. Although He has gone up on high, and taken His seat by the Father's throne, He has not left us comfortless. The better translation is, "I will not leave you *orphans*." He did not leave Joseph when they cast him into prison; "God was with him." When Daniel was cast into the den of lions, they had to put the Almighty in with him. They were so bound together that they could not be separated, and so God went down into the den with Daniel.

If we have got Christ with us, we can do all things. Do not let us be thinking how weak we are. Let us lift up our eyes to Him and think of Him as our Elder Brother, who has all power given to Him in heaven and on earth. He says: "Lo, I am with you always, even unto the end of the world." Some of our children and friends leave us, and it is a very sad hour. But, thank God, the believer and Christ shall never be separated! He is with us here, and we shall be with Him in person by and by, and shall see Him in His beauty. Not only is He with us, but He has sent us the Holy Ghost. Let us honor the Holy Ghost by acknowledging that He is here in our midst. He has power to give sight to the blind and liberty to the captive, and to open the ears of the deaf that they may hear the glorious words of the gospel.

6. The "I Will" of Resurrection

Then there is another *I will* in John 6:40; it occurs four times in the chapter: "I will raise him up at the last day."

I rejoice to think that I have a Savior who has power over death. My blessed Master holds the keys of death and hell. I pity the poor unbeliever and infidel. They have no hope in the resurrection; but every child of God can open that chapter and read the promise, and his heart ought to leap within him for joy as he reads it.

You know the tradesman generally puts the best specimen of his wares in the window to show us the quality of his stock. And so, when Christ was down here, He gave us a specimen of what He could do. He raised three from the dead, that we might know what power He had. There was (1) Jairus's daughter, (2) the widow's son, and (3) Lazarus of Bethany. He raised all three of them, so that every doubt might be swept away from our hearts.

How dark and gloomy this world would be if we had no hope in the resurrection; but now, when we lay our little children down in the grave, although it is in sorrow, it is not without hope. We have seen them pass away, we have seen them in the terrible struggle with death; but there has been one star to illumine the darkness and gloom—the thought that though the happy circle has been broken on earth, it shall be completed again in yon world of heavenly light. You that have lost a loved one, rejoice as you read this "I will"! Those who have died in Christ shall come forth again by and by. The darkness shall flee away, and the morning light of the resurrection shall dawn upon us. It is only a little while, and He who has said it shall come; His voice shall be heard in the grave—"I will raise him up at the last day." Precious promise! Precious *I will*!

I had an unsaved brother for whom I was very anxious. For fourteen long years I tried to lead that brother to "the Lamb of God, which taketh away the sin of the world." He was the Benjamin of the family, born a few weeks after my father's death. When he was seventeen he had a long run of typhoid fever, and he never fully recovered from it.

I did everything I could to bring him to Christ. He was a young man of considerable promise. I know no one who could sit down and discuss against the divinity of Christ like that man. I was not any match for him in argument. Day by day I preached to him as best I knew how.

I think I never loved a man on earth as I loved that brother. I never knew what it was to love a father, because he died before I remember. I loved my brother so much, perhaps, because he was sickly, and that drew my love and sympathy toward him; and oh, how my heart yearned for his salvation!

After preaching one night, I said, "Now if any of this audience would like to take up his cross and follow Christ, I would like him to rise," and I cannot tell you what a thrill of joy filled my soul when that brother of mine arose. It seemed the happiest night of my life. I was full of joy and thankfulness, and afterward my brother and I worked together for a time, and talked of the gospel, and in the summer we sat upon the hillside and talked of that old home.

After a year had passed I went to Chicago, and he was to go with me. He bid me good-bye, and I said, "Well, Samuel, I will see you in a few days, and I will only say good-bye till then."

A few days after a telegram came saying, "Samuel is dead." I had to travel a thousand miles to bury him, and I got more comfort out of that promise, "I will raise him up at the last day," than anything else in the Bible. How it cheered me! How it lighted up my path! And as I went into the room and looked upon the lovely face of that brother, how that passage ran through my soul: "Thy brother shall rise again." I said, "Thank God for that promise." It was worth more than the world to me.

When we laid him in the grave, it seemed as if I could hear the voice of Jesus Christ saying, "Thy brother shall rise again." Blessed promise of the resurrection! Blessed "I will!" "I will raise him up at the last day."

7. The "I Will" of Glory

Now the next "I will" is in John 17:24: "Father, I will that they also, whom thou hast given Me, be with Me where I am."

This was in His last prayer in the guest chamber, on the last night before He was crucified and died that terrible death on Calvary. Many a believer's countenance begins to light up at the thought that he shall see the King in His beauty by and by. Yes; there is a glorious day before us in the future. Some think that on the first day we are converted we have got everything. To be sure, we get salvation for the past and peace for the present; but then there is the glory for the future in store. That's what kept Paul rejoicing. He said, "These light afflictions, these few stripes, these few brickbats and stones that they throw at me—why, the glory that is beyond excels them so much that I count them as nothing, nothing at all, so that I may win Christ." And so, when things go against us, let us cheer up; let us remember that the night will soon pass away and the morning dawn upon us. Death never comes there. It is banished from that heavenly land. Sickness, and pain, and sorrow come not there to mar that grand and glorious home where we shall be by and by with the Master. God's family will be all together there. Glorious future, my friends! Yes, glorious day! And it may be a great deal nearer than many of us think. During these few days we are here, let us stand steadfast and firm, and by and by we shall be in the unbroken circle in yon world of light and have the King in our midst.

Prevailing Prayer

What Hinders It?

CONTENTS

Prefatory Note

The two first and essential means of grace are the Word of God and prayer. By these comes conversion; for we are born again by the Word of God, which liveth and abideth forever; and whosoever shall call upon the name of the Lord shall be saved.

By these also we grow; for we are exhorted to desire the sincere milk of the Word that we may grow thereby, and we cannot grow in grace and in the knowledge of the Lord Jesus Christ except we also speak to Him in prayer.

It is by the Word that the Father sanctifies us; but we are also bidden to watch and pray, lest we enter into temptation.

These two means of grace must be used in their right proportion. If we read the Word and do not pray, we may become puffed up with knowledge, without the love that buildeth up. If we pray without reading the Word, we shall be ignorant of the mind and will of God, and become mystical and fanatical, and liable to be blown about by every wind of doctrine.

The following chapters relate especially to prayer; but in order that our prayers may be for such things as are according to the will of God, they must be based upon the revelation of His own will to us; for of Him, and through Him, and to Him are all things;

it is only by hearing His Word, in which we learn His purposes toward us and toward the world, that we can pray acceptably, praying in the Holy Ghost, asking those things which are pleasing in His sight.

These addresses are not to be regarded as exhaustive but suggestive. This great subject has been the theme of prophets and apostles, and of all good men in all ages of the world; my desire in sending for this little volume is to encourage God's children to seek by prayer "to move the Arm that moves the world."

1

The Prayers of the Bible

Those who have left the deepest impression on this sin-cursed earth have been men and women of prayer. You will find that prayer has been the mighty power that has moved not only God, but man. Abraham was a man of prayer, and angels came down from heaven to converse with him. Jacob's prayer was answered in the wonderful interview at Peniel that resulted in his having such a mighty blessing and in softening the heart of his brother Esau; the child Samuel was given in answer to Hannah's prayer; Elijah's prayer closed up the heavens for three years and six months, and he prayed again and the heavens gave rain.

The apostle James tells us that the prophet Elijah was a man "subject to like passions as we are" (James 5:17). I am thankful that those men and women who were so mighty in prayer were just like ourselves. We are apt to think that those prophets and mighty men and women of old time were different from what we are. To be sure they lived in a much darker age, but they were of like passions with ourselves.

We read that on another occasion Elijah brought down fire on Mount Carmel. The prophets of Baal cried long and loud, but no answer came. The God of Elijah heard and answered his prayer. Let us remember that the God of Elijah still lives. The prophet was translated and went up to heaven, but his God still lives, and we have the same access to Him that Elijah had. We have the same warrant to go to God and ask the fire from heaven to come down and consume our lusts and passions—to burn up our dross and let Christ shine through us.

Elisha prayed, and life came back to a dead child. Many of our children are dead in trespasses and sins. Let us do as Elisha did; let us entreat God to raise them up in answer to our prayers.

Manasseh, the king, was a wicked man, and had done everything he could against the God of his father; yet in Babylon, when he cried to God, his cry was heard, and he was taken out of prison and put on the throne at Jerusalem. Surely if God gave heed to the prayer of wicked Manasseh, He will hear ours in the time of our distress. Is not this a time of distress with a great number of our fellowmen? Are there not many among us whose hearts are burdened? As we go to the throne of grace, let us remember that GOD ANSWERS PRAYER.

Look, again, at Samson. He prayed, and his strength came back so that he slew more at his death than during his life. He was a restored backslider, and he had power with God. If those who have been backsliders will but return to God, they will see how quickly God will answer prayer.

Job prayed, and his captivity was turned. Light came in the place of darkness, and God lifted him up above the height of his former prosperity—in answer to prayer.

Daniel prayed to God, and Gabriel came to tell him that he was a man greatly beloved of God. Three times that message came to him from heaven in answer to prayer. The secrets of heaven were imparted to him, and he was told that God's Son was going to be cut off for the sins of His people. We find also that Cornelius prayed, and Peter was sent to tell him words whereby he and his should be saved. In answer to prayer this great blessing came upon him and his household. Peter had gone up to the housetop to pray in the afternoon when he had that wonderful vision of the sheet let down from heaven. It was when prayer was made without ceasing unto God for Peter that the angel was sent to deliver him.

So all through the Scriptures you will find that when believing prayer went up to God, the answer came down. I think it would be a very interesting study to go right through the Bible and see what has happened while God's people have been on their knees calling upon Him. Certainly the study would greatly strengthen our faith—showing, as it would, how wonderfully God has heard and delivered when the cry has gone up to Him for help.

Look at Paul and Silas in the prison at Philippi. As they prayed and sang praises, the place was shaken, and the jailer was converted. Probably that one conversion has done more than any other recorded in the Bible to bring people into the kingdom of God. How many have been blessed in seeking to answer the question, "What must I do to be saved?" It was the prayer of those two godly men that brought the jailer to his knees, and that brought blessing to him and his family.

You remember how Stephen, as he prayed and looked up, saw the heavens opened, and the Son of Man at the right hand of God; the light of heaven fell on his face so that it shone. Remember, too, how the face of Moses shone as he came down from the Mount; he had been in communion with God. So when we get really into communion with God, He lifts up His countenance upon us; and instead of our having gloomy looks, our faces will shine, because God has heard and answered our prayers.

Jesus, as a Man of Prayer

I want to call special attention to Christ as an example for us in all things; in nothing more than in prayer. We read that Christ prayed to His Father for everything. Every great crisis in His life was preceded by prayer. Let me quote a few passages. I never noticed till a few years ago that Christ was praying at His baptism. As He prayed, the heaven was opened, and the Holy Ghost descended on Him. Another great event in His life was His transfiguration. "And as He prayed, the fashion of His countenance was altered, and His raiment was white and glistering" (Luke 9:29).

We read in Luke 6:12, "It came to pass in those days, that he went out into a mountain to pray, and continued all night in prayer to God." This is the only place where it is recorded that the Savior spent a whole night in prayer. What was about to take place? When He came down from the mountain, He gathered His disciples around Him and preached that great discourse known as the Sermon on the Mount—the most wonderful sermon that has ever been preached to mortal men. Probably no sermon has done so much good, and it was preceded by a night of prayer. If our sermons are going to reach the hearts and consciences of the people, we must be much in prayer to God, that there may be power with the Word.

In the Gospel of John we read that Jesus, at the grave of Lazarus, lifted up His eyes to heaven, and said: "Father, I thank Thee that Thou hast heard Me. And I knew that Thou hearest Me always: but because of the people which stand by I said it, that they may believe that Thou hast sent Me" (11:41–42). Notice, that before He spoke the dead to life, He spoke to His Father. If our spiritually dead ones are to be raised, we must first get power with God. The reason we so often fail in moving our fellowmen is that we try to win them without first getting power with God. Jesus was in communion with His Father, and so He could be assured that His prayers were heard.

We read also in John 12:27–28 that He prayed to the Father. I think this is one of the saddest chapters in the whole Bible. He was about to leave the Jewish nation and to make atonement for the sin of the world. Hear what He says: "Now is My soul troubled, and what shall I say? Father, save Me from this hour: but for this cause came I unto this hour" (v. 27). He was almost under the shadow of the cross; the iniquities of mankind were about to be laid upon Him; one of His twelve disciples was going to deny Him and swear he never knew Him; another was to sell Him for thirty pieces of silver; all were to forsake Him and flee. His soul was exceeding sorrowful, and He prayed; when His soul was troubled, God spoke to Him. Then in the garden of Gethsemane, while He prayed, an angel appeared to strengthen Him. In answer to His cry, "Father, glorify Thy name," He heard a voice coming down from the glory—"I have both glorified it, and will glorify it again" (v. 28).

Another memorable prayer of our Lord was in the garden of Gethsemane: "He was withdrawn from them about a stone's cast, and kneeled down, and prayed" (Luke 22:41). I would draw your attention to the recorded fact that four times the answer came right down from heaven while the Savior prayed to God. The first time was at His baptism, when the heavens were opened, and the Spirit descended upon Him in answer to His prayer. Again, on the Mount of Transfiguration, God appeared and spoke to Him. Then when the Greeks came desiring to see Him, the voice of God was heard responding to His call; and again, when He cried to the Father in the midst of His agony, a direct response was given. These things are recorded, I doubt not, that we may be encouraged to pray.

We read that His disciples came to Him and said, "Lord, teach us to pray." It is not recorded that He taught them how to preach. I have often said that I would rather know how to pray like Daniel than to preach like Gabriel. If you get love into your soul, so that the grace of God may come down in answer to prayer, there will be no trouble about reaching the people. It is not by eloquent sermons that perishing souls are going to be reached; we need the power of God in order that the blessing may come down.

The prayer our Lord taught His disciples is commonly called the Lord's Prayer. I think that the Lord's prayer, more properly, is that in John 17. That is the longest prayer on record that Jesus made. You can read it slowly and carefully in about four or five minutes. I think we may learn a lesson here. Our Master's prayers were short when offered in public; when He was alone with God, that was a different thing, and He could spend the whole night in communion with His Father. My experience is that those who pray most in their closets generally make short prayers in public. Long prayers are too often not prayers at all, and they weary the people. How short the publican's prayer was: "God be merciful to me a sinner!" The Syrophoenician woman's was shorter still: "Lord help me!" She went right to the mark, and she got what she wanted. The prayer of the thief on the cross was a short one: "Lord, remember me when Thou comest into Thy kingdom!" Peter's prayer was, "Lord, save me, or I perish!" So, if you go through the Scriptures, you will find that the prayers that brought immediate answers were generally brief. Let our prayers be to the point, just telling God what we want.

In the prayer of our Lord, in John 17, we find that He made seven requests—one for Himself, four for His disciples around Him, and two for the disciples of succeeding ages. Six times in that one prayer He repeated that God had sent Him. The world looked upon Him as an imposter; He wanted them to know that He was heaven-sent. He speaks of the world nine times, and makes mention of His disciples and those who believe on Him fifty times.

Christ's last prayer on the cross was a short one: "Father, forgive them; for they know not what they do." I believe that prayer was answered. We find that right there in front of the cross, a Roman centurion was converted. It was probably in answer to the Savior's prayer. The conversion of the thief, I believe, was in answer to that prayer of our blessed Lord. Saul of Tarsus may have heard it, and the words may have followed him as he traveled to Damascus; so that when the Lord spoke to him on the way, he may have recognized the voice. One thing we do know; that on the day of

Pentecost some of the enemies of the Lord were converted. Surely that was in answer to the prayer, "Father, forgive them!"

Men of God Are Men of Prayer

Hence we see that prayer holds a high place among the exercises of a spiritual life. All God's people have been praying people. Look, for instance, at Baxter! He stained his study walls with praying breath; after he was anointed with the unction of the Holy Ghost, he sent a river of living water over Kidderminster and converted hundreds. Luther and his companions were men of such mighty pleading with God that they broke the spell of ages, and laid nations subdued at the foot of the cross. John Knox grasped all Scotland in his strong arms of faith; his prayers terrified tyrants. Whitefield, after much holy, faithful closet-pleading, went to the devil's fair and took more than a thousand souls out of the paw of the lion in one day. See a praying Wesley turn more than ten thousand souls to the Lord! Look at the praying Finney, whose prayers, faith, sermons, and writings have shaken this whole country and sent a wave of blessing through the churches on both sides of the sea.

Dr. Guthrie thus speaks of prayer and its necessity:

The first true sign of spiritual life, prayer, is also the means of maintaining it. Man can as well live physically without breathing, as spiritually without praying. There is a class of animals—the cetaceous, neither fish nor seafowl—that inhabit the deep. It is their home, they never leave it for the shore; yet, though swimming beneath its waves, and sounding its darkest depths, they have ever and anon to rise to the surface that they may breathe the air. Without that, these monarchs of the deep could not exist in the dense element in which they live, and move, and have their being. And something like what is imposed on them by a physical necessity, the Christian has to do by a spiritual one. It is by ever and anon ascending up to God, by rising through prayer into a loftier, purer region for supplies of divine grace, that he maintains his spiritual life. Prevent these animals from rising to the surface, and they die for want of breath; prevent the Christian from rising to God, and he dies for want of prayer. "Give me children," cried Rachel, "or else I die." "Let me breathe," says a man gasping, "or else I die." "Let me pray," says the Christian, "or else I die."

"Since I began," said Dr. Payson when a student, "to beg God's blessing on my studies, I have done more in one week than in the whole year before." Luther, when most pressed with work, said, "I have so much to do that I cannot get on without three hours a day praying." And not only do theologians think and speak highly of prayer; men of all ranks and positions in life have felt the same. General Havelock rose at four o'clock, if the hour for marching was six, rather than lose the precious privilege of communion with God before setting out. Sir Matthew Hale said: "If I omit praying and reading God's Word in the morning, nothing goes well all day."

"A great part of my time," said McCheyne, "is spent in getting my heart in tune for prayer. It is the link that connects earth with heaven."

A comprehensive view of the subject will show that there are nine elements which are essential to true prayer. The first is *adoration*; we cannot meet God on a level at the start. We must approach Him as One far beyond our reach or sight. The next is *confession*; sin must be put out of the way. We cannot have any communion with God while there is any transgression between us. If there stands some wrong you have done a man, you cannot expect that man's favor until you go to him and confess the fault. *Restitution* is another; we have to make good the wrong, wherever possible. *Thanksgiving* is the next; we must be thankful for what God has done for us already. Then comes *forgiveness*, and then *unity*; and then for prayer, such as these things produce, there must be *faith*. Thus influenced, we shall be ready to offer direct *petition*. We hear a good deal of praying that is just exhorting, and if you did not see the man's eyes closed, you would suppose he was preaching. Then, much that is called prayer is simply finding fault. There needs to be more petition in our prayers. After all these, there must come *submission*. While praying, we must be ready to accept the will of God.

We shall consider these nine elements in detail, closing our inquiries by giving incidents illustrative of the certainty of our receiving, under such conditions, answers to prayer.

The Hour of Prayer

Lord, what a change within us one short hour
Spent in Thy presence will prevail to make!
What heavy burdens from our bosoms take;
What parched grounds refresh as with a shower.

We kneel—and all around us seems to lower;
We rise—and all, the distant and the near,
Stands forth in sunny outline brave and clear;
We kneel: how weak!—we rise: how full of power!

Why, therefore, should we do ourselves this wrong,
Or others—that we are not always strong?
That we are ever overborne with care;
That we should ever weak or heartless be,
Anxious or troubled, while with us is prayer,
And joy, and strength, and courage, are with Thee?

Richard Trench

2

Adoration

For Moody, it was crucial for Christians to acknowledge God while also being thankful for His gifts. Prayer that does not begin with a recognition of God's holiness cannot properly pray that the name of the Father be "hallowed," or held in reverence before all creation. To pray as a disciple of Christ is to "give [God] His right place." Beginning prayer with adoration demands more than opening one's prayers with praise before moving on to petition. Rather, to quote Extreme, it demands "more than words to show you feel that your love for me is real."* It demands that we learn to take our "right place before God—in the dust" so that we may "put God in His right place." Positioning ourselves rightly before God clarifies two basic theological convictions that undergird prayer. First, God is holy and worthy of our praise. Second, human flourishing is dependent upon a right relationship with God that highlights the necessity of humility before God. Prayer gestures toward this right relationship but does not guarantee

---

* Extreme, "More Than Words," *Pornograffitti*, track 5 (A & M, 1990), compact disc.

it because it is possible for prayer to be self-aggrandizing rather than expressing true humility (Matt. 6:5–8; Luke 18:9–14). For Christians to articulate faithful theological convictions through prayer, they must position themselves rightly before God.

———※———

Adoration has been defined as the act of rendering divine honor, including in it reverence, esteem, and love. It literally signifies to apply the hand to the mouth, "to kiss the hand." In Eastern countries this is one of the great marks of respect and submission. The importance of coming before God in this spirit is great; therefore it is so often impressed upon us in the Word of God.

The Rev. Newman Hall, in his work on the Lord's Prayer, says:

Man's worship, apart from revelation, has been uniformly characterized by selfishness. We come to God either to thank Him for benefits already received, or to implore still further benefits: food, raiment, health, safety, comfort. Like Jacob at Bethel, we are disposed to make the worship we render to God correlative with "food to eat, and raiment to put on." This style of petition, in which self generally precedes and predominates, if it does not altogether absorb our supplications, is not only seen in the votaries of false systems, but in the majority of the prayers of professed Christians. Our prayers are like the Parthian horsemen, who ride one way while they look another; we seem to go toward God, but, indeed, reflect upon ourselves. And this may be the reason why many times our prayers are sent forth, like the raven out of Noah's ark, and never return. But when we make the glory of God the chief end of our devotion, they go forth like the dove, and return to us again with an olive branch.

Let me refer you to a passage in the prophecies of Daniel. He was one of the men who knew how to pray; his prayer brought

the blessing of heaven upon himself and upon his people. He
says:

> I set my face unto the LORD God, to seek by prayer and supplications,
> with fasting, and sackcloth, and ashes; and I prayed unto the LORD
> my God, and made my confession, and said, O LORD, the great and
> dreadful God, keeping the covenant and mercy to them that love
> Him, and to them that keep His commandments[!] (Dan. 9:3–4)

The thought I want to call special attention to is conveyed in the
words, "Lord, the great and dreadful God!" Daniel took his right
place before God—in the dust; he put God in His right place. It was
when Abraham was on his face, prostrate before God, that God
spoke to him. Holiness belongs to God; sinfulness belongs to us.

Brooks, that grand old Puritan writer, says:

> A person of real holiness is much affected and taken up in the ad-
> miration of the holiness of God. Unholy persons may be somewhat
> affected and taken with the other excellences of God; it is only
> holy souls that are taken and affected with His holiness. The more
> holy any are, the more deeply are they affected by this. To the holy
> angels, the holiness of God is the sparkling diamond in the ring
> of glory. But unholy persons are affected and taken with anything
> rather than with this. Nothing strikes the sinner into such a damp
> as a discourse on the holiness of God; it is as the handwriting on
> the wall; nothing makes the head and heart of a sinner to ache like
> a sermon upon the Holy One; nothing galls and gripes, nothing
> stings and terrifies unsanctified ones, like a lively setting forth of
> the holiness of God. But to holy souls there are no discourses that
> do more suit and satisfy them, that do more delight and content
> them, that do more please and profit them, than those that do
> most fully and powerfully discover God to be glorious in holiness.

So, in coming before God, we must adore and reverence His
name.

The same thing is brought out in Isaiah 6:1–3:

> In the year that king Uzziah died I saw also the LORD sitting upon a throne, high and lifted up, and his train filled the temple. Above it stood the seraphims: each one had six wings; with twain he covered his face, and with twain he covered his feet, and with twain he did fly. And one cried unto another, and said, Holy, holy, holy, is the LORD of hosts: the whole earth is full of His glory.

A Sense of God's Holiness Needed

When we see the holiness of God, we shall adore and magnify Him. Moses had to learn the same lesson. God told him to take his shoes from off his feet, for the place whereon he stood was holy ground. When we hear men trying to make out that they are holy, and speaking about their holiness, they make light of the holiness of God. It is His holiness that we need to think and speak about; when we do that, we shall be prostrate in the dust. You remember, also, how it was with Peter. When Christ made Himself known to him, he said, "Depart from me, for I am a sinful man, O Lord!" A sight of God is enough to show us how holy He is, and how unholy we are.

We find that Job, too, had to be taught the same lesson. "Then Job answered the LORD, and said: Behold, I am vile; what shall I answer thee? I will lay mine hand upon my mouth" (Job 40:3–4).

As you hear Job discussing with his friends, you would think he was one of the holiest men who ever lived. He was eyes to the blind and feet to the lame; he fed the hungry and clothed the naked. What a wonderfully good man he was! It was all I, I, I. At last God said to him, "Gird up your loins like a man, and I will put a few questions to you." The moment that God revealed Himself, Job changed his language. He saw his own vileness and God's purity. He said, "I have heard of Thee by the hearing of the ear: but now mine eye seeth Thee. Wherefore I abhor myself, and repent in dust and ashes" (42:5–6).

The same thing is seen in the cases of those who came to our Lord in the days of His flesh; those who came aright, seeking and obtaining the blessing, manifested a lively sense of His infinite superiority to themselves. The centurion, of whom we read in Matthew 8, said: "Lord, I am not worthy that Thou shouldest come under my roof"; Jairus "worshiped Him," as he presented his request; the leper, in the Gospel of Mark, came "kneeling down to Him"; the Syrophoenician woman "came and fell at His feet"; the man full of leprosy "seeing Jesus, fell on his face." So, too, the beloved disciple, speaking of the feeling they had concerning Him when they were abiding with Him as their Lord, said: "We beheld His glory, the glory as of the only begotten of the Father, full of grace and truth" (John 1:14). However intimate their companionship, and tender their love, they reverenced as much as they communed and adored as much as they loved.

We may say of every act of prayer as George Herbert says of public worship:

> When once thy foot enters the church, be bare;
> God is more than thou; for thou art there
> Only by His permission. Then beware,
> And make thyself all reverence and fear.
> Kneeling ne'er spoiled silk stocking; quit thy state,
> All equal are within the church's gate.

The wise man says:

> Keep thy foot when thou goest to the house of God, and be more ready to hear, than to give the sacrifice of fools: for they consider not that they do evil. Be not rash with thy mouth, and let not thine heart be hasty to utter any thing before God: for God is in heaven, and thou upon earth: therefore let thy words be few. (Eccles. 5:1–2)

If we are struggling to live a higher life, and to know something of God's holiness and purity, what we need is to be brought into contact with Him, that He may reveal Himself. Then we shall take our place before Him as those men of old were constrained to do. We shall hallow His Name—as the Master taught His disciples, when He said, "Hallowed be Thy name." When I think of the irreverence of the present time, it seems to me that we have fallen on evil days.

Let us, as Christians, when we draw near to God in prayer, give Him His right place. "Let us have grace, whereby we may serve God acceptably with reverence and godly fear: for our God is a consuming fire" (Heb. 12:28–29).

The Trinity

Thou dear and great mysterious Three,
    Forever be adored;
For all the endless grace we see
    In our Redeemer stored.
The Father's ancient grace we sing,
    That chose us in our Head;
Ordaining Christ, our God and King,
    To suffer in our stead.
The sacred Son, in equal strains,
    With reverence we address,
For all His grace, and dying pains,
    And splendid righteousness.
With tuneful tongue, the Holy Ghost,
    For His great work we praise,
Whose power inspires the blood-bought host
    Their grateful voice to raise.
Thus the Eternal Three in One
    We join to praise, for grace
And endless glory through the Son,
    As shining from His face.

3

Confession

The confession of sin marks one out as a member of God's people. As John writes, "If we confess our sins, He is faithful and just to forgive us our sins, and to cleanse us from all unrighteousness" (1 John 1:9). The "if . . . then" structure here is not intended to convey cause and effect, as if we must confess all our sins in order to be forgiven for those sins. Rather, the confession of sin is offered as "proof" that one's reception of God's forgiveness is warranted. Confession of sin is generally inconvenient. To put it another way, there are often negative consequences associated with confession that most of us would likely opt to avoid. As such, "confession implies humility, and this, in God's sight, is of great price." To live without confession, to hide our rebellions rather than acknowledging them, or to call "evil good, and good evil" (Isa. 5:20) is to reject the wisdom and Word of God and to chart our own course. In confession, we entrust ourselves not to the mercy of other Christians or the world, which may too often be lacking, but to the loving discipline of our benevolent Father. In confession we avoid "the cold and dead formalism in the professing church" cultivated as we continue our rebellion so that we may "be clear and right before God" and prepared to point the world to Him.

———✳———

Another element in true prayer is confession. I do not want Christian friends to think that I am talking to the unsaved. I think we, as Christians, have a good many sins to confess.

If you go back to the Scripture records, you will find that the men who lived nearest to God, and had most power with Him, were those who confessed their sins and failures. Daniel, as we have seen, confessed his sins and those of his people (Dan. 9:3–19). Yet there is nothing recorded against Daniel. He was one of the best men then on the face of the earth, yet his confession of sin is one of the deepest and most humble on record. Brooks, referring to Daniel's confession, says:

> In these words you have seven circumstances that Daniel useth in confessing of his and the people's sins; and all to heighten and aggravate them. First, "We have sinned;" secondly, "We have committed iniquity;" thirdly, "We have done wickedly;" fourthly, "We have rebelled against thee;" fifthly, "We have departed from Thy precepts;" sixthly, "We have not hearkened unto Thy servants;" seventhly, "Nor our princes, nor all the people of the land." These seven aggravations which Daniel reckons up in his confession are worthy our most serious consideration.

Job was no doubt a holy man, a mighty prince, yet he had to fall in the dust and confess his sins. So you will find it all through the Scriptures. When Isaiah saw the purity and holiness of God, he beheld himself in his true light, and he exclaimed, "Woe is me! for I am undone; because I am a man of unclean lips" (Isa. 6:5).

I firmly believe that the Church of God will have to confess her own sins before there can be any great work of grace. There must

256

be a deeper work among God's believing people. I sometimes think it is about time to give up preaching to the ungodly and preach to those who profess to be Christians. If we had a higher standard of life in the Church of God, there would be thousands more flocking into the kingdom. So it was in the past; when God's believing children turned away from their sins and their idols, the fear of God fell upon the people roundabout. Take up the history of Israel, and you will find that when they put away their strange gods, God visited the nation, and there came a mighty work of grace.

Judgment of Sin in the Church

What we want in these days is a true and deep revival in the Church of God. I have little sympathy with the idea that God is going to reach the masses by a cold and formal Church. The judgment of God must begin with us. You notice that when Daniel got that wonderful answer to prayer recorded in the ninth chapter, he was confessing his sin. That is one of the best chapters on prayer in the whole Bible. We read:

> And whiles I was speaking, and praying, and confessing my sin and the sin of my people Israel, and presenting my supplication before the Lord my God for the holy mountain of my God; Yea, whiles I was speaking in prayer, even the man Gabriel, whom I had seen in the vision at the beginning, being caused to fly swiftly, touched me about the time of the evening oblation. And he informed me, and talked with me, and said, O Daniel, I am now come forth to give thee skill and understanding. (Dan. 9:20–22)

So also when Job was confessing his sin, God turned his captivity and heard his prayer. God will hear our prayer and turn our captivity when we take our true place before Him and confess and forsake our transgressions. It was when Isaiah cried out before the Lord, "I am undone," that the blessing came; the live coal was taken from the altar and put upon his lips, and he went out to write one of the most wonderful books the world has ever seen. What a blessing it has been to the Church!

It was when David said, "I have sinned!" that God dealt in mercy with him. "I acknowledge my sin unto Thee, and mine iniquity have I not hid. I said, I will confess my transgressions unto the LORD; and Thou forgavest the iniquity of my sin" (Ps. 32:5). Notice how David made a very similar confession to that of the prodigal in Luke 15 in Psalm 51:3–4: "I acknowledge my transgressions: and my sin is ever before me. Against Thee, Thee only, have I sinned, and done this evil in Thy sight[!]" There is no difference between the king and the beggar when the Spirit of God comes into the heart and convicts of sin.

Richard Sibbes quaintly says of confession:

This is the way to give glory to God: when we have laid open our souls to God, and laid as much against ourselves as the devil could do that way, for let us think what the devil would lay to our charge at the hour of death and the day of judgment. He would lay hard to our charge this and that—let us accuse ourselves as he would, and as he will ere long. The more we accuse and judge ourselves, and set up a tribunal in our hearts, certainly there will follow an incredible ease. Jonah was cast into the sea, and there was an ease in the ship; Achan was stoned, and the plague was stayed. Out with Jonah, out with Achan; and there will follow ease and quiet in the soul presently. Conscience will receive wonderful ease.

It must needs be so; for when God is honored, conscience is purified. God is honored by confession of sin every way. It honors His omniscience, that He is all-seeing; that He sees our sins and searches our hearts—our secrets are not hid from Him. It honors His power. What makes us confess our sins, but that we are afraid of His power, lest He should execute it? And what makes us confess our sins, but that we know there is mercy with Him that He may be feared, and that there is pardon for sin? We would not confess our sins else. With men it is, confess, and have execution; but with God, confess, and have mercy. It is His own protestation. We should never lay open our sins but for mercy. So it honors God; and when He is honored, He honors the soul with inward peace and tranquility.

Old Thomas Fuller says: "Man's owning his weakness is the only stock for God thereon to graft the grace of His assistance."

Confession implies humility, and this, in God's sight, is of great price.

A farmer went with his son into a wheat field, to see if it was ready for the harvest. "See, father," exclaimed the boy, "how straight these stems hold up their heads! They must be the best ones. Those that hang their heads down, I am sure cannot be good for much." The farmer plucked a stalk of each kind and said: "See here, foolish child! This stalk that stood so straight is light-headed, and almost good for nothing; while this that hung its head so modestly is full of the most beautiful grain."

Outspokenness is needful and powerful, both with God and man. We need to be honest and frank with ourselves. A soldier said in a revival meeting: "My fellow soldiers, I am not excited; I am *convinced*—that is all. I feel that I ought to be a Christian; that I ought to say so, to tell you so, and to ask you to come with me; and now if there is a call for sinners seeking Christ to come forward, I for one shall go—not to make a show, for I have nothing but sin to show. I do not go because I want to—I would rather keep my seat; but going will be telling the truth. I ought to be a Christian, I want to be a Christian; and going forward for prayers is just telling the truth about it." More than a score went with him.

Speaking of Pharaoh's words, "Entreat the Lord that He may take away the frogs from me," Mr. Spurgeon says:

A fatal flaw is manifest in that prayer. *It contains no confession of sin.* He says not, "I have rebelled against the Lord; entreat that I may find forgiveness!" Nothing of the kind; he loves sin as much as ever. A prayer without penitence is a prayer without acceptance. If no tear has fallen upon it, it is withered. Thou must come to God as a sinner through a Savior, but by no other way. He who comes to God like the Pharisee, with, "God, I thank Thee that I am not as other men are," never draws near to God at all; but he who cries, "God be merciful to me a sinner," has come to God by the way which God has Himself appointed. There must be confession of sin before God, or our prayer is faulty.

If this confession of sin is deep among believers, it will be so among the ungodly also. I never knew it to fail. I am now anxious that God should revive His work in the hearts of His children, so that we may see the exceeding sinfulness of sin. There are a great many fathers and mothers who are anxious for the conversion of their children. I have had as many as fifty messages from parents come to me within a single week, wondering why their children are not saved and asking prayer for them. I venture to say that, as a rule, the fault lies at our own door. There may be something in our lives that stands in the way. It may be there is some secret sin that keeps back the blessing. David lived in the awful sin into which he fell for many months before Nathan made his appearance. Let us pray God to come into our hearts and make His power felt. If it is a right eye, let us pluck it out; if it is a right hand, let us cut it off; that we may have power with God and with man.

Lack of Power in the Church

Why is it that so many of our children are wandering off into the drinking saloons and drifting away into infidelity—going down to a dishonored grave? There seems to be very little power in the Christianity of the present time. Many godly parents find that their children are going astray. Does it arise from some secret sin clinging around the heart? There is a passage of God's Word that is often quoted, but in ninety-nine cases out of a hundred those who quote it stop at the wrong place. In Isaiah 59:1 we read: "Behold, the

LORD's hand is not shortened, that it cannot save, neither His ear heavy, that it cannot hear." There they stop. Of course God's hand is not shortened, and His ear is not heavy; but we ought to read the next verses: "Your iniquities have separated between you and your God, and your sins have hid His face from you, that He will not hear. For your hands are defiled with blood, and your fingers with iniquity; your lips have spoken lies, your tongue hath muttered perverseness" (vv. 2–3). As Matthew Henry says, "It was owing to themselves—they stood in their own light, they shut their own door. God was coming toward them in the way of mercy, and they hindered Him. '*Your iniquities have kept good things from you.*'"

Bear in mind that if we are regarding iniquity in our hearts, or living on a mere empty profession, we have no claim to expect that our prayers will be answered. There is not one solitary promise for us. I sometimes tremble when I hear people quote promises, and say that God is bound to fulfill those promises to them, when all the time there is something in their own lives which they are not willing to give up. It is well for us to search our hearts and find out why it is that our prayers are not answered.

That is a very solemn passage in Isaiah 1:10–13:

> Hear the word of the LORD, ye rulers of Sodom; give ear unto the law of our God, ye people of Gomorrah. To what purpose is the multitude of your sacrifices unto Me? saith the Lord: I am full of the burnt offerings of rams, and the fat of fed beasts; and I delight not in the blood of bullocks, or of lambs, or of he goats. When ye come to appear before Me, who hath required this at your hand, to tread My courts? Bring no more vain oblations; incense is an abomination unto Me; the new moons and sabbaths, the calling of assemblies, I cannot away with; it is iniquity, even the solemn meeting.

"Even the solemn meeting"—think of that! If God does not get our heart-services, He will have none of it; it is an abomination to Him.

Your new moons and your appointed feasts My soul hateth: they are a trouble unto Me; I am weary to bear them. And when ye spread forth your hands, I will hide Mine eyes from you: yea, when ye make many prayers, I will not hear: your hands are full of blood. Wash you, make you clean; put away the evil of your doings from before Mine eyes; cease to do evil; learn to do well; seek judgment, relieve the oppressed, judge the fatherless, plead for the widow.

Come now, and let us reason together, saith the LORD: though your sins be as scarlet, they shall be as white as snow; though they be red like crimson, they shall be as wool. (vv. 14–18)

In Proverbs 28:9 we read: "He that turneth away his ear from hearing the law, even his prayer shall be abomination." Think of that! It may shock some of us to think that our prayers are an abomination to God, yet if any are living in known sin, this is what God's Word says about them. If we are not willing to turn from sin and obey God's law, we have no right to expect that He will answer our prayers. Unconfessed sin is unforgiven sin, and unforgiven sin is the darkest, foulest thing on this sin-cursed earth. You cannot find a case in the Bible where a man has been honest in dealing with sin, but God has been honest with him and blessed him. The prayer of the humble and the contrite heart is a delight to God. There is no sound that goes up from this sin-cursed earth so sweet to His ear as the prayer of the man who is walking uprightly.

Let me call attention to that prayer of David, in Psalm 139:23–24: "Search me, O, God, and know my heart; try me, and know my thoughts: and see if there be any wicked way in me, and lead me in the way everlasting!" I wish all my readers would commit these verses to memory. If we should all honestly make this prayer once every day there would be a good deal of change in our lives. "Search *me*"—not my neighbor. It is so easy to pray for other people but so hard to get home to ourselves. I am afraid that we who are busy in the Lord's work are very often in danger of neglecting our vineyard. In this psalm, David got home to himself.

There is a difference between God searching me and my searching myself. I may search my heart, and pronounce it all right, but when God searches me as with a lighted candle, a good many things will come to light that perhaps I knew nothing about.

"Try *me*." David was tried when he fell by taking his eye off from the God of his father Abraham. "Know *my* thoughts." God looks at the thoughts. Are our thoughts pure? Have we in our hearts thoughts against God or against His people—against anyone in the world? If we have, we are not right in the sight of God. Oh, may God search us, every one! I do not know any better prayer that we can make than this prayer of David. One of the most solemn things in the Scripture history is that when holy men—better men than we are—were tested and tried, they were found to be as weak as water away from God.

Let us be sure that we are right. Isaac Ambrose, in his work on "Self Trial," has the following pithy words:

Now and then propose we to our hearts these two questions: 1. "Heart, how dost thou?"—a few words, but a very serious question. You know this is the first question and the first salute that we use to one another—How do you do? I would to God we sometimes thus spoke to our hearts: "Heart, how dost thou? How is it with thee, for thy spiritual state?" 2. "Heart, what wilt thou do?" or, "Heart, what dost thou think will become of thee and me?"—as that dying Roman once said: "Poor, wretched, miserable soul, whither art thou and I going—and what will become of thee, when thou and I shall part?"

This very thing does Moses propose to Israel, though in other terms, "Oh that they would consider their latter end!"—and oh that we would put this question constantly to our hearts, to consider and debate upon! "Commune with your own hearts," said David; that is, debate the matter betwixt you and your hearts to the very utmost. Let your hearts be so put to it in communing with them, as that they may speak their very bottom. Commune—or hold a serious communication and clear intelligence and acquaintance—with your own hearts.

It was the confession of a divine, sensible of his neglect, and especially of the difficulty of this duty:

I have lived forty years and somewhat more, and carried my heart in my bosom all this while, and yet my heart and I are as great strangers, and as utterly unacquainted, as if we had never come near one another. Nay, I know not my heart; I have forgotten my heart. Alas! alas! that I could be grieved at the very heart, that my poor heart and I have been so unacquainted! We are fallen into an Athenian age, spending our time in nothing more than in telling or hearing news. How go things here? How there? How in one place? How in another? But who is there that is inquisitive? How are things with my poor heart? Weigh but in the balance of a serious consideration, what time we have spent in this duty, and what time otherwise; and for many scores and hundreds of hours or days that we owe to our hearts in this duty, can we write fifty? Or where there should have been fifty vessels full of this duty, can we find twenty, or ten? Oh, the days, months, years, we bestow upon sin, vanity, the affairs of this world, while we afford not a minute in converse with our own hearts concerning their case!

Confess Self-Seeking as Sin

If there is anything in our lives that is wrong, let us ask God to show it to us. Have we been selfish? Have we been more jealous of our own reputation than of the honor of God? Elijah thought he was very jealous for the honor of God; but it turned out that it was his own honor after all—self was really at the bottom of it. One of the saddest things, I think, that Christ had to meet with in His disciples was this very thing; there was a constant struggle between them as to who should be the greatest, instead of each one taking the humblest place and being least in his own estimation.

We are told in proof of this, that:

And He came to Capernaum: and being in the house He asked them, What was it that ye disputed among yourselves by the way?

But they held their peace: for by the way they had disputed among themselves, who should be the greatest. And He sat down, and called the twelve, and saith unto them, If any man desire to be first, the same shall be last of all, and servant of all. And He took a child, and set him in the midst of them: and when He had taken him in His arms, He said unto them, Whosoever shall receive one of such children in My name, receiveth Me: and whosoever shall receive Me, receiveth not Me, but Him that sent Me. (Mark 9:33–37)

Soon after:

And James and John, the sons of Zebedee, come unto Him, saying, Master, we would that Thou shouldest do for us whatsoever we shall desire. And He said unto them, What would ye that I should do for you? They said unto Him, Grant unto us that we may sit, one on Thy right hand, and the other on Thy left hand, in Thy glory. But Jesus said unto them, Ye know not what ye ask: can ye drink of the cup that I drink of? and be baptized with the baptism that I am baptized with? And they said unto Him, We can.

And Jesus said unto them, Ye shall indeed drink of the cup that I drink of; and with the baptism that I am baptized withal shall ye be baptized: But to sit on My right hand and on My left hand is not mine to give; but it shall be given to them for whom it is prepared. And when the ten heard it, they began to be much displeased with James and John.

But Jesus called them to Him, and saith unto them, Ye know that they which are accounted to rule over the Gentiles exercise lordship over them; and their great ones exercise authority upon them. But so shall it not be among you: but whosoever will be great among you, shall be your minister: And whosoever of you will be the chiefest, shall be servant of all. For even the Son of man came not to be ministered unto, but to minister, and to give His life a ransom for many. (10:35–45)

The latter words were spoken in the third year of His ministry. Three years the disciples had been with Him; they had listened to the words that fell from His lips, yet they had failed to learn this lesson of humility. The most humiliating thing that happened among the chosen twelve occurred on the night of our Lord's betrayal, when Judas sold Him and Peter denied Him. If there was any place where there should have been an absence of these thoughts, it was at the Supper table. Yet we find that when Christ instituted that blessed memorial, there was a debate going on among His disciples who should be the greatest. Think of that!— right under the cross, when the Master was "exceeding sorrowful, even unto death," was already tasting the bitterness of Calvary, and the horrors of that dark hour were gathering upon His soul.

I think if God searches us, we will find a good many things in our lives for us to confess. If we are tried and tested by God's law, there will be many, many things that will have to be changed. I ask again: Are we selfish or jealous? Are we willing to hear of others being used of God more than we are? Are our Methodist friends willing to hear of a great revival of God's work among the Baptists? Would it rejoice their souls to hear of such efforts being blessed? Are Baptists willing to hear of a reviving of God's work in the Methodist, Congregational, or other churches? If we are full of narrow, party, and sectarian feelings, there will be many things to be laid aside. Let us pray to God to search us, and try us, and see if there be any evil way in us. If these holy and good men felt that they were faulty, should we not tremble and endeavor to find out if there is anything in our lives that God would have us get rid of?

Once again, let me call your attention to the prayer of David contained in Psalm 51. A friend of mine told me some years ago that he repeated this prayer as his own every week. I think it would be a good thing if we offered up these petitions frequently; let them go right up from our hearts. If we have been proud, or irritable, or lacking in patience, shall we not at once confess it? Is it not time that we began at home and got our lives straightened out? See how quickly the ungodly will then begin to inquire the way of life! Let those of us who are parents set our own houses in order, and be filled with Christ's Spirit; then it will not be long before our children will be inquiring what they must do to get the same Spirit. I believe that today, by its lukewarmness and formality, the Christian Church is making more infidels than all the books that infidels ever wrote. I do not fear infidel lectures half so much as the cold and dead formalism in the professing Church at the present time. One prayer meeting like that the disciples had on the day of Pentecost would shake the whole infidel fraternity.

What we want is to get hold of God in prayer. You are not going to reach the masses by great sermons. We want to "move the Arm that moves the world." To do that, we must be clear and right before God.

> For if our heart condemn us, God is greater than our heart, and knoweth all things. Beloved, if our heart condemn us not, then have we confidence toward God. And whatsoever we ask, we receive of Him, because we keep His commandments, and do those things that are pleasing in His sight. (1 John 3:20–22)

Confession

No, not despairingly
　　Come I to Thee;
No, not distrustingly
　　Bend I the knee;
Sin hath gone over me,
Yet is this still my plea,
　　Jesus hath died.
Ah, mine iniquity
　　Crimson has been;
Infinite, infinite,
　　Sin upon sin;
Sin of not loving Thee,
Sin of not trusting Thee.
　　Infinite sin.

Lord, I confess to Thee
Sadly my sin;
All I am, tell I Thee,
All I have been.
Purge Thou my sin away,
Wash Thou my soul this day;
Lord, make me clean!

Dr. H. Bonar

4

Restitution

As we confess, we open ourselves up to recognizing and taking responsibility for that damage. As Moody writes, "If we have taken anything from any man, if we have in any way defrauded a man, let us not only confess it but do all we can to make restitution. If we have misrepresented anyone—if we have started some slander, or some false report about him—let us do all in our power to undo the wrong." Whereas confession is the acknowledgment of our sin, restitution involves making amends for wrong done. For Moody, restitution was a natural extension of confession. Whether or not Moody would have connected the dots between restitution and the issues related to making those formerly enslaved whole after the Civil War is unclear. It seems likely, however, that Moody's interest in restitution was, in part, motivated by his sensitivity to poverty and the trappings of worldly wealth. Restitution was not only a way of showing genuine repentance but also of offering material assistance to those one has wronged and freeing oneself from the burden of enjoying the benefits of unrighteousness.

———————*———————

A third element of successful prayer is *restitution*. If I have at any time taken what does not belong to me, and am not willing to make restitution, my prayers will not go very far toward heaven. It is a singular thing, but I have never touched on this subject in my addresses without hearing of immediate results. A man once told me that I would not need to dwell on this point at a meeting I was about to address, as probably there would be no one present that would need to make restitution. But I think if the Spirit of God searches our hearts, we shall most of us find a good many things have to be done that we never thought of before.

After Zacchaeus met with Christ, things looked altogether different. I venture to say that the idea of making restitution never entered into his mind before. He thought, probably, that morning that he was a perfectly honest man. But when the Lord came and spoke to him, he saw himself in an altogether different light. Notice how short his speech was. The only thing put on record that he said was this: "Behold, Lord, the half of my goods I give to the poor; and if I have taken anything from any man by false accusation, I restore him fourfold" (Luke 19:8). A short speech; but how the words have come ringing down through the ages!

By making that remark he confessed his sin—that he had been dishonest. Besides that, he showed that he knew the requirements of the law of Moses. If a man had taken what did not belong to him, he was not only to return it but to multiply it by four. I think that men in this dispensation ought to be fully as honest as men under the law. I am getting so tired and sick of your mere sentimentalism that does not straighten out a man's life. We may sing our hymns and psalms, and offer prayers, but they will be an abomination to God unless we are willing to be thoroughly straightforward in our daily life. Nothing will give Christianity such a hold upon the world as to have God's believing people begin to act in this way. Zacchaeus had probably more influence in Jericho after he made restitution than any other man in it.

Finney, in his lectures to professing Christians, says:

> One reason for the requirement, "Be not conformed to this world," is the immense, salutary, and instantaneous influence it would have, if everybody would do business on the principles of the gospel. Turn the tables over, and let Christians do business one year on gospel principles. It would shake the world! It would ring louder than thunder. Let the ungodly see professing Christians in every bargain consulting the good of the person they are trading with—seeking not their own wealth, but every man another's wealth—living above the world—setting no value on the world any further than it would be the means of glorifying God; what do you think would be the effect? It would cover the world with confusion of face, and overwhelm them with conviction of sin.

Finney makes one grand mark of genuine repentance to be restitution.

> The thief has not repented who keeps the money he stole. He may have conviction, but no repentance. If he had repentance, he would go and give back the money. If you have cheated any one, and do not restore what you have taken unjustly; or if you have injured any one, and do not set about to undo the wrong you have done, as far as in you lies, you have not truly repented.

In Exodus 22 we read: "If a man shall steal an ox, or a sheep, and kill it, or sell it; he shall restore five oxen for an ox, and four sheep for a sheep" (v. 1). And again:

> If a man shall cause a field or vineyard to be eaten, and shall put in his beast, and shall feed in another man's field; of the best of his own field, and of the best of his own vineyard shall he make restitution.

If fire break out, and catch in thorns, so that the stacks of corn, or the standing corn, or the field, be consumed therewith, he that kindled the fire shall surely make restitution. (vv. 5–6)

Or turn to Leviticus, where the law of the trespass-offering is laid down—the same point is there insisted on with equal clearness and force:

If a soul sin, and commit a trespass against the Lord, and lie unto his neighbour in that which was delivered him to keep, or in fellowship, or in a thing taken away by violence, or hath deceived his neighbour; or have found that which was lost, and lieth concerning it, and sweareth falsely; in any of all these that a man doeth, sinning therein: Then it shall be, because he hath sinned, and is guilty, that he shall restore that which he took violently away, or the thing which he hath deceitfully gotten, or that which was delivered him to keep, or the lost thing which he found, or all that about which he hath sworn falsely; he shall even restore it in the principal, and shall add the fifth part more thereto, and give it unto him to whom it appertaineth, in the day of his trespass offering. (6:2–5)

The same thing is repeated in Numbers, where we read:

And the LORD spake unto Moses, saying, Speak unto the children of Israel, When a man or woman shall commit any sin that men commit, to do a trespass against the LORD, and that person be guilty; then they shall confess their sin which they have done: and he shall recompense his trespass with the principal thereof, and add unto it the fifth part thereof, and give it unto him against whom he hath trespassed. But if the man have no kinsman to recompense the trespass unto, let the trespass be recompensed unto the LORD, even to the priest; beside the ram of the atonement, whereby an atonement shall be made for him. (5:5–8)

These were the laws that God laid down for His people, and I believe their principle is as binding today as it was then. If we have taken anything from any man, if we have in any way defrauded a man, let us not only confess it but do all we can to make restitution. If we have misrepresented anyone—if we have started some slander, or some false report about him—let us do all in our power to undo the wrong. It is in reference to a practical righteousness such as this that God says in Isaiah:

> Behold, ye fast for strife and debate, and to smite with the fist of wickedness: ye shall not fast as ye do this day, to make your voice to be heard on high.
>
> Is it such a fast that I have chosen? a day for a man to afflict his soul? is it to bow down his head as a bulrush, and to spread sackcloth and ashes under him? wilt thou call this a fast, and an acceptable day to the LORD?
>
> Is not this the fast that I have chosen? to loose the bands of wickedness, to undo the heavy burdens, and to let the oppressed go free, and that ye break every yoke?
>
> Is it not to deal thy bread to the hungry, and that thou bring the poor that are cast out to thy house? when thou seest the naked, that thou cover him; and that thou hide not thyself from thine own flesh?
>
> Then shall thy light break forth as the morning, and thine health shall spring forth speedily: and thy righteousness shall go before thee; the glory of the LORD shall be thy reward.
>
> Then shalt thou call, and the LORD shall answer; thou shalt cry, and He shall say, Here I am. If thou take away from the midst of thee the yoke, the putting forth of the finger, and speaking vanity. (58:4–9)

Trapp, in his comment on Zacchaeus, says:

> Sultan Selymus could tell his councillor Pyrrhus, who persuaded him to bestow the great wealth he had taken from the Persian merchants upon some notable hospital for relief of the poor, that God hates robbery for burnt-offering. The dying Turk commanded it rather to be restored to the right owners, which was

done accordingly, to the great shame of many Christians, who mind nothing less than restitution. When Henry III of England had sent the Friar Minors a load of frieze to clothe them, they returned the same with this message, "that he ought not to give alms of what he had rent from the poor; neither would they accept of that abominable gift." Master Latimer saith, "If ye make no restitution of goods detained, ye shall cough in hell, and the devils shall laugh at you." Henry VII, in his last will and testament, after the disposition of his soul and body, devised and willed restitution should be made of all such moneys as had unjustly been levied by his officers. Queen Mary restored again all ecclesiastical livings assumed to the crown, saying that she set more by the salvation of her own soul, than she did by ten kingdoms. A bull came also from the Pope, at the same time, that others should do the like, but none did. Latimer tells us that the first day he preached about restitution, one came and gave him £20 to restore; the next day another brought him £30; another time another gave him £200.

Mr. Bradford, hearing Latimer on that subject, was struck in the heart for one dash of the pen which he had made without the knowledge of his master, and could never be quiet till, by the advice of Mr. Latimer, restitution was made, for which he did willingly forego all the private and certain patrimony which he had on earth. "I, myself," saith Mr. Burroughs, "knew one man who had wronged another but of five shillings, and fifty years after could not be quiet till he had restored it."

True Repentance Requires Restitution

If there is true repentance it will bring forth fruit. If we have done wrong to someone, we should never ask God to forgive us until we are willing to make restitution. If I have done any man a great injustice and can make it good, I need not ask God to forgive me until I am willing to do so. Suppose I have taken something that does not belong to me. I cannot expect forgiveness until I make restitution. I remember preaching in an Eastern city, and a fine-looking man came up to me at the close. He was in great distress of mind. "The fact is," he said, "I am a defaulter. I have taken money that belonged to my employers. How can I become a Christian without restoring it?"

"Have you got the money?" He told me he had not got it all. He had taken about $1,500, and he still had about $900. He said, "Could I not take that money and go into business, and make enough to pay them back?" I told him that was a delusion of Satan, that he could not expect to prosper on stolen money; that he should restore all he had, and go and ask his employers to have mercy upon him, and forgive him. "But they will put me in prison," he said. "Can you not give me any help?"

"No; you must restore the money before you can expect to get any help from God." "It is pretty hard," he said. "Yes, it is hard; but the great mistake was in doing the wrong at first." His burden became so heavy that it was, in fact, unbearable. He handed me the money—$950 and some cents—and asked me to take it back to his employers. I told them the story, and said that he wanted mercy from them, not justice. The tears trickled down the cheeks of these two men, and they said, "Forgive him! Yes, we will be glad to forgive him." I went downstairs and brought him up. After he had confessed his guilt and been forgiven, we all fell down on our knees and had a blessed prayer meeting. God met us and blessed us there.

There was another friend of mine who had come to Christ and was trying to consecrate himself and his wealth to God. He had formerly had transactions with the government and had taken advantage of them. This thing came to memory, and his conscience troubled him. He had a terrible struggle; his conscience kept rising up and smiting him. At last he drew a check for $1,500 and sent it to the treasury of the government. He told me he received such a blessing after he had done it. That is bringing forth fruits meet for repentance. I believe a great many men are crying to God for light; and they are not getting it because they are not honest.

A man came to one of our meetings, when this subject was touched upon. The memory of a dishonest transaction flashed into his mind. He saw at once how it was that his prayers were not answered but "returned into his own bosom," as the Scripture phrase puts it. He left the meeting, took the train, and went to a distant city, where he had defrauded his employer years before. He went straight to this man, confessed the wrong, and offered to make restitution. Then he remembered another transaction in which he had failed to meet the just demands upon him; he at once made arrangements to have a large amount repaid. He came back to the place where we were holding the meetings, and God blessed him wonderfully in his own soul. I have not met a man for a long time who seemed to have received such a blessing.

Some years ago, in the north of England, a woman came to one of the meetings and appeared to be very anxious about her soul. For some time she did not seem to be able to get peace. The truth was, she was covering up one thing that she was not willing to confess. At last, the burden was too great, and she said to a worker: "I never go down on my knees to pray, but a few bottles of wine keep coming up before my mind." It appeared that years before, when she was housekeeper, she had taken some bottles of wine belonging to her employer. The worker said: "Why do you not make restitution?" The woman replied that the man was dead; and besides, she did not know how much it was worth. "Are there any heirs living to whom you can make restitution?" She said there was a son living at some distance, but she thought it would be a very humiliating thing, so she kept back for some time. At last she felt as if she must have a clear conscience at any cost, so she took the train and went to the place where the son of her employer resided. She took five pounds with her; she did not exactly know what the wine was worth, but that would cover it at any rate. The man said he did not want the money, but she replied, "I do not want it; it has burnt my pocket long enough." So he agreed to take half of it, and give it to some charitable object. Then she came back, and

I think she was one of the happiest mortals I have ever met with. She said she could not tell whether she was in the body or out of it—such a blessing had come to her soul.

It may be that there is something in our lives that needs straightening out; something that happened perhaps twenty years ago, and that has been forgotten till the Spirit of God brought it to our remembrance. If we are not willing to make restitution, we cannot expect God to give us great blessing. Perhaps that is the reason so many of our prayers are not answered.

Perfect Cleansing

Who would be cleansed from every sin,
Must to God's holy altar bring
 The whole of life—its joys, its tears,
 Its hopes, its loves, its powers, its years,
The will, and every cherished thing!
Must make this sweeping sacrifice—
 Choose God, and dare reproach and shame,
 And boldly stand in storm or flame
For Him who paid redemption's price;
Then trust (not struggle to believe),
 And trusting wait, nor doubt, but pray
That in His own good time He'll say,
"Thy faith hath saved thee; now receive."
His time is when the soul brings all,
 Is all upon His altar lain;
 When pride and self-conceit are slain,
And crucified with Christ, we fall
Helpless upon His word, and lie;
 When, faithful to His word, we feel
 The cleansing touch, the Spirit's seal,
And know that He does sanctify.

A. T. Allis

5

Thanksgiving

The next thing I would mention as an element of prayer is *thanksgiving*. We ought to be more thankful for what we get from God. Perhaps some of you mothers have a child in your family who is constantly complaining—never thankful. You know that there is not much pleasure in doing anything for a child like that. If you meet with a beggar who is always grumbling, and never seems to be thankful for what you give, you very soon shut the door in his face altogether. Ingratitude is about the hardest thing we have to meet with. The great English poet William Shakespeare says:

> Blow, blow, thou winter wind—
> Thou art not so unkind
>   As man's ingratitude;
> Thy tooth is not so keen,
> Because thou art not seen,
>   Although thy breath be rude.

We cannot speak too plainly of this evil, which so demeans those who are guilty of it. Even in Christians there is but too much of it to be seen. Here we are, getting blessings from God day after day; yet how little praise and thanksgiving there is in the Church of God! Gurnall, in his *Christian Armor*, referring to the words, "In everything give thanks," says:

Praise is comely for the upright. "An unthankful saint" carries a contradiction with it. Evil and Unthankful are twins that live and die together; as any one ceaseth to be evil, he begins to be thankful. It is that which God expects at your hands; He made you for this end. When the vote passed in heaven for your being—yea, happy being in Christ!—it was upon this account, that you should be a name and a praise to Him on earth in time, and in heaven to eternity. Should God miss this, He would fail of one main part of His design. What prompts Him to bestow every mercy, but to afford you matter to compose a song for His praise? "They are My people, children that will not lie; so He was their Savior."

He looks for fair dealing at your hands. Whom may a father trust with his reputation, if not his child? Where can a prince expect honor, if not among his favorites? Your state is such that the least mercy you have is more than all the world besides. Thou, Christian, and thy few brethren, divide heaven and earth among you! What hath God that He withholds from you? Sun, moon and stars are set up to give you light; sea and land have their treasures for your use; others are encroachers upon them; you are the rightful heirs to them; they groan that any others should be served by them. The angels, bad and good, minister unto you; the evil, against their will, are forced like scullions when they tempt you, to scour and brighten your graces, and make way for your greater comforts; the good angels are servants to your heavenly Father, and disdain not to carry you in their arms. Your God withholds not Himself from you; He is your portion—Father, Husband, Friend. God is His own happiness, and admits you to enjoy Him. Oh, what honor is this, for the subject to drink in his prince's cup! "Thou shalt make them drink of the river of Thy pleasures." And all this is not the purchase of your sweat and blood; the feast is paid for by Another, only He expects your thanks to the Founder.

No sin-offering is imposed under the Gospel; thank-offerings are all He looks for.

Charnock, in discoursing on *Spiritual Worship*, says:

The praise of God is the choicest sacrifice and worship, under a dispensation of redeeming grace. This is the prime and eternal part of worship under the Gospel. The Psalmist, speaking of the Gospel times, spurs on to this kind of worship: "Sing unto the Lord a new song; let the children of Zion be joyful in their King; let the saints be joyful in glory; let them sing aloud upon their beds; let the high praises of God be in their mouth." He begins and ends Psalm 149 with *Praise ye the* LORD! That cannot be a spiritual and evangelical worship that hath nothing of the praise of God in the heart. The consideration of God's adorable perfections discovered in the Gospel will make us come to Him with more seriousness, beg blessings of Him with more confidence, fly to Him with a winged faith and love, and more spiritually glorify Him in our attendances upon Him.

Praise Is United in Prayer

There is a great deal more said in the Bible about praise than prayer; yet how few praise-meetings there are! David, in his psalms, always mixes praise with prayer. Solomon prevailed much with God in prayer at the dedication of the temple; but it was the voice of praise which brought down the glory that filled the house, for we read:

And it came to pass, when the priests were come out of the holy place: (for all the priests that were present were sanctified, and did not then wait by course:

Also the Levites which were the singers, all of them of Asaph, of Heman, of Jeduthun, with their sons and their brethren, being arrayed in white linen, having cymbals and psalteries and harps, stood at the east end of the altar, and with them an hundred and twenty priests sounding with trumpets:)

It came even to pass, as the trumpeters and singers were as one, to make one sound to be heard in praising and thanking the LORD; and when they lifted up their voice with the trumpets and cymbals and instruments of musick, and praised the LORD, saying, For He is good; for His mercy endureth for ever: that then the house was filled with a cloud, even the house of the LORD; so that the priests could not stand to minister by reason of the cloud: for the glory of the LORD had filled the house of God. (2 Chron. 5:11–14)

We read, too, of Jehoshaphat, that he gained the victory over the hosts of Ammon and Moab through praise, which was excited by faith and thankfulness to God.

And they rose early in the morning, and went forth into the wilderness of Tekoa: and as they went forth, Jehoshaphat stood and said, Hear me, O Judah, and ye inhabitants of Jerusalem; Believe in the LORD your God, so shall ye be established; believe His prophets, so shall ye prosper.

And when he had consulted with the people, he appointed singers unto the LORD, and that should praise the beauty of holiness, as they went out before the army, and to say, Praise the LORD; for His mercy endureth for ever.

And when they began to sing and to praise, the LORD set ambushments against the children of Ammon, Moab, and mount Seir, which were come against Judah; and they were smitten. (2 Chron. 20:20–22)

It is said that in a time of great despondency among the first settlers in New England, it was proposed in one of their public assemblies to proclaim a fast. An old farmer arose; spoke of their provoking heaven with their complaints, reviewed their measures, showed that they had much to be thankful for, and moved that instead of appointing a day of fasting, they should appoint a day of thanksgiving. This was done; and the custom has been continued ever since.

However great our difficulties, or deep even our sorrows, there is room for thankfulness. Thomas Adams has said:

> Lay up in the ark of thy memory not only the pot of manna, the bread of life; but even Aaron's rod, the very scourge of correction, wherewith thou hast been bettered. Blessed be the Lord, not only giving, but taking away, saith Job. God who sees there is no walking upon roses to heaven, puts His children into the way of discipline; and by the fire of correction eats out the rust of corruption. God sends trouble, then bids us call upon Him; promiseth our deliverance; and lastly, the all He requires of us is to glorify Him. "Call upon Me in the day of trouble; I will deliver thee, and thou shalt glorify Me."

Like the nightingale, we can sing in the night, and say with John Newton:

> Since all that I meet shall work for my good,
> The bitter is sweet, the medicine food;
> Though painful at present, 'twill cease before long,
> And then—oh, how pleasant!—the conqueror's song.

Among all the apostles none suffered so much as Paul; but none of them do we find so often giving thanks as he. Take his letter to the Philippians. Remember what he suffered at Philippi; how they laid many stripes upon him and cast him into prison. Yet every chapter in that epistle speaks of rejoicing and giving thanks. There is that well-known passage: "Be careful for nothing, but in everything, by prayer and supplication, with thanksgiving, let your requests be made known unto God" (Phil. 4:6). As someone has said, there are here three precious ideas: "Careful for nothing, prayerful for everything, and thankful for anything." We always get more by being thankful for what God has done for us. Paul says again: "We give thanks to God, the Father of our Lord Jesus Christ, praying always for you" (Col. 1:3). So he was constantly giving thanks. Take up any one of his epistles, and you will find them full of praise to God.

Even if nothing else called for thankfulness, it would always be an ample cause for it that Jesus Christ loved us and gave Himself for us. A farmer was once found kneeling at a soldier's grave near Nashville. Someone came to him and said: "Why do you pay so much attention to this grave? Was your son buried here?" "No," he said. "During the war my family were all sick, I knew not how to leave them. I was drafted. One of my neighbors came over and said: 'I will go for you; I have no family.' He went off. He was wounded at Chickamauga. He was carried to the hospital, and there died. And, sir, I have come a great many miles, that I might write over his grave these words, '*He died for me.*'"

This the believer can always say of his blessed Savior, and in the fact may well rejoice. "By Him therefore, let us offer the sacrifice of praise continually, that is, the fruit of our lips, giving thanks to His name" (Heb. 13:15).

The Praise of God

Speak, lips of mine!
   And tell abroad
   The praises of my God.
Speak, stammering tongue!
   In gladdest tone,
   Make His high praises known.
Speak, sea and earth!
   Heaven's utmost star,
   Speak from your realms afar!
Take up the note,
   And send it round
   Creation's farthest bound.

Speak, heaven of heavens!
  Wherein our God
  Has made His bright abode.
Speak, angels, speak!
  In songs proclaim
  His everlasting name.
Speak, son of dust!
  Thy flesh He took
  And heaven for thee forsook.
Speak, child of death!
  Thy death He died,
  Bless thou the Crucified.

Dr. H. Bonar

6

Forgiveness

Christian unity requires forgiveness. Unity was in short supply in Moody's day, particularly following the Civil War. Christians were divided along the issues of slavery and reparations, resulting in segregated congregations and fissures between Christians in the North and South. Beyond slavery, Moody was also concerned with the deepening divide between the rich and the poor. As God's people became increasingly embedded in American culture, they needed to be reminded of the power of forgiveness. The tensions between God's people would not be solved by leaning into American politics but by showcasing God's forgiveness even for the most heinous of sins.

The next thing is perhaps the most difficult of all to deal with—*forgiveness*. I believe this is keeping more people from having power with God than any other thing—they are not willing to cultivate the spirit of forgiveness. If we allow the root of bitterness to spring up in our hearts against someone, our prayer will not be answered. It may not be an easy thing to live in sweet fellowship with all those with whom we come in contact, but that is what the grace of God is given to us for.

The disciples' prayer is a test of sonship; if we can pray it all from the heart, we have good reason to think that we have been born of God. No man can call God Father but by the Spirit. Though this prayer has been such a blessing to the world, I believe it has been a great snare; many stumble over it into perdition. They do not weigh its meaning, nor take its facts right into their hearts. I have no sympathy with the idea of universal sonship—that all men are the sons of God. The Bible teaches very plainly that we are adopted into the family of God. If all were sons, God would not need to adopt any. We are all God's by creation; but when people teach that any man can say, "Our Father which art in heaven," whether he is born of God or not, I think that is contrary to Scripture. "As many as are led by the Spirit of God, they are the sons of God" (Rom. 8:14). Sonship in the family is the privilege of the believer. "In this the children of God are manifest, and the children of the devil," says 1 John 3:10. If we are doing the will of God, that is a very good sign that we are born of God. If we have no desire to do that will, how can we call God "Our Father?"

Another thing. We cannot really pray for God's kingdom to come until we are in it. If we should pray for the coming of God's kingdom while we are rebelling against Him, we are only seeking our own condemnation. No unrenewed man really wants God's will to be done on the earth. You might write over the door of every unsaved man's house, and over his place of business, "God's will is not done here."

If the nations were really to put up this prayer, all their armies could be discharged. They tell us there are some twelve millions of men in the standing armies of Europe alone. But men do not want God's will done on earth as it is in heaven; that is the trouble.

Now let us come to the part I want to dwell upon: "Forgive us our trespasses, as we forgive them that trespass against us." This is the only part of the prayer that Christ explained. "For if ye forgive men their trespasses, your heavenly Father will also forgive you: but if ye forgive not men their trespasses, neither will your Father forgive your trespasses" (Matt. 6:14–15).

Notice that when you go into the door of God's kingdom, you go in through the door of forgiveness. I never knew of a man getting a blessing in his own soul if he was not willing to forgive others. If we are unwilling to forgive others, God cannot forgive us. I do not know how language could be more plain than it is in these words of our Lord. I firmly believe a great many prayers are not answered because we are not willing to forgive someone. Let your mind go back over the past and through the circle of your acquaintance; are there any against whom you are cherishing hard feelings? Is there any root of bitterness springing up against someone who has perhaps injured you? It may be that for months or years you have been nursing this unforgiving spirit; how can *you* ask God to forgive you? If I am not willing to forgive those who may have committed some single offense against me, what a mean, contemptible thing it would be for me to ask God to forgive the ten thousand sins of which I have been guilty!

But Christ goes still further. He says: "Therefore if thou bring thy gift to the altar, and there rememberest that thy brother hath ought against thee; leave there thy gift before the altar, and go thy way; first be reconciled to thy brother, and then come and offer thy gift" (5:23–24). It may be that you are saying: "I do not know that I have anything against anyone." Has anyone anything against you? Is there someone who thinks you have done them wrong? Perhaps you have not, but it may be they think you have. I will tell you what I would do before I go to sleep tonight: I would go and see them, and have the question settled. You will find that you will be greatly blessed in the very act.

Supposing you are in the right and they are in the wrong; you may win your brother or sister. May God root out of all our hearts this unforgiving spirit.

A gentleman came to me some time ago and wanted me to talk to his wife about her soul. That woman seemed as anxious as any person I ever met, and I thought it would not take long to lead her into the light, but it seemed that the longer I talked with her, the more her darkness increased. I went to see her again the next day, and found her in still greater darkness of soul. I thought there must be something in the way that I had not discovered, and I asked her to repeat with me this disciples' prayer. I thought if she could say this prayer from the heart, the Lord would meet her in peace. I began to repeat it sentence after sentence, and she repeated it after me until I came to this petition: "Forgive us our trespasses, as we forgive them that trespass against us." There she stopped. I repeated it the second time, and waited for her to say it after me; she said she could not do it. "What is the trouble?"

She replied, "There is one woman I never will forgive." "Oh," I said, "I have got at your difficulty; it is no use my going on to pray, for your prayers will not go higher than my head. God says He will not forgive you unless you forgive others. If you do not forgive this woman, God will never forgive you. That is the decree of heaven." She said, "Do you mean to say that I cannot be forgiven until I have forgiven her?" "No, I do not say it; the Lord says it, and that is far better authority." Said she, "Then I will never be forgiven." I left the house without having made any impression on her. A few years after, I heard that this woman was in an asylum for the insane. I believe this spirit of unforgiveness drove her mad.

Forgiveness Brings Joy

If there is someone who has aught against you, go at once and be reconciled. If you have aught against anyone, write to them a letter, telling them that you forgive them, and so have this thing off your conscience. I remember being in the inquiry room some years ago; I was in one corner of the room, talking to a young lady. There seemed to be something in the way, but I could not find out what it was. At last I said, "Is there not someone you do not forgive?" She looked up at me, and said, "What made you ask that? Has anyone told you about me?" "No," I said, "but I thought perhaps that might be the case, as you have not received forgiveness yourself." "Well," she said, pointing to another corner of the room, where there was a young lady sitting, "I have had trouble with that young lady; we have not spoken to each other for a long time." "Oh," I said, "it is all plain to me now; you cannot be forgiven until you are willing to forgive her."

It was a great struggle. But then you know, the greater the cross the greater the blessing. It is human to err, but it is Christlike to forgive and be forgiven. At last this young lady said: "I will go and forgive her." Strange to say, the same conflict was going on in the mind of the lady in the other part of the room. They both came to their right mind about the same time. They met each other in the middle of the floor. The one tried to say that she forgave the other, but they could not finish; so they rushed into each other's arms. Then the four of us—the two seekers and the two workers—got down on our knees together, and we had a grand meeting. These two went away rejoicing.

Dear friend, is this the reason why your prayers are not answered? Is there some friend, some member of your family, someone in the church, you have not forgiven? We sometimes hear of members of the same church who have not spoken to each other for years. How can we expect God to forgive when this is the case? I remember one town that Mr. Sankey and myself visited. For a week it seemed as if we were beating the air; there was no power in the meetings. At last I said one day that perhaps there was someone cultivating this unforgiving spirit. The chairman of our committee, who was sitting next to me, got up and left the meeting right in view of the audience. The arrow had hit the mark and gone home to the heart of the chairman of the committee. He had had trouble with someone for about six months. He at once hunted up this man and asked him to forgive him. He came to me with tears in his eyes and said: "I thank God you ever came here." That night the inquiry room was thronged. The chairman became one of the best workers I have ever known, and he has been active in Christian service ever since.

Several years ago the Church of England sent a devoted missionary to New Zealand. After a few years of toil and success, he was one Sabbath holding a communion service in a district where the converts had not long since been savages. As the missionary was conducting the service, he observed one of the men, just as he was about to kneel at the rail, suddenly start to his feet and hastily go to the opposite end of the church. By and by he returned, and calmly took his place. After service the clergyman took him on one side, and asked the reason for his strange behavior. He replied: "As I was about to kneel I recognized in the man next to me the chief of a neighboring tribe, who had murdered my father and drunk his blood; and I had sworn by all the gods that I would slay that man at the first opportunity. The impulse to have my revenge at the first almost overpowered me, and I rushed away, as you saw me, to escape the power of it. As I stood at the other end of the room and considered the object of our meeting, I thought of Him who prayed for His own murderers: 'Father, forgive them, for they know not what they do.' And I felt that I could forgive the murderer of my father, and came and knelt down at his side."

As one has said: "There is an ugly kind of forgiveness in the world—a kind of hedgehog forgiveness, shot out like quills. Men take one who has offended, and set him down before the blow-pipe of their indignation, and scorch him, and burn his fault into him; and when they have kneaded him sufficiently with their fists, then they forgive him." The father of Frederick the Great, on his deathbed, was warned by M. Roloff, his spiritual adviser, that he was bound to forgive his enemies. He was quite troubled, and after a moment's pause said to the queen: "You, Feekin, may write to your brother (the king of England) *after I am dead*, and tell him that I forgave him, and died at peace with him." "It would be better," M. Roloff mildly suggested, "that your majesty should write at once." "No," was the stern reply. "Write after I am dead. That will be safer."

Another story tells of a man who, supposing he was about to die, expressed his forgiveness to one who had injured him, but added: "Now you mind, if I get well, the old grudge holds good." My friends, that is not forgiveness at all. I believe true forgiveness includes forgetting the offense—putting it entirely away out of our hearts and memories. As Matthew Henry says:

> We do not forgive our offending brother aright nor acceptably, if we do not forgive him from the heart, for it is that God looks at. No malice must be harbored there, nor ill-will to any; no projects of revenge must be hatched there, nor desires of it, as there are in many who outwardly appear peaceful and reconciled. We must from the heart desire and seek the welfare of those who have offended us.

God Forgives and Forgets

If God's forgiveness were like that often shown by us, it would not be worth much. Supposing God said: "I will forgive you, but I will never forget it; all through eternity I will keep reminding you of it," we should not feel that to be forgiveness at all. Notice what God says: "I will remember their sin no more." In Ezekiel 18:22 it is said that not one of our sins shall be mentioned; is not that like God? I do like to preach this forgiveness—the sweet truth that sin is blotted out for time and eternity, and shall never once be mentioned against us. In another Scripture we read: "Their sins and iniquities will I remember no more" (Heb. 10:17). Then when you turn to Hebrews 11, and read God's roll of honor, you find that not one of the sins of any of those men of faith is mentioned. Abraham is spoken of as the man of faith, but it is not told how he denied his wife down in Egypt; all that had been forgiven. Moses was kept out of the promised land because he lost patience, but this is not mentioned in the New Testament, though his name appears in the apostle's roll of honor. Samson, too, is named, but his sins are not brought up again. Why, we even read of "righteous Lot"; he did not look much like a righteous man in the Old Testament story, but he has been forgiven, and God has made him "righteous." If we are once forgiven by God, our sins will be remembered against us no more. This is God's eternal decree.

Brooks says of God's pardon granted to His people:

When God pardons sin, He takes it sheer away; that if it should be sought for, yet it could not be found; as the prophet Jeremiah speaks: "In those days, and in that time, saith the Lord, the iniquity of Israel shall be sought for, and there shall be none; and the sins of Judah, and they shall not be found; for I will pardon them whom I reserve." As David, when he saw in Mephibosheth the features of his friend Jonathan, took no notice of his lameness, or any other defect or deformity; so God, beholding in His people the glorious image of His Son, winks at all their faults and deformities, which made Luther say, "Do with me what thou wilt, since Thou hast pardoned my sin." And what is it to pardon sin, but not to mention sin?

We read in the Gospel of Matthew: "If thy brother shall trespass against thee, go and tell him his fault between thee and him alone: if he shall hear thee, thou hast gained thy brother" (18:15). Then a little further on we read that Peter comes to Christ and says: "How oft shall my brother sin against me, and I forgive him? Till seven times?" Jesus replied, "I say not unto thee, until seven times; but, until seventy times seven" (vv. 21–22). Peter did not seem to think that he was in danger of falling into sin; his question was, How often should I forgive my brother? But very soon we hear that Peter has fallen. I can imagine that when he did fall, the sweet thought came to him of what the Master had said about forgiving until seventy times seven. The voice of sin may be loud, but the voice of forgiveness is louder.

Let us enter into David's experience, when he said:

> Blessed is he whose transgression is forgiven, whose sin is covered. Blessed is the man unto whom the LORD imputeth not iniquity, and in whose spirit there is no guile. When I kept silence, my bones waxed old through my roaring all the day long. For day and night Thy hand was heavy upon me; my moisture is turned into the drought of summer. I acknowledge my sin unto Thee, and mine iniquity have I not hid. I said, I will confess my transgressions unto the LORD; and Thou forgavest the iniquity of my sin. (Ps. 32:1–5)

David could look below, above, behind, and before; to the past, present, and future; and know that all was well. Let us make up our minds that we will not rest until this question of sin is forever settled, so that we can look up and claim God as our forgiving Father. Let us be willing to forgive others, that we may be able to claim forgiveness from God, remembering the words of the Lord Jesus, how He said: "If ye forgive men their trespasses, your heavenly Father will also forgive you; but if ye forgive not men their trespasses, neither will your Father forgive your trespasses" (Matt. 6:14–15).

> Now, oh joy! my sins are pardoned!
>   Now I can and do believe! .
> All I have, and am, and shall be,
>   To my precious Lord I give;
> He roused my deathly slumbers,
>   He dispersed my soul's dark night;
> Whispered peace, and drew me to Him
>   Made Himself my chief delight.
>
> Let the babe forget its mother,
>   Let the bridegroom slight his bride;

True to Him, I'll love none other,
    Cleaving closely to His side.
Jesus, hear my soul's confession;
    Weak am I, but strength is Thine;
On Thine arms for strength and succor,
    Calmly may my soul recline!

Albert Midlane

7

Unity

Moody viewed Christian unity as a sign that God's people loved one another. It signaled the church's commitment to God's purposes and a willingness to set aside disagreements to focus on the gospel. With the deep divisions created by slavery, the Civil War, and the ongoing treatment of Black people, particularly Black Christians, in the South, unity was no simple task. Beyond issues of race, Moody was also concerned with economic divisions. For instance, Moody critiqued the so-called mission churches, which he viewed as encouraging the wealthy to give to the poor while keeping the poor at arm's length.

Unity was not a trite or trivial aspiration. Unity would be hard won. It signaled the actual state and nature of the church. God's people cannot be divided even if, at times, they find themselves at odds with one another. Division is a problem because it does not represent the reality of Jews and Gentiles united in Christ who demonstrate the "manifold wisdom of God" (Eph. 3:10).

The next thing we need to have, if we would get our prayers answered, is *unity*. If we do not love one another, we certainly shall not have much power with God in prayer. One of the saddest things in the present day is the division in God's Church. You notice that when the power of God came upon the early church, it was when they were all of one accord. I believe the blessing of Pentecost never would have been given but for that spirit of unity. If they had been divided and quarreling among themselves, do you think the Holy Ghost would have come, and those thousands been converted? I have noticed in our work, that if we have gone to a town where three churches were united in it, we have had greater blessing than if only one church was in sympathy. And if there have been twelve churches united, the blessing has multiplied fourfold; it has always been in proportion to the spirit of unity that has been manifested. Where there are bickerings and divisions, and where the spirit of unity is absent, there is very little blessing and praise.

Dr. Guthrie thus illustrates this fact; he says:

> Separate the atoms which make the hammer, and each would fall on the stone as a snowflake; but welded into one, and wielded by the firm arm of the quarry man, it will break the massive rocks asunder. Divide the waters of Niagara into distinct and individual drops, and they would be no more than falling rain, but in their united body they would quench the fires of Vesuvius, and have some to spare for the volcanoes of other mountains.

History tells us that it was agreed upon by both armies of the Romans and the Albans to put the trial of all to the issue of a battle betwixt six brethren—three on the one side, the sons of Curatius, and three on the other, the sons of Horatius. While the Curatii were united, though all three sorely wounded, they killed two of the Heratii. The third began to take to his heels, though not hurt at all; and when he saw them follow slowly, one after another, because of wounds and heavy armor, he fell upon them singly, and slew all three. It is the cunning sleight of the devil to divide us that he may destroy us.

We ought to endure much and sacrifice much, rather than permit discord and division to prevail in our hearts. Martin Luther says:

> When two goats meet upon a narrow bridge over deep water, how do they behave? Neither of them can turn back again, neither can pass the other, because the bridge is too narrow; if they should thrust one another they might both fall into the water and be drowned. Nature, then, has taught them that if the one lays himself down and permits the other to go over him, both remain unhurt. Even so people should rather endure to be trod upon than to fall into debate and discord one with another.

Cawdray says: "As in music, if the harmony of tones be not complete they are offensive to the cultivated ear; so if Christians disagree among themselves they are unacceptable to God."

There are diversities of gifts—that is clearly taught—but there is one Spirit. If we have all been redeemed with the same blood, we ought to see eye to eye in spiritual things. Paul writes: "Now there are diversities of gifts, but the same Spirit. And there are differences of administrations, but the same Lord" (1 Cor. 12:4–5).

Where there is union, I do not believe any power, earthly or infernal, can stand before the work. When the church, the pulpit, and the pew get united, and God's people are all of one mind, Christianity is like a red-hot ball rolling over the earth, and all the hosts of death and hell cannot stand before it. I believe that men will then come flocking into the kingdom by hundreds and thousands. "By this," says Christ, "shall all men know that ye are My disciples, if ye have love one to another." If only we love one another, and pray for one another, there will be success. God will not disappoint us.

There can be no real separation or division in the true Church of Christ; they are redeemed by one price and indwelt by one

299

Spirit. If I belong to the family of God, I have been bought with the same blood, though I may not belong to the same sect or party as another. What we want to do is to get these miserable sectarian walls taken away. Our weakness has been in our division; and what we need is that there should be no schism or division among those who love the Lord Jesus Christ. In the first epistle to the Corinthians we read of the first symptoms of sectarianism coming into the early church:

> Now I beseech you, brethren, by the name of our Lord Jesus Christ, that ye all speak the same thing, and that there be no division among you; but that ye be perfectly joined together in the same mind and in the same judgment.
>
> For it hath been declared unto me of you, my brethren, by them which are of the house of Chloe, that there are contentions among you. Now this I say, that every one of you saith, I am of Paul; and I of Apollos; and I of Cephas; and I of Christ. Is Christ divided? Was Paul crucified for you? Or were ye baptized in the name of Paul? (1:10–13)

Notice how one said, "I am of Paul," and another, "I am of Apollos," and another, "I am of Cephas." Apollos was a young orator, and the people had been carried away by his eloquence. Some said Cephas, or Peter, was of the regular apostolic line, because he had been with the Lord, and Paul had not. So they were divided, and Paul wrote this letter in order to settle the question. Jenkyn, in his commentary on the epistle of Jude, says:

> The partakers of a "common salvation" who here agree in one way to heaven, and who expect to be hereafter in one heaven, should be of one heart. It is the apostle's inference in Ephesians. What an amazing misery is it, that they who agree in common faith should disagree like common foes! That Christians should live as if faith had banished love! This common faith should allay and temper our spirits in all our differences. This should moderate our minds,

300

though there is inequality in earthly relations. What a powerful motive was that of Joseph's brethren to him to forgive their sin, they being both his brethren, and the servants of the God of his fathers! Though our own breath cannot blow out the taper of contention, oh, yet let the blood of Christ extinguish it!

Division in the Church Deplored

What a strange state of things Paul, Cephas, and Apollos would find if they would come to the world today! The little tree that sprang up at Corinth has grown up into a tree like Nebuchadnezzar's, with many of the fowls of heaven gathered into it. Suppose Paul and Cephas were to come down to us now, they would hear at once about our Churchmen and Dissenters. "A dissenter!" says Paul. "What is that?" "We have a Church of England, and there are those who dissent from the Church." "Oh, indeed! Are there two classes of Christians here, then?" "I am sorry to say there are a good many more divisions. The Dissenters themselves are split up. There are Wesleyans, Baptists, Presbyterians, Independents, and so on; even these are all divided up." "Is it possible," says Paul, "that there are so many divisions?" "Yes; the Church of England is pretty well divided itself. There is the Broad Church, the High Church, the Low Church, and the High-Lows. Then there is the Lutheran Church; and away in Russia they have the Greek Church, and so on." I declare I do not know what Paul and Cephas would think if they came back to the world; they would find a strange state of things. It is one of the most humiliating things in the present day to see how God's family is divided up. If we love the Lord Jesus Christ the burden of our hearts will be that God may bring us closer together, so that we may love one another and rise above all party feeling.

In repairing a church in one of the Boston wards, the inscription upon the wall behind the pulpit was covered up. Upon the first Sabbath after repairs, a little five-year-old whispered to her mother: "I know why God told the paint men to cover that pretty verse up. It was because the people did not love one another." The inscription was, "A new commandment I give unto you, that ye love one another."

A Boston minister says he once preached on "The Recognition of Friends in the Future," and was told after service by a hearer that it would be more to the point to preach about the recognition of friends here, as he had been in the church twenty years and did not know any of its members.

I was in a little town some time ago, when one night as I came out of the meeting, I saw another building where the people were coming out. I said to a friend, "Have you got two churches here?" "Oh, yes." "How do you get on?" "Oh, we get on very well." "I am glad to hear that. Was your brother minister at the meeting?" "Oh, no, we don't have anything to do with each other. We find that is the best way." And they called that "getting on very well." Oh, may God make us of one heart and of one mind! Let our hearts be like drops of water flowing together. Unity among the people of God is a sort of foretaste of heaven. There we shall not find any Baptists, or Methodists, or Congregationalists, or Episcopalians; we shall all be one in Christ. We leave all our party names behind us when we leave this earth. Oh, that the Spirit of God may speedily sweep away all these miserable walls that we have been building up!

Did you ever notice that the last prayer Jesus Christ made on earth, before they led Him away to Calvary, was that His disciples might all be one? He could look down the stream of time and see that divisions would come—how Satan would try to divide the flock of God. Nothing will silence infidels so quickly as Christians everywhere being united. Then our testimony will have weight with the ungodly and the careless. But when they see how Christians are divided, they will not believe their testimony. The Holy Spirit is grieved, and there is little power where there is no unity.

If I thought I had one drop of sectarian blood in my veins, I would let it out before I went to bed; if I had one sectarian hair in my head, I would pull it out. Let us get right to the heart of Jesus Christ; then our prayers will be acceptable to God and showers of blessings will descend.

Union

Let party names no more be known
   Among the ransomed throng;
For Jesus claims them for His own;
   To Him they all belong.
One in their covenant Head and King,
   They should be one in heart;
Of one salvation all should sing,
   Each claiming his own part.
One bread, one family, one rock,
   One building, formed by love,
One fold, one Shepherd, yea, one flock,
   They shall be one above.

Joseph Irons

8

Faith

Faith is the foundation for prayer. Praying while expecting nothing suggests that God is somehow incapable or unwilling to provide for our needs or redirect our desires. For Moody, faith involves our conviction that God will act on our behalf. God may not give us exactly what we pray for, but we believe God will give us exactly what we need.

———※———

Another element is *faith*. It is as important for us to know how to pray as it is to know how to work. We are not told that Jesus ever taught His disciples how to preach, but He taught them how to pray. He wanted them to have power with God; then He knew they would have power with man. In James 1:5–6 we read: "If any of you lack wisdom, let him ask of God . . . and it shall be given him. But let him ask in faith, nothing wavering." So faith is the golden key that unlocks the treasures of heaven. It was the shield that David took when he met Goliath on the field; he believed that

God was going to deliver the Philistines into his hands. Someone has said that faith could lead Christ about anywhere; wherever He found it He honored it. Unbelief sees something in God's hand and says, "I cannot get it." Faith sees it and says, "I will have it."

The new life begins with faith; then we have only to go on building on that foundation. "Therefore I say unto you, What things soever ye desire, when ye pray, believe that ye receive them, and ye shall have them" (Mark 11:24). But bear in mind, we must be in earnest when we go to God.

I do not know of a more vivid illustration of the cry of distress for help going up to God, in all the earnestness of deeply realized need, than the following story supplies.

Carl Steinman, who visited Mount Hecla, Iceland, just before the great eruption in 1845, after a repose of eighty years, narrowly escaped death by venturing into the smoking crater against the earnest entreaty of his guide. On the brink of the yawning gulf he was prostrated by a convulsion of the summit, and held there by blocks of lava upon his feet. He graphically writes:

Oh, the horrors of that awful realization! There, over the mouth of a black and heated abyss, I was held suspended, a helpless and conscious prisoner, to be hurled downward by the next great throe of trembling Nature! "Help! help! help!—for the love of God, help!" I shrieked, in the very agony of my despair.

I had nothing to rely upon but the mercy of heaven; and I prayed to God as I had never prayed before, for the forgiveness of my sins, that they might not follow me to judgment. All at once I heard a shout, and, looking around, I beheld, with feelings that cannot be described, my faithful guide hastening down the sides of the crater to my relief.

"I warned you!" said he. "You did!" cried I, "but forgive me, and save me, for I am perishing!" "I will save you, or perish with you!"

The earth trembled, and the rocks parted—one of them rolling down the chasm with a dull, booming sound. I sprang forward; I seized a hand of the guide, and the next moment we had both fallen, locked in each other's arms, upon the solid earth above. I was free, but still upon the verge of the pit.

Bishop Hall, in a well-known extract, thus puts the point of earnestness in its relation to the prayer of faith.

An arrow, if it be drawn up but a little way, goes not far; but, if it be pulled up to the head, flies swiftly and pierces deep. Thus prayer, if it be only dribbled forth from careless lips, falls at our feet. It is the strength of ejaculation and strong desire which sends it to heaven, and makes it pierce the clouds. It is not the arithmetic of our prayers, how many they are; nor the rhetoric of our prayers, how eloquent they be; nor the geometry of our prayers, how long they be; nor the music of our prayers, how sweet our voice may be; nor the logic of our prayers, how argumentative they may be; nor the method of our prayers, how orderly they may be; nor even the divinity of our prayers, how good the doctrine may be—which God cares for. He looks not for the horny knees which James is said to have had through the assiduity of prayer. We might be like Bartholomew, who is said to have had a hundred prayers for the morning, and as many for the evening, and all might be of no avail. Fervency of spirit is that which availeth much.

Archbishop Leighton says:

It is not the gilded paper and good writing of a petition that prevails with a king, but the moving sense of it. And to that King who discerns the heart, heart-sense is the sense of all, and that which He only regards. He listens to hear what that speaks, and takes all as nothing where that is silent. All other excellence in prayer is but the outside and fashion of it. This is the life of it.

Brooks says:

As a painted fire is no fire, a dead man no man, so a cold prayer is no prayer. In a painted fire there is no heat, in a dead man there is no life; so in a cold prayer there is no omnipotency, no devotion, no blessing. Cold prayers are as arrows without heads, as swords without edges, as birds without wings; they pierce not, they cut not, they fly not up to heaven. Cold prayers do always freeze before they get to heaven. Oh that Christians would chide themselves out of their cold prayers, and chide themselves into a better and warmer frame of spirit, when they make their supplications to the Lord!

Take the case of the Syrophoenician woman (Matt. 15:22–28; Mark 7:24–30). When she called to the Master, it seemed for a time as if He were deaf to her request. The disciples wanted her to be sent away. Although they were with Christ for three years, and sat at His feet, yet they did not know how full of grace His heart was. Think of Christ sending away a poor sinner who had come to Him for mercy! Can you conceive such a thing? Never once did it occur. This poor woman put herself in the place of her child. "Lord, help me!" she said. I think when we get so far as that in the earnest desire to have our friends blessed—when we put ourselves in their place—God will soon hear our prayer.

Having Faith for Others

I remember, a number of years ago at a meeting, I asked all those who wished to be prayed for to come forward and kneel or take seats in front. Among those who came was a woman. I thought by her looks that she must be a Christian, but she knelt down with the others. I said: "You are a Christian, are you not?" She said she had been one for so many years. "Did you understand the invitation? I asked those only who wanted to become Christians." I shall never forget the look on her face as she replied, "I have a son who has gone far away; I thought I would take his place today, and see if God would not bless him." Thank God for such a mother as that!

The Syrophoenician woman did the same thing—"Lord, help *me!*" It was a short prayer, but it went right to the heart of the Son of God. He tried her faith, however. He said: "It is not meet to take the children's bread and cast it to dogs." She replied: "Truth, Lord: yet the dogs eat of the crumbs which fall from their masters' table." "O woman, great is thy faith!" What a eulogy He paid to her! Her story will never be forgotten as long as the Church is on the earth. He honored her faith and gave her all she asked for. Every one can say, "Lord, help me!" We all need help. As Christians, do we need more grace, more love, more purity of life, more righteousness? Then let us make this prayer today. I want God to help me to preach better and to live better, to be more like the Son of God. The golden chains of faith link us right to the throne of God, and the grace of heaven flows down into our souls.

I do not know but that woman was a great sinner; still, the Lord heard her cry. It may be that up to this hour you have been living in sin; but if you will cry, "Lord, help me!" He will answer your prayer, if it is an honest one. Very often when we cry to God we do not really mean anything. You mothers understand that. Your children have two voices. When they ask you for anything, you can soon tell if the cry is a make-believe one or not. If it is, you do not give any heed to it; but if it is a real cry for help, how quickly you respond! The cry of distress always brings relief. Your child is playing around, and says, "Mamma, I want some bread," but goes on playing. You know that he or she is not very hungry; so you let it alone. But, by and by, the child drops the toys and comes tugging at your dress. "Mamma, I am so hungry!" Then you know that the cry is a real one; you soon go to the pantry and get some bread. When we are in earnest for the bread of heaven, we will get it. This woman was terribly in earnest; therefore her petition was answered.

I remember hearing of a boy brought up in an English alms-house. He had never learned to read or write, except that he could read the letters of the alphabet. One day a man of God came there, and told the children that if they prayed to God in their trouble, He would send them help. After a time, this boy was apprenticed to a farmer. One day he was sent out into the fields to look after some sheep. He was having rather a hard time, so he remembered what the preacher had said, and he thought he would pray to God about it. Someone going by the field heard a voice behind the hedge. They looked to see whose it was, and saw the little fellow on his knees, saying, "A, B, C, D," and so on. The man said, "My boy, what are you doing?" He looked up and said he was praying. "Why, that is not praying; it is only saying the alphabet." He said he did not know just how to pray, but a man once came to the poorhouse, who told them that if they called upon God, He would help them. So he thought that if he named over the letters of the alphabet, God would take them and put together into a prayer, and give him what he wanted. The little fellow was really praying. Sometimes, when your child talks, your friends cannot understand what he says; but the mother understands very well. So if our prayer comes right from the heart, God understands our language. It is a delusion of the devil to think we cannot pray; we can, if we really want anything. It is not the most beautiful or the most eloquent language that brings down the answer; it is the cry that goes up from a burdened heart. When this poor Gentile woman cried out, "Lord, help me!" the cry flashed over the divine wires and the blessing came. So you can pray if you will; it is the desire, the wish of the heart, that God delights to hear and to answer.

Expect to Receive When You Pray

Then we must *expect* to receive a blessing. When the centurion wanted Christ to heal his servant, he thought he was not worthy to go and ask the Lord himself, so he sent his friends to make the petition. He sent out messengers to meet the Master, and say, "Lord, trouble not Thyself: for I am not worthy that Thou shouldest enter under my roof: wherefore neither thought I myself worthy to come unto Thee: but say in a word, and my servant shall be healed" (Luke 7:6–7). Jesus said to the Jews, "I have not found so great faith, no, not in Israel" (v. 9). He marveled at the faith of this centurion; it pleased Him, so that He healed the servant then and there (Matt. 8:5–13). Faith brought the answer.

In John we read of a nobleman whose child was sick. The father fell on his knees before the Master, and said, "Sir, come down ere my child die" (John 4:49). Here you have both earnestness and faith; and the Lord answered the prayer at once. The nobleman's son began to amend that very hour. Christ honored the man's faith.

In his case there was nothing to rest upon but the bare word of Christ, but this was enough. It is well to bear always in mind that the object of faith is not the creature but the Creator; not the instrument but the Hand that wields it.

Richard Sibbes puts it for us thus:

> The object in believing is God, and Christ as Mediator. We must have both to found our faith upon. We cannot believe in God, except we believe in Christ. For God must be satisfied by God; and by Him that is God must that satisfaction be applied—the Spirit of God—by working faith in the heart, and for raising it up when it is dejected. All is supernatural in faith. The things we believe are above nature; the promises are above nature; the worker of it, the Holy Ghost, is above nature; and everything in faith is above nature. There must be a God in whom we believe, and a God through whom we may know that Christ is God—not only by that which Christ hath done, the miracles, which none could do but God, but also by what is done to Him. And two things are done to Him, which show that He is God—that is, faith and prayer. We must believe only in God, and pray only to God; but Christ is the object of both these. Here He is set forth as the object of faith, and of prayer in that of Saint Stephen, "Lord Jesus, receive my spirit." And, therefore, He is God; for that is done unto Him which is proper and peculiar only to God. Oh, what a strong foundation, what bottom and basis our faith hath! There is God the Father, Son and Holy Ghost, and Christ the Mediator. That our

faith may be supported, we have Him to believe on who supports heaven and earth.

There is nothing that can lie in the way of the accomplishment of any of God's promises, but it is conquerable by faith.

As Samuel Rutherford says, commenting on the case of the Syrophoenician woman:

> See the sweet use of faith under a sad temptation; faith trafficketh with Christ and heaven in the dark, upon plain trust and credit, without seeing any surety of dawn: Blessed are they that have not seen, and yet have believed. And the reason is because faith is sinewed and boned with spiritual courage; so as to keep a barred city against hell, yea, and to stand under impossibilities; and here is a weak woman, though not as a woman, yet as a believer, standing out against Him who is "the Mighty God, the Father of Ages, the Prince of Peace." Faith only standeth out, and overcometh the sword, the world, and all afflictions. This is our victory, whereby one man overcometh the great and vast world.

Bishop Ryle has said of Christ's intercession as the ground and sureness of our faith:

> The bank note without a signature at the bottom is nothing but a worthless piece of paper. The stroke of a pen confers on it all its value. The prayer of a poor child of Adam is a feeble thing in itself, but once indorsed by the hand of the Lord Jesus, it availeth much. There was an officer in the city of Rome who was appointed to have his doors always open, in order to receive any Roman citizen who applied to him for help. Just so the ear of the Lord Jesus is ever open to the cry of all who want mercy and grace. It is His office to help them. Their prayer is His delight.

Reader, think of this. Is not this encouragement?

Let us close this chapter by referring to some of our Lord's own words concerning faith in its relation to prayer:

And when He saw a fig tree in the way, He came to it, and found nothing thereon, but leaves only, and said unto it, Let no fruit grow on thee henceforward for ever. And presently the fig tree withered away.

And when the disciples saw it, they marvelled, saying, How soon is the fig tree withered away! Jesus answered and said unto them, Verily I say unto you, If ye have faith, and doubt not, ye shall not only do this which is done to the fig tree, but also if ye shall say unto this mountain, Be thou removed, and be thou cast into the sea; it shall be done. And all things, whatsoever ye shall ask in prayer, believing, ye shall receive. (Matt. 21:19–22)

So again our Lord says:

Verily, verily, I say unto you, he that believeth on Me, the works that I do shall he do also; and greater works than these shall he do; because I go unto My Father. And whatsoever ye shall ask in My name, that will I do, that the Father may be glorified in the Son. If ye shall ask any thing in My name, I will do it. (John 14:12–14)

If ye abide in Me, and My words abide in you, ye shall ask what ye will, and it shall be done unto you. (15:7)

And in that day ye shall ask Me nothing. Verily, verily, I say unto you, Whatsoever ye shall ask the Father in My name, He will give it you. Hitherto have ye asked nothing in My name: ask, and ye shall receive, that your joy may be full. (16:23–24)

Have Faith in God

Have faith in God, for He who reigns on high
Hath borne thy grief, and hears the suppliant's sigh;
Still to His arms, thine only refuge, fly,
	Have faith in God!
Fear not to call on Him, O soul distressed!

Thy sorrow's whisper woos thee to His breast;
He who is oftenest there is oftenest blest.
    Have faith in God!
Lean not on Egypt's reeds; slake not thy thirst
At earthly cisterns. Seek the Kingdom first.
Though man and Satan fright thee with their worst,
    Have faith in God!
Go, tell Him all! The sigh thy bosom heaves
Is heard in heaven. Strength and peace He gives,
Who gave Himself for thee. Our Jesus lives;
    Have faith in God!

Anna Shipton

9

Petition

Moody encouraged those who pray to come with specific requests. Prayer certainly involves more than presenting a wish list to God, yet asking God for His power and assistance need not turn God into a resource rather than a ruler. When we approach God with our requests, we acknowledge that we need Him. We need His guidance, grace, power, and presence. Moody believed God's people were being hindered by not asking God to provide and to act. By not asking, we're assuming we can do what needs to be done without God. For Moody, prayer was a time of encounter. It was a moment when God and His people met together. He desired to see God's people ask Him for His assistance and wait for God to respond.

The next element in prayer that I notice is *petition*. How often we go to prayer meetings without really asking for anything! Our prayers go all round the world, without anything definite being asked for.

We do not expect anything. Many people would be greatly surprised if God did answer their prayers. I remember hearing of a very eloquent man who was leading a meeting in prayer. There was not a single definite petition in the whole. A poor, earnest woman shouted out: "Ask Him summat, man!" How often you hear what is called prayer without any asking. "Ask, and ye shall receive."

I believe if we put all the stumbling blocks out of the way, God will answer our petitions. If we put away sin and come into His presence with pure hands, as He has commanded us to come, our prayers will have power with Him. In Luke's Gospel we have as a grand supplement to the disciples' prayer, "Ask, and it shall be given you; seek, and ye shall find; knock, and it shall be opened unto you" (11:9). Some people think God does not like to be troubled with our constant coming and asking. The only way to trouble God is not to come at all. He encourages us to come to Him repeatedly, and press our claims.

I believe you will find three kinds of Christians in the Church today. The first are those who *ask*; the second those who *seek*; and the third those who *knock*. "Teacher," said a bright, earnest-faced boy, "why is it that so many prayers are unanswered? I do not understand. The Bible says, 'Ask, and ye shall receive; seek, and ye shall find; knock, and it shall be opened unto you'; but it seems to me a great many knock and are not admitted."

"Did you never sit by your cheerful parlor fire," said the teacher, "on some dark evening, and hear a loud knocking at the door? Going to answer the summons, have you not sometimes looked out into the darkness, seeing nothing but hearing the pattering feet of some mischievous boy, who knocked but did not wish to enter and therefore ran away? Thus is it often with us. We ask for blessings but do not really expect them; we knock but do not mean to enter; we fear that Jesus will not hear us, will not fulfill His promises, will not admit us; and so we go away."

"Ah, I see," said the earnest-faced boy, his eyes shining with the new light dawning in his soul: "Jesus cannot be expected to answer runaway knocks. He has never promised it. I mean to keep knocking, knocking, until He *cannot help opening the door.*"

Too often we knock at mercy's door and then run away, instead of waiting for an entrance and an answer. Thus we act as if we were afraid of having our prayers answered.

A great many people pray in that way; they do not wait for the answer. Our Lord teaches us here that we are not only to ask, but we are to wait for the answer; if it does not come, we must seek to find out the reason. I believe that we get a good many blessings just by asking; others we do not get, because there may be something in our lives that needs to be brought to light. When Daniel began to pray in Babylon for the deliverance of his people, he sought to find out what the trouble was, and why God had turned away His face from them. So there may be something in our lives that is keeping back the blessing; if there is, we want to find it out. Someone, speaking on this subject, has said: "We are to ask with a beggar's humility, to seek with a servant's carefulness, and to knock with the confidence of a friend."

Never Be Discouraged in Prayer

How often people become discouraged and say they do not know whether or not God does answer prayer! In the parable of the importunate widow, Christ teaches us how we are not only to pray and seek, but to find. If the unjust judge heard the petition of the poor woman who pushed her claims, how much more will our heavenly Father hear our cry! A good many years ago a man in the state of New Jersey was condemned to be hung. Every possible influence was brought to bear upon the governor to have the man reprieved; but he stood firm and refused to alter the sentence. One morning the wife of the condemned man, with her ten children, went to see the governor. When he came to his office, they all fell on their faces before him and besought him to have mercy on the husband—the father. The governor's heart was moved, and he at once wrote out a reprieve. The importunity of the wife and children saved the life of the man, just as the woman in the parable, who, pressing her claims, induced the unjust judge to grant her request.

It was this that brought the answer to the prayer of blind Bartimaeus. The people, and even the disciples, tried to hush him into silence; but he only cried out the louder, "Thou Son of David, have mercy on me!"

Prayer is hardly ever mentioned in the Bible alone; it is prayer and earnestness; prayer and watchfulness; prayer and thanksgiving. It is an instructive fact that throughout Scripture prayer is always linked with something else. Bartimaeus was in earnest, and the Lord heard his cry.

Then the highest type of Christian is the one who has got clear beyond asking and seeking, and keeps knocking till the answer comes. If we knock, God has promised to open the door and grant our request. It may be years before the answer comes; He may keep us knocking, but He has promised that the answer will come.

I will tell you what I think it means to knock. A number of years ago, when we were having meetings in a certain city, it came to a point where there seemed to be very little power. We called together all the mothers, and asked them to meet and pray for their children. About fifteen hundred mothers came together and poured out their hearts to God in prayer. One mother said: "I wish you would pray for my two boys. They have gone off on a drunken spree; and it seems as if my heart would break." She was a widowed mother. A few mothers gathered together, and said: "Let us have a prayer meeting for these boys." They cried to God for these two wandering boys; and now see how God answered their prayer.

That day these two brothers had planned to meet at the corner of the street where our meetings were being held. They were going to spend the night in debauchery and sin. About seven o'clock the first one came to the appointed place; he saw the people going into the meeting. As it was a stormy night, he thought he would go in for a little while. The Word of God reached him, and he went into the inquiry room, where he gave his heart to the Savior.

The other brother waited at the corner until the meeting broke up, expecting his brother to come; he did not know that he had been in the meeting. There was a young men's meeting in the church nearby, and this brother thought he would like to see what was going on; so he followed the crowd into the meeting. He also was impressed with what he heard, and was the first one to go into the inquiry room, where he found peace. While this was happening, the first one had gone home to cheer his mother's heart with the good news. He found her on her knees. She had been knocking at the mercy seat. While she was doing so, her boy came in and told her that her prayers had been answered; his soul was saved. It was not long before the other brother came in and told his story—how he, too, had been blessed.

On the following Monday night, the first to get up at the young converts' meeting was one of these brothers, who told the story of their conversion. No sooner had he taken his seat, than the other jumped up and said: "All that my brother has told you is true, for I am his brother. The Lord has indeed met us and blessed us."

I heard of a wife in England who had an unconverted husband. She resolved that she would pray every day for twelve months for his conversion. Every day at twelve o'clock she went to her room alone and cried to God. Her husband would not allow her to speak to him on the subject, but she could speak to God on his behalf. It may be that you have a friend who does not wish to be spoken with about his salvation; you can do as this woman did—go and pray to God about it. The twelve months passed away, and there was no sign of his yielding. She resolved to pray for six months longer; so every day she went alone and prayed for the conversion of her husband. The six months passed, and still there was no sign, no answer. The question arose in her mind, could she give him up? "No," she said; "I will pray for him as long as God gives me breath." That very day, when he came home to dinner, instead of going into the dining room he went upstairs. She waited, and waited, and waited; but he did not come down to dinner. Finally she went to his room, and found him on his knees crying to God to have mercy upon him. God convicted him of sin; he not only became a Christian, but the Word of God had free course and was glorified in him. God used him mightily. That was God answering the prayers of this Christian wife; she knocked, and knocked, till the answer came.

Be Encouraged—God Is Faithful

I heard something the other day that cheered me greatly. Prayer has been made for a man for about forty years, but there was no sign of any answer. It seemed as though he was going down to his grave as one of the most self-righteous men on the face of the earth. Conviction came in one night. In the morning he sent for the members of his family and said to his daughter: "I want you to pray for me. Pray that God would forgive my sins; my whole life has been nothing but sin—sin." And all this conviction came in one night. What we want is to press our case right up to the throne of God. I have often known cases of men who came to our meetings, and although they could not hear a word that was said, it seemed as though some unseen power laid hold of them, so that they were convicted and converted then and there.

I remember at one place where we were holding meetings, a wife came to the first meeting and asked me to talk with her husband. "He is not interested," she said, "but I am in hopes he will become so." I talked with him, and I think I hardly ever spoke to a man who seemed to be so self-righteous. It looked as though I might as well have talked to an iron post, he seemed to be so encased in self-righteousness. I said to his wife that he was not at all interested. She said, "I told you that, but I am interested for him." All the thirty days we were there that wife never gave him up. I must confess she had ten times more faith for him than I had. I had spoken to him several times, but I could see no ray of hope. The last night but two the man came to me and said: "Would you see me in another room?" I went aside with him, and asked him what was the trouble. He said, "I am the greatest sinner in the state of Vermont." "How is that?" I said. "Is there any particular sin you have been guilty of?" I must confess I thought he had committed some awful crime, which he was covering up, and that he now wanted to make confession.

"My whole life," he said, "has been nothing but sin. God has shown it to me today." He asked the Lord to have mercy on him, and he went home rejoicing in the assurance of sins forgiven. There was a man convicted and converted in answer to prayer. So if you are anxious about the conversion of some relative, or some friend, make up your mind that you will give God no rest, day or night, till He grants your petition. He can reach them, wherever they are—at their places of business, in their homes, or anywhere—and bring them to His feet.

Dr. Austin Phelps, in his "Still Hour," says:

The prospect of gaining an object will always affect thus the expression of intense desire. The feeling which will become spontaneous with a Christian under the influence of such a trust is this: I come to my devotions this morning on an errand of real life. This is no romance, and no farce. I do not come here to go through a form of words; I have no hopeless desires to express. I have an object to gain; I have an end to accomplish. This is a business in which I am about to engage. An astronomer does not turn his telescope to the skies with a more reasonable hope of penetrating those distant heavens, than I have of reaching the mind of God by lifting up my heart at the throne of grace. This is the privilege of my calling of God in Christ Jesus. Even my faltering voice is now to be heard in heaven; and it is to put forth a new power there, the results of which only God can know, and only eternity can develop. Therefore, O Lord, Thy servant findeth it in his heart to pray this prayer unto Thee!

Jeremy Taylor says:

Easiness of desire is a great enemy to the success of a good man's prayer. It must be an intent, zealous, busy, operative prayer; for consider what a huge indecency it is that a man should speak to God for a thing that he values not! Our prayers upbraid our spirits when we beg tamely for those things for which we ought to die, which are more precious than imperial sceptres, richer than the spoils of the sea, or the treasures of Indian hills.

Dr. Patton, in his work on "Remarkable Answers to Prayer," says:

Jesus bids us seek. Imagine a mother seeking a lost child. She looks through the house, and along the streets, then searches the fields and woods, and examines the riverbanks. A wise neighbor meets her and says: "Seek on, look everywhere; search every accessible place. You will not find, indeed; but then seeking is a good thing. It puts the mind on the stretch; it fixes the attention; it aids observation; it makes the idea of the child very real. And then, after a while, you will cease to want your child." The words of Christ are, "Knock, and it shall be opened unto you." Imagine a man knocking at the door of a house, long and loud. After he has done this for an hour, a window opens, and the occupant of the house puts out his head and says: "That is right, my friend; I shall not open the door, but keep on knocking—it is excellent exercise, and you will be the healthier for it. Knock away till sundown; and then come again, and knock all tomorrow. After some days thus spent you will attain to a state of mind in which you will no longer care to come in." Is this what Jesus intended us to understand, when He said—"Ask, and ye shall receive; seek, and ye shall find; knock, and it shall be opened unto you?" No doubt one would thus soon cease to ask, to seek, and to knock; but would it not be from disgust?

Nothing is more pleasing to our Father in heaven than direct, importunate, and persevering prayer. Two Christian ladies, whose husbands were unconverted, feeling their great danger, agreed to spend one hour each day in united prayer for their salvation. This was continued for seven years, when they debated whether they should pray longer, so useless did their prayers appear. They decided to persevere till death, and, if their husbands went to destruction, it should be laden with prayers. In renewed strength, they prayed three years longer, when one of them was awakened in the night by her husband, who was in great distress for sin. As soon as the day dawned, she hastened, with joy, to tell her praying companion that God was about to answer their prayers. What was her surprise to meet her friend coming to her on the same errand! Thus ten years of united and persevering prayer was crowned with the conversion of both husbands on the same day.

We cannot be too frequent in our requests; God will not weary of His children's prayers. Sir Walter Raleigh asked a favor of Queen Elizabeth, to which she replied, "Raleigh, when will you leave off begging?" "When your Majesty leaves off giving," he replied. So long must we continue praying.

Mr. George Muller, in a recent address given by him in Calcutta, said that in 1844 five individuals were laid on his heart, and he began to pray for them. Eighteen months passed away before one of them was converted. He prayed on for five years more, and another was converted. At the end of twelve years and a half, a third was converted. And now for forty years he had been praying for the other two, without missing one single day on any account whatever; but they were not yet converted. He felt encouraged, however, to continue in prayer; and he was sure of receiving an answer in relation to the two who were still resisting the Spirit.

"To See His Face"

Sweet is the precious gift of prayer,
To bow before a throne of grace;

To leave our every burden there,
    And gain new strength to run our race;
To gird our heavenly armor on,
Depending on the Lord alone.
And sweet the whisper of His love,
    When conscience sinks beneath its load,
That bids our guilty fears remove,
    And points to Christ's atoning blood;
Oh, then 'tis sweet indeed to know
God can be just and gracious too.
But oh, to see our Savior's face!
    From sin and sorrow to be freed!
To dwell in His divine embrace—
    This will be sweeter far indeed!
The fairest form of earthly bliss
Is less than nought, compared with this.

Unknown

10

Submission

Christians need to avoid the impression that God is a genie in a lamp. Prayer does not obligate God to grant our wishes. Instead, prayer is a moment of submission. It is not simply that we agree to do as God asks but set aside our own interests, ambitions, and desires in order to adopt God's desires. For Moody, a willingness to submit to God's will is a prerequisite for prayer. We do not pray with the intention of convincing God that our way would be best. Instead, we approach prayer knowing that God's will and way are far better than our own.

Another essential element in prayer is *submission*. All true prayer must be offered in full submission to God. After we have made our requests known to Him, our language should be, "Thy will be done." I would a thousand times rather that God's will should be done than my own. I cannot see into the future as God can; therefore, it is a good deal better to let Him choose for me than to choose for myself. I know His mind about spiritual things. His will is that I should be sanctified; so I can with confidence pray to God for that, and expect an answer to my prayers. But when it comes to temporal matters, it is different; what I ask for may not be God's purpose concerning me.

As one has well put it:

> Depend upon it, prayer does not mean that I am to bring God down to my thoughts and my purposes, and bend His government according to my foolish, silly, and sometimes sinful notions. Prayer means that I am to be raised up into feeling, into union and design with Him; that I am to enter into His counsel, and carry out His purpose fully. I am afraid sometimes we think of prayer as altogether of an opposite character, as if thereby we persuaded or influenced our Father in heaven to do whatever comes into our own minds, and whatever would accomplish our foolish, weak-sighted purposes. I am quite convinced of this, that God knows better what is best for me and for the world than I can possibly know; and even though it were in my power to say, "*My* will be done," I would rather say to Him, "*Thy* will be done."

It is reported of a woman, who, being sick, was asked whether she was willing to live or die, that she answered, "Which God pleases." "But," said one, "if God should refer it to you, which would you choose?" "Truly," replied she, "I would refer it to Him again." Thus that man obtains his will of God, whose will is subjected to God.

Mr. Spurgeon remarks on this subject,

> The believing man resorts to God at all times, that he may keep up his fellowship with the divine mind. Prayer is not a soliloquy, but a dialogue; not an introspection, but a looking toward the hills, whence cometh our help. There is a relief in unburdening the mind to a sympathetic friend, and faith feels this abundantly; but there is more than this in prayer. When an obedient activity has gone to

the full length of its line, and yet the needful thing is not reached, then the hand of God is trusted in to go beyond us, just as before it was relied upon to go with us. Faith has no desire to have its own will, when that will is not in accordance with the mind of God; for such a desire would at bottom be the impulse of an unbelief which did not rely upon God's judgment as our best guide. Faith knows that God's will is the highest good, and that anything which is beneficial to us will be granted to our petitions.

History informs us that the Tusculani, a people of Italy, offended the Romans, whose power was infinitely superior to theirs; Camillus, at the head of a considerable army, was on his march to subdue them. Conscious of their inability to cope with such an enemy, they took the following method to appease him: they declined all thoughts of resistance, set open their gates, and every man applied himself to his proper business, resolving to submit where they knew it was in vain to contend. Camillus, entering their city, was struck with the wisdom and candor of their conduct, and addressed himself to them in these words: "You only, of all people, have found out the true method of abating the Roman fury; and your submission has proved your best defense. Upon these terms, we can no more find in our heart to injure you than upon other terms you could have found power to oppose us." The chief magistrate replied: "We have so sincerely repented of our former folly, that in confidence of that satisfaction to a generous enemy, we are not afraid to acknowledge our fault."

Pray for Personal Submission

In view of the difficulty of bringing our hearts to this complete submission to the divine will, we may well adopt Fenelon's prayer: "O God, take my heart, for I cannot give it; and when Thou hast it, keep it; for I cannot keep it for Thee; and save me in spite of myself." Some of the best men the world has ever seen have made great mistakes on this point. Moses could pray for Israel, and could prevail with God; but God did not answer his petition for himself. He asked that God would take him over Jordan, that he might see Lebanon; and after the forty years' wandering in the wilderness, he desired to go into the promised land; but the Lord did not grant his desire. Was that a sign that God did not love him? By no means. He was a man greatly beloved of God, like Daniel; and yet God did not answer this prayer of his. Your child says, "I want this or that," but you do not grant the request, because you know that it will be the ruin of the child to give him everything he wants. Moses wished to enter the promised land, but the Lord had something else in store for him. As someone has said, God kissed away his soul and took him home to Himself. "God buried him"—the greatest honor ever paid to mortal man.

Fifteen hundred years afterward God answered the prayer of Moses; He allowed him to go into the promised land and to get a glimpse of the coming glory. On the Mount of Transfiguration, with Elijah, the great prophet, and with Peter, James, and John, he heard the voice come from the throne of God: "This is My beloved Son; hear ye Him." That was better than to have gone over Jordan, as Joshua did, and to sojourn for thirty years in the land of Canaan. So when our prayers for earthly things are not answered, let us submit to the will of God and know that it is all right. When one inquired of a deaf and dumb boy why he thought he was born deaf and dumb, taking the chalk he wrote upon the board, "Even so, Father; for so it seemed good in Thy sight."

John Brown, of Haddington, once said:

No doubt I have met with trials like others; but yet so kind has God been to me, that I think if He were to give me as many years as I have lived in the world, I would not desire one single circumstance in my lot changed, except that I wish there had been less sin. It might be written on my coffin, "Here lies one of the cares of

Providence, who early lost both father and mother, and yet never wanted for the care of either."

Elijah was mighty in prayer; he brought fire down from heaven on his sacrifice, and his petitions brought rain on the thirsty land. He stood fearlessly before King Ahab in the power of prayer. Yet we find him sitting under a juniper tree like a coward, asking God that He would let him die. The Lord loved him too well for that; He was going to take him up to heaven in a chariot of fire. So we must not allow the devil to take advantage of us, and make us believe that God does not love us because He does not grant all our petitions in the time and way we would have Him do.

As Moses takes up more room in the Old Testament than any other character, so it is with Paul in the New Testament; except, perhaps, the Lord Himself. Yet Paul did not know how to pray for himself. He besought the Lord to take away "the thorn in the flesh." His request was not granted; but the Lord bestowed upon him a greater blessing. He gave him more grace. It may be we have some trial—some thorn in the flesh. If it is not God's will to take it away, let us ask Him to give us more grace in order to bear it. We find that Paul gloried in his reverses and his infirmities because all the more the power of God rested upon him. It may be there are some of us who feel as if everything is against us. May God give us grace to take Paul's platform and say: "All things work together for good to them that love God." So when we pray to God we must be submissive, and say, "Thy will be done."

In the Gospel of John we read: "If ye" (that "if" is a mountain to begin with); "If ye abide in Me, and My words abide in you, ye shall ask what ye will, and it shall be done unto you" (15:7). The latter part is often quoted, but not the first. Why, there is very little abiding in Christ nowadays! You go and visit Him once in a while; but that is all. If Christ is in my heart, of course I will not ask anything that is against His will. And how many of us have God's Word abiding in us? We must have a warrant for our prayers.

If we have some great desire, we must search the Scriptures to find if it be right to ask it. There are many things we want that are not good for us; and many other things we desire to avoid are really our best blessings. A friend of mine was shaving one morning, and his little boy, not four years old, asked him for his razor, and said he wanted to whittle with it. When he found he could not get it, he began to cry as if his heart would break. I am afraid that there are a great many of us who are praying for razors. John Bunyan blessed God for that Bedford jail more than for anything else that happened to him in this life. We never pray for affliction, and yet it is often the best thing we could ask.

Afflictions Turned into Blessings

Dyer says:

> Afflictions are blessings to us when we can bless God for afflictions. Suffering has kept many from sinning. God had one Son without sin; but He never had any without sorrow. Fiery trials make golden Christians; sanctified afflictions are spiritual promotions.

Rutherford beautifully writes, in reference to the value of sanctified trial, and the wisdom of submitting in it to God's will:

> Oh, what owe I to the file, to the hammer, to the furnace of my Lord Jesus, who hath now let me see how good the wheat of Christ is that goeth through His mill and His oven, to be made bread for His own table! Grace tried is better than grace; and it is more than grace; it is glory in its infancy. I now see that Godliness is more than the outside, and this world's passements and their bushings. Who knoweth the truth of grace without a trial? Oh, how little getteth Christ of us, but that which He winneth (to speak so) with much toil and pains! And how soon would faith freeze without a cross! How many dumb crosses have been laid upon my back, that had never a tongue to speak the sweetness of Christ, as this hath! When

Christ blesseth His own crosses with a tongue, they breathe out Christ's love, wisdom, kindness, and care for us. Why should I start at the plough of my Lord, that maketh deep furrows on my soul? I know that He is no idle husbandman; He purposeth a crop. Oh that this white, withered lea-ground were made fertile to bear a crop for Him, by whom it is so painfully drest, and that this fallow ground were broken up! Why was I (a fool!) grieved that He put His garland and His rose upon my head—the glory and honor of His faithful witnesses? I desire now to make no more pleas with Christ. Verily He hath not put me to a loss by what I suffer; He oweth me nothing; for in my bonds how sweet and comfortable have the thoughts of Him been to me, wherein I find a sufficient recompense of reward! How blind are my adversaries who sent me to a banqueting house, to a house of wine, to the lovely feasts of my lovely Lord Jesus, and not to a prison, or place of exile!

We may close our remarks on this subject by a reference to the words of the prophet Jeremiah, in Lamentations, where he says:

The LORD is good unto them that wait for Him, to the soul that seeketh Him. It is good that a man should both hope and quietly wait for the salvation of the LORD. It is good for a man that he bear the yoke in his youth.

He sitteth alone and keepeth silence, because he hath borne it upon him. He putteth his mouth in the dust; if so be there may be hope. He giveth his cheek to him that smiteth him: he is filled full with reproach.

For the LORD will not cast off for ever: but though He cause grief, yet will He have compassion according to the multitude of His mercies. For He doth not afflict willingly nor grieve the children of men. . . .

Who is he that saith, and it cometh to pass, when the LORD commandeth it not? Out of the mouth of the most High proceedeth not evil and good? Wherefore doth a living man complain, a man for the punishment of his sins? Let us search and try our ways, and turn again to the LORD. (3:25–33, 37–41)

Submission

Hear me, my God, and if my lip hath dared
    To murmur 'neath Thy Hand, oh, teach me now
To feel each inmost thought before Thee bared,
    And this rebellious will in faith to bow.
Though I wept wildly o'er the ruined shrine,
    Where earthly idols held Thy place alone,
Now purify and make this temple Thine,
    And teach me, Lord, to say, "Thy will be done!"
What can I bring to offer that is mine?
    A youth of sorrow, and a life of sin.
    What can I lay upon Thy hallowed shrine,
    One hope of pardon for the past to win?
While thus a suppliant at Thy feet I bow,
    Still dare I lift to Thee my tearful eyes,
I plead the promise of Thy word, that Thou
    A broken, contrite heart will not despise.
What shall I bring? A bruised spirit, Lord,
    Worn with the contest, pining now for rest,
And yearning for Thy peace, as some poor bird,
    'Mid the wild tempest, seeks its mother's breast,
My sacrifice, the Lamb who died for me;
    I plead the merits of Thy sinless Son;
I bring Thy promises; I trust in Thee;
    In love Thou smitest; Lord, "Thy will be done!"

Author Unknown

11

Answered Prayers

In John 15:7, we find who have their prayers answered: "If ye abide in Me, and My words abide in you, ye shall ask what ye will, and it shall be done unto you." Now in James 4:3, we find some spoken of whose prayers were not answered: "Ye ask, and receive not, because ye ask amiss." There are a great many prayers not answered because there is not the right motive; we have not complied with the Word of God; we ask amiss. It is a good thing that our prayers are not answered when we ask amiss.

If our prayers are not answered, it may be that we have prayed without the right motive, or that we have not prayed according to the Scriptures. So let us not be discouraged, or give up praying, although our prayers are not answered in the way we want them.

A man once went to George Muller and said he wanted him to pray for a certain thing. The man stated that he had asked God a great many times to grant him his request, but He had not seen fit to do it. Mr. Muller took out his notebook and showed the man the name of a person for whom, he said, he had prayed for twenty-four years. The prayer, Muller added, was not answered yet; but the Lord had given him assurance that that person was going to be converted, and his faith rested there.

We sometimes find that our prayers are answered right away while we are praying; at other times the answer is delayed. But especially when men pray for mercy, how quickly the answer comes! Look at Paul, when he cried, "O Lord, what wilt Thou have me to do?" The answer came at once. Then the publican who went up to the temple to pray—he got an immediate answer. The thief on the cross prayed, "Lord, remember me when Thou comest into Thy kingdom!" and the answer came immediately—then and there. There are many cases of a similar kind in the Bible, but there are also others who prayed long and often. The Lord delights in hearing His children make their requests known unto Him—telling their troubles all out to Him; and then we should wait for His time. We do not know when that is.

There was a mother in Connecticut who had a son in the army, and it almost broke her heart when he left, because he was not a Christian. Day after day she lifted up her voice in prayer for her boy. She afterward learned that he had been taken to the hospital and there died, but she could not find out anything about how he had died. Years passed, and one day a friend came to see some member of the family on business. There was a picture of the soldier boy upon the wall. He looked at it, and said, "Did you know that young man?" The mother said, "That young man was my son. He died in the late war." The man replied, "I knew him very well; he was in my company." The mother then asked, "Do you know anything about his end?" The man said, "I was in the hospital, and he died a most peaceful death, triumphant in the faith." The mother had given up hope of ever hearing of her boy, but before she went hence she had the satisfaction of knowing that her prayers had prevailed with God.

I think we shall find a great many of our prayers that we thought unanswered answered when we get to heaven. If it is the true prayer of faith, God will not disappoint us. Let us not doubt God. On one occasion, at a meeting I attended, a gentleman pointed out an individual and said, "Do you see that man over there? That is one of the leaders of an infidel club." I sat down beside him, when the infidel said, "I am not a Christian. You have been humbugging these people long enough, and making some of these old women believe that you get answers to prayer. Try it on me." I prayed, and when I got up, the infidel said with a good deal of sarcasm, "I am not converted; God has not answered your prayer!" I said, "But you may be converted yet." Sometime afterward I received a letter from a friend, stating that he had been converted and was at work in the meetings.

Jeremiah prayed, and said: "Ah Lord GOD! Behold, Thou hast made the heaven and the earth by Thy great power and stretched out arm, and there is nothing too hard for Thee" (Jer. 32:17). Nothing is too hard for God; that is a good thing to take for a motto. I believe this is a time of great blessing in the world, and we may expect great things. While the blessing is falling all around, let us arise and share in it. God has said, "Call unto Me, and I will answer thee, and show thee great and mighty things, which thou knowest not" (33:3). Now let us call on the Lord, and let us pray that it may be done for Christ's sake—not our own.

Always Ask "For Christ's Sake"

At a Christian convention a number of years ago, a leading man got up and spoke—his subject being "For Christ's Sake"—and he threw new light upon that passage. I had never seen it in that way before. When the war broke out the gentleman's only son had enlisted, and he never saw a company of soldiers but his heart went right out after them. They started a Soldiers' Home in the city where that gentleman lived, and he gladly went on the committee, and acted as president. Some time afterward he said to his wife, "I have given so much time to these soldiers that I have neglected my business," and he went down to his office with the fixed determination that he would not be disturbed by any soldiers that day. The door opened soon after, and he saw a soldier entering. He never minded him, but kept on writing; and the poor fellow stood for some time. At last the soldier put down an old soiled piece of paper on which there was writing. The gentleman observed that it was the handwriting of his son, and he seized the letter at once and read it. It was something to this effect: "Dear Father, this young man belongs to my company. He has lost his health in defense of his country, and he is on his way home to his mother to die. Treat him kindly for Charlie's sake." The gentleman at once dropped his work and took the soldier to his house, where he was kindly cared for until he was able to be sent home to his mother; then he took him to the station, and sent him home with a "God bless you, for Charlie's sake!"

Let our prayers, then, be for Christ's sake. If we want our sons and daughters converted, let us pray that it be done for Christ's sake. If that is the motive, our prayers will be answered. If God gave up Christ for the world, what will He not give us? If He gave Christ to the murderers and blasphemers, and the rebels of a world lying in wickedness and sin, what would He not give to those who go to Him for Christ's sake? Let our prayer be that God may advance His work, not for our glory—not for our sake—but for the sake of His beloved Son whom He hath sent.

So let us remember that when we pray we ought to expect an answer. Let us be looking for it. I remember at the close of a meeting in one of our Southern cities near the close of the war, a man came up to me weeping and trembling. I thought something I had said had aroused him, and I began to question him as to what it was. I found, however, that he could not tell a word of what I had said. "My friend," said I, "what is the trouble?" He put his hand into his pocket, and brought out a letter, all soiled, as if his tears had fallen on it. "I got that letter," he said, "from my sister last night. She tells me that every night she goes on her knees and prays to God for me. I think I am the worst man in all the army of the Cumberland. I have been perfectly wretched today." That sister was six hundred miles away, but she had brought her brother to his knees in answer to her earnest, believing prayer. It was a hard case, but God heard and answered the prayer of this godly sister, so that the man was as clay in the hands of the potter. He was soon brought into the kingdom of God—all through his sister's prayers.

I went off some thirty miles to another place, where I told this story. A young man, a lieutenant in the army, sprang to his feet and said, "That reminds me of the last letter I got from my mother. She told me that every night as the sun went down she prayed for me. She begged of me, when I got her letter, to go away alone, and yield myself to God. I put the letter in my pocket, thinking there would be plenty of time." He went on to say that the next news that came from home was that his mother was gone. He went out into the woods alone and cried to his mother's God to have mercy upon him. As he stood in the meeting with his face shining, that lieutenant said: "My mother's prayers are answered, and my only regret is that she did not live to know it; but I will meet her by and by." So, though we may not live to see the answer to our prayers, if we cry mightily to God, the answer will come.

In Scotland, a good many years ago, there lived a man with his wife and three children—two girls and a boy. He was in the habit of getting drunk, and thus losing his situation. At last, he said he would take Johnnie and go off to America, where he would be away from his old associates, and where he could commence life over again. He took the little fellow, seven years old, and went away. Soon after he arrived in America, he went into a saloon and got drunk. He got separated from his boy in the streets, and he has never been seen by his friends since. The little fellow was placed in an institution, and afterward apprenticed in Massachusetts. After he had been there some time, he became discontented and went off to sea; finally, he came to Chicago to work on the lakes. He had been a roving spirit, had gone over sea and land, and now he was in Chicago. When the vessel came into port, one time, he was invited to a gospel meeting. The joyful sound of the gospel reached him, and he became a Christian.

After he had been a Christian a little while, he became very anxious to find his mother. He wrote to different places in Scotland but could not find out where she was. One day he read in the psalms, "No good thing will He withhold from them that walk uprightly." He closed his Bible, got down on his knees, and said: "O God, I have been trying to walk uprightly for months past; help me to find my mother." It came into his mind to write back to the place in Massachusetts from which he had run away years before. It turned out that a letter from Scotland had been waiting for him there for seven years. He wrote at once to the place in Scotland, and found that his mother was still living; the answer came back immediately. I would like you to have seen him when he got that letter. He brought it to me; and the tears flowed so that he could scarcely read it. His sister had written on behalf of the mother; she had been so overcome by the tidings of her long-lost boy that she could not write.

The sister said that all the nineteen years he had been away, his mother had prayed to God day and night that he might be saved, and that she might live to know what had become of him and see him once more. Now, said the sister, she was so overjoyed, not only that he was alive but that he had become a Christian. It was not long before the mother and sisters came out to Chicago to meet him.

I mention this incident to show how God answers prayer. This mother cried to God for nineteen long years. It must have seemed to her sometimes as though God did not mean to give her the desire of her heart, but she kept praying, and at last the answer came.

A Prayer Meeting Testimony

The following personal testimony was publicly given at one of our meetings lately held in London, and may serve to help and encourage readers of these pages.

———*———

I want you to understand, my friends, that what I state is not what I did, but what God did. *God only could have done it!* I had given it up as a bad job, long before. But it is of God's great mercy that I am standing here tonight, to tell you that Christ is able to save *to the uttermost* all that come to God through Him.

The reading of those "requests" [for the salvation of inebriates] touched me very deeply indeed. They seemed to be an echo of many a request for prayer which has been made for me. And, from my knowledge of society generally, and of human nature, I know that in a very great number of families there is need of some such request.

Therefore if what I may tell you will cheer any Christian heart, encourage any godly father and mother to go on praying for their sons, or assist any man or woman who has felt himself or herself beyond the reach of hope, I shall thank God for it.

I had very good opportunities. My parents loved the Lord Jesus, and did their best to train me up in the right path; and for some time I thought myself that I should be a Christian. But I got away from Christ, and turned further and further away from God and all good influences.

It was at a public school where I first learned to drink. Many a time at seventeen I drank to excess, but I had an amount of self-respect that kept me from going thoroughly to the bad till I was about twenty-three; but from then till I was twenty-six, I went steadily downhill. At Cambridge I went on further and further in drinking, until I lost all self-respect, and voluntarily chose the worst of companions.

I strayed further and further from God, until my friends, those who were Christians and those who were not, considered, and told me that there was very little hope for me. I had been pleaded with by all sorts of people, but I "hated reproof." I hated everything that savored of religion, and I sneered at every bit of good advice, or any kind word offered me in that way.

My father and mother both died without seeing me brought to the Lord. They prayed for me all the time they lived, and at the very last my mother asked me if I would not follow her to be with her in heaven. To quiet and soothe her, I said I would. But I did not mean it; and I thought, when she had passed away, that she knew now my real feelings. After her death I went from bad to worse, and plunged deeper and deeper into vice. Drink got a stronger hold of me, and I went lower and lower down. I was never "in the gutter," in the acceptation in which that term is generally understood; but I was as low in my soul as any man who lives in one of the common lodging-houses.

I went from Cambridge first to a town in the north, where I was articled to a solicitor; and then to London. While I was in the north, Messrs. Moody and Sankey came to the town I lived in; and an aunt of mine, who was still praying for me after my mother's death, came and said to me, "I have a favor to ask of you." She had been very kind to me, and I knew what she wanted. She said, "It is to go and hear Messrs. Moody and Sankey." "Very good," I said; "it is a bargain. I will go and hear the men; but you are never to ask me again. You will promise that?" "Yes," she said, "I do." I went, and kept, as I thought, most religiously my share of the bargain.

I waited until the sermon was over, and I saw Mr. Moody coming down from the pulpit. Earnest prayer had been offered for me, and there had been an understanding between my aunt and him that the sermon should apply to me, and that he would come and speak to me immediately afterward. We met Mr. Moody in the aisle, and I thought that I had done a very clever thing when I walked round my aunt, before Mr. Moody could address me, and out of the building.

I wandered further from God after that; and I do not think that I bent my knees in prayer for between two and three years. I went to London, and things grew worse and worse. At times I tried to pull up. I made any number of resolutions. I promised myself and my friends not to touch the drink. I kept my resolutions for some days, and, on one occasion, for six months; but the temptation came with stronger force than ever, and swept me further and further from the pathway of virtue. When in London I neglected my business and everything I ought to have done, and sank deeper into sin.

One of my boon companions said to me, "If you don't pull up, you will kill yourself." "How is that?" I asked. "You are killing yourself, for you can't drink so much as you used to." "Well," I replied, "I can't help it, then." I got to such a state that I did not think there was any possible help for me.

The recital of these things pains me; and as I relate them, God forbid that I should feel anything but shame. I am telling you these things because we have a Savior; and if the Lord Jesus Christ saved even me, He is able also to save you. Affairs went on in this manner until, at last, I lost all control over myself.

I had been drinking and playing billiards one day, and in the evening I returned to my lodgings. I thought that I would sit there awhile, and then go out again, as usual. Before going out, I began to think, and the thought struck me, "How will all this end?" "Oh," I thought to myself, "what is the use of that? I know how it will end—in my eternal destruction, body and soul!" I felt I was killing myself—my body; and I knew too well what would be the result to my soul. I thought it impossible for me to be saved. But the thought came to me very strongly, "Is there any way of escape?" "No," I said; "I have made any number of resolutions. I have done all I could to keep clear of drink, but I can't. It is impossible."

All Things Are Possible with God

Just at that moment the words came into my mind, from God's own Word—words that I had not remembered since I was a boy: "With men this is impossible; but with God all things are possible." And then I saw, in a flash, that what I had just admitted, as I had done hundreds of times before, to be an impossibility, was the one thing that God had pledged Himself to do, if I would go to Him. All the difficulties came up in my way—my companions, my surroundings of all sorts, and my temptations; but I just looked up and thought, "It is possible with God."

I went down on my knees there and then, in my room, and began to ask God to do the impossible. As soon as I prayed to Him, with very stammering utterance—I had not prayed for nearly three years—I thought, "Now, then, God will help me." I took hold of His truth, I don't know how. It was nine days before I knew how, and before I had any assurance, or peace and rest, to my soul. I got up, there and then, with the hope that God would save me. I took it to be the truth, and I ultimately proved it; for which I praise God.

I thought the best thing I could do would be to go and get somebody to talk to me about my soul, and tell me how to be saved; for I was a perfect heathen, though I had been brought up so well. I went out and hunted about London; and it shows how little I knew of religious people and places of worship, that I could not find a Wesleyan chapel. My mother and father were Wesleyans, and I thought I would find a place belonging to their denomination; but I could not. I searched an hour and a half; and that night I was in the most utter, abject misery of body and soul any man can think of or conceive.

I came home to my lodgings and went upstairs, and thought to myself, "I will not go to bed till I am saved." But I was so ill from drinking—I had not had my usual amount of food in the evening; and the reaction was so tremendous, that I felt I must go to bed (although I dared not), or I should be in a very serious condition in the morning.

I knew how I should be in the morning, thinking, "What a fool I was last night!" when I would wake up moderately fresh, and go off to drink again, as I had often done. But again I thought, "God can do the impossible. He will do that which I cannot do myself." And I prayed to the Lord to let me wake up in much the same condition as that in which I went to bed, feeling the weight of my sins and my misery. Then I went to sleep. The first thing in the morning, as soon as I remembered where I was, I thought, "Has the conviction left me?" No; I was more miserable than before, and—it seemed strange, though it was natural—I got up, and thanked the Lord because He had kept me anxious about my soul.

Have you ever felt like that? Perhaps after some meeting or conversation with some Christian, or reading the Word of God, you have gone to your room miserable and "almost persuaded."

I went on for eight or nine days seeking the Lord. On the Saturday morning I had to go and tell the clerks. That was hard. I did it with the tears running down my cheeks. A man does not like to cry before other men. Anyway, I told them I wanted to become, and meant to become, a Christian. The Lord helped me with that promise, "With God all things are possible."

A skeptic dropped his head and said nothing. Another fellow, with whom I played billiards, said, "I wish I had the pluck to say so myself!" My words were received in a different way from what I thought they would be. But the very man who had told me that I was killing myself with drink spent an hour and a half trying to get me to drink, saying that I "had the blues, and was out of sorts; and that a glass of brandy or whisky would do me good." He tried to get me to drink; and I turned upon him at last and said, "You remember what you said to me; I am trying to get away from drink, and not to touch it again." When I think of that I am reminded of the words of God Himself: "The tender mercies of the wicked are cruel" (Prov. 12:10).

And now the Lord drew me on until the little thread became a cable, by which my soul could swing. He drew me nearer; until I found that He was my Savior. Truly He is "able to save to the uttermost all that come unto God by Him."

I must not forget to tell you that I went down before God in my misery, my helplessness, and my sin, and owned to Him that it was impossible that I should be saved; that it was impossible for me to keep clear of drink; but from that night to this moment, I have never had the slightest desire for drink.

It was a hard struggle indeed to give up smoking. But God, in His great wisdom, knew that I must have come to grief if I had to fight single-handed against the overwhelming desire I had for drink; and He took that desire, too, clean away. From that day to this the Lord has kept me away from drink and made me hate it most bitterly. I simply said that I had not any strength; nor have I now; but it is the Lord Jesus who "is able also to save them to the uttermost that come unto God by Him."

If there is any one hearing me who has given up all hope, come to the Savior! That is His name, for "He shall save His people from their sins." Wherever I have gone, since then, I have found Him to be my Savior. God forbid that I should glory! It would be glorying in my shame. It is to my shame that I speak thus of myself; but oh, the Savior is able to save, and He will save!

Christian friends, continue to pray. You may go to heaven before your sons are brought home. My parents did; and my sisters prayed for me for years and years. But now I can help others on their way to Zion. Praise the Lord for all His mercy to me!

Remember, "with God all things are possible." And then you may say like St. Paul, "I can do all things through Christ which strengtheneth me" (Phil. 4:13).

Look Up

O soul most desolate, look up! For thee
    One faithful voice doth promise sure relief.
Whate'er thy sin, whate'er thy sorrow be,
    Tell all to Jesus. He looketh where
The weary-hearted weep, and draweth near
    To listen fondly to the half-formed prayer,
Or read the silent pleading of a tear.
Lose not thy privilege, O silent soul;
    Pour out thy sorrow at thy Savior's feet.
What outcast spurns the hand that gives the dole?
    Oh, let Him hear thy voice; to Him thy voice is sweet.

A. S.

Notes

1. Mark A. Noll, *The Civil War as a Theological Crisis* (Chapel Hill: University of North Carolina Press, 2006), 59.

2. James F. Findlay, *Dwight L. Moody: American Evangelist, 1837–1899* (Eugene, OR: Wipf and Stock, 1969), 85.

3. Findlay, *Dwight L. Moody*, 86.

4. Alfred D. Chandler, *The Visible Hand: The Managerial Revolution in American Business* (Cambridge: Harvard University Press, 1977).

5. Rosanne Currarino, *The Labor Question in America: Economic Democracy in the Gilded Age* (Urbana: University of Illinois Press, 2011), 11.

6. Edward J. Blum, "'To Doubt This Would Be to Doubt God': Reconstruction and the Decline of Providential Confidence," in *Apocalypse and the Millennium in the American Civil War Era*, edited by Ben Wright and Zachary W. Dresser (Baton Rouge: Louisiana State University, 2013), 245.

7. Mark A. Noll, *America's Book: The Rise and Decline of a Bible Civilization, 1794–1911* (Oxford: Oxford University Press, 2022), 475.

8. Noll, *America's Book*, 544.

9. Dwight L. Moody to Mr. Cooke of Northfield (MFP, Correspondence with Northfield Citizens, 1), D. L. Moody Family Papers, Moody Center Archives, Northfield, MA, https://archives.moodycenter.org/digital/collection/p17348coll1 /id/513/rec/1.

10. William Revell Moody, *The Life of Dwight L. Moody* (Chicago: Revell, 1900), 38.

11. Revell Moody, *Life of Dwight L. Moody*, 37.

12. Kevin Belmonte, *D. L. Moody* (Nashville: Thomas Nelson, 2010), 35.

13. For further discussion, see Findlay, *Dwight L. Moody*, 89.

14. Dwight L. Moody, *The Men of the Bible* (Chicago: Bible Institute Colportage Association, 1898), 23.

15. Stanley Gundry, *Love Them In: The Life and Theology of Dwight Moody* (Grand Rapids: Baker, 1976), 10.

16. Revell Moody, *Life of Dwight L. Moody*, 93.

17. A. T. Rowe, *D. L. Moody: The Soul Winner* (Anderson, IN: Gospel Trumpet Company, 1927), 83.

Notes

18. Edwin Hodder, *The Life and Work of the Seventh Earl of Shaftesbury, K. G.* (London: Cassell & Company, 1890), 689.

19. Dwight L. Moody to Daniel W. Whittle (TMC, Correspondence with Daniel W. Whittle, 1), Powell Family Collection, Binder 1, Moody Center Archives, Northfield, MA, https://archives.moodycenter.org/digital/collection/p17348coll1/id/60/rec/2.

20. As quoted in Lyle W. Dorsett, *A Passion for Souls: The Life of D. L. Moody* (Chicago: Moody, 1997), 185.

21. Sermon notes on deliverance (Deliverance to the Captive 1), Special Collections, Yale Divinity School Library, Moody Center Archives, Northfield, MA, https://archives.moodycenter.org/digital/collection/p17348coll4/id/188/rec/10.

22. Dorsett, *Passion for Souls*, 116.

23. As quoted in Dorsett, *Passion for Souls*, 128.

24. Gregg Quiggle, "An Analysis of Dwight Moody's Urban Social Vision," PhD thesis (Open University, 2010), 108, https://oro.open.ac.uk/54492/.

25. Revell Moody, *Life of Dwight L. Moody*, 146.

26. Revell Moody, *Life of Dwight L. Moody*, 147.

27. Revell Moody, *Life of Dwight L. Moody*, 149.

28. R. A. Torrey, *Why God Used D. L. Moody* (Chicago: Revell, 1923), 53.

29. Quiggle, "Analysis of Dwight Moody's Urban Social Vision," 241.

30. "Our Augusta Letter," *Atlanta Constitution*, May 4, 1876, 1, https://www.newspapers.com/article/the-atlanta-constitution-our-augusta-let/115869929/.

31. Edward J. Blum, *Reforging the White Republic: Race, Religion, and American Nationalism 1865–1898* (Baton Rouge: Louisiana State University Press, 2005), 143–44.

32. While Blum suggests that Moody no longer tolerated segregation at his revivals (Blum, *Reforging the White Republic*, 144), there is evidence that Moody continued the practice after expressing his frustration in 1895. See Gregg Quiggle, *Bread and Bibles: D. L. Moody's Evangelism and Social Action* (Chicago: Moody, 2024).

33. "Mr. Moody's Wise Course," *Savannah Morning News*, March 7, 1886.

34. "Mr. Moody's Wise Course."

35. Quiggle, "Analysis of Dwight Moody's Urban Social Vision," 261.

36. Blum, *Reforging the White Republic*, 123.

37. Blum, "'To Doubt This Would Be to Doubt God': Reconstruction and the Decline of Providential Confidence," 225.

38. *Hand-Book of the Northfield Seminary and the Mt. Hermon School* (Chicago: Revell, 1889), 12.

39. Noll, *America's Book*, 540.

40. Findlay, *Dwight L. Moody*, 313.

41. D. L. Moody, *To the Work! To the Work! Exhortations to Christians* (Chicago: Revell, 1884), 3.

42. Kevin J. Vanhoozer and Owen Strachan, *The Pastor as Public Theologian: Reclaiming a Lost Vision* (Grand Rapids: Baker, 2015), 17.

43. Revell Moody, *Life of Dwight L. Moody*, 497.

44. Torrey, *Why God Used D. L. Moody*, 54.

45. Revell Moody, *Life of Dwight L. Moody*, 367.

DWIGHT L. MOODY (1837–1899) was a highly acclaimed late-nineteenth-century evangelist and preacher. Among other schools and institutions, he founded the Moody Bible Institute of Chicago in 1886 and the Bible Institute Colportage Association, now Moody Publishers, in 1894. He is author of several books, including *Christ in You* and *Spiritual Power*.

JAMES SPENCER serves as president of the D. L. Moody Center, an independent nonprofit organization in Northfield, Massachusetts, and is host of *Useful to God with Dr. James Spencer*, a weekly podcast and radio program on KLTT Colorado.